Jack C. Ferguson
732 Donna Drive
Vestavia, AL 35226
Email: jfergus732@yahoo.com

The Newspaper Boy

Youth

Youth is not a time of life; it is a state of mind . . . it is a matter of the will, a quality of the imagination, a vigor of the emotions; it is the freshness of the deep springs of life . . . .

Samuel Ullman
Birmingham, Alabama
1840–1924

For my good friend Jack Ferguson with every good wish —

Jany 29, 2018

The Newspaper Boy

Coming of Age in Birmingham, Alabama,
During the Civil Rights Era

A Memoir

by Chervis Isom

THE WORKING WRITER
{DISCOVERY <2013> GROUP}

Lyrics taken from the songs of Hank Williams, "I Saw the Light" and "I'm So Lonesome I Could Cry," are used with permission of his daughter, Jett Williams, and for which the author offers his thanks and appreciation.

Permission to use the poem *Youth* is granted by Samuel Ullman's great-grandson, B. G. Minisman.

Book and Jacket Design
by Travis Bryant

First Hardcover Edition
0 1 2 3 4 5 6 7 8 9

ISBN 978-1-940524-03-0

The Working Writer Discovery Group is a limited edition publisher offering innovative opportunities for "working writers" (those who must keep a day job so as to write for their calling). Our purpose is to introduce and market unheralded authors, who have, in their own voices, sought to elevate the cultural values of dignity, compassion, and charity in an increasingly complex technological world.

Follow the development of the hopes and aspirations of our writers, editors, booksellers, and readers by visiting www.workingwriter.com. Join us in our mission to foster a greater awareness of the unique gifts of writers at work in your own backyard . . . through the very old, but highly stable technology of the written word in book form.

In Memoriam, September 15, 1963

Denise McNair, 11
Addie May Collins, 14
Cynthia Morris Wesley, 14
Carole Robertson, 14
Virgil Ware, 13
Johnny Robinson, 16

The extraordinary events of 1963 in Birmingham—the change of city government; the Civil Rights Movement; the children's marches; the deaths of six innocent children (on Sunday, September the fifteenth), and then, in November on the twenty-second, the assassination of President John Kennedy in Dallas—all combine to mark 1963 as a watershed year in our continuing American saga. Now, fifty years from these and other extraordinary events, it is fitting and proper that we recognize and memorialize the tragic events of that year while celebrating the victory of right over might, as the laws of segregation were repealed in our city. And in my own life, the year 2013 marks the fiftieth anniversary of my marriage to Martha Green Isom, the mother of our children, Hugo and Natalie. We pray that our grandchildren will discover the life of promise and hope set in motion all those years ago in a city we are proud to call home. Birmingham, Alabama.

To My Friends
Vernon E. and Helen Bjordal Miller

To My Grandchildren
Clint McCullough Isom, age 15; Jacob Hoke ("Jake") Sansom, age 15;
Virginia Mackenzie ("Maxie") Sansom, age 11
Frances Lanier Isom, age 10

To The Honored Memory of —
My law partner and mentor, Abe Berkowitz, and
My father, Hewlett Chervis Isom, Sr.

Table of Contents

Preface

I had no way to know it at the time (back in April of 1965), but the arc of my life was about to change as a result of a job interview with a lawyer named Abe Berkowitz, a name I knew only because of his letters to the editor of the local newspaper.

Though his letters had been published a few years earlier, during the period of American history we now call the Civil Rights Era, I had remembered this "A. Berkowitz" as the one person who stood out as exceptionally courageous during those troubled times, when a faceless Ku Klux Klan was busy operating behind the scenes in the political life of our city. Birmingham in the late fifties and early sixties was by all measures a tough town, and it took a tough man to be willing to offer his candid, contrarian views to the public through the local newspaper, placing his name at the conclusion of his letters

Frankly, after all these many years, I can't remember how long I sat before Mr. Berkowitz's desk in a stupor that April 1965—how long I sat before finally finding my tongue when he asked me what I now call "the question." Nor do I recall exactly how I answered the question, but I did manage to tell him something of my background and my moral evolution (though I had no intention of doing so until he put me on the spot). One thing is certain, however, that job interview for a summer position with Mr. Berkowitz in 1965 (a job I didn't get) marked the third time the newspaper would shape the course of my life.

The first time was as a teenager, when over a course of five years (1952-1957) my worldview would radically change as a result of my single-minded devotion to my daily newspaper delivery routes. You see, I didn't simply deliver those papers; I would lock onto and consume every word of the headline stories, taking in all the existential horrors of those years: the War in Korea, the Cold War, the fear of communism, and the looming threat of increasingly violent racial tensions across the South.

And the second time my life was changed by the newspaper was when I met Vernon and Helen Miller. Had it not been for my morning *Post-Herald* route I would never have met this delightful and intelligent couple from the Far North who had moved into my territory and quickly became my favorite customers ("territory" being a word I use to describe a location far broader than one limited to mere geographical boundaries. I also use it to suggest "the territory of the heart.")

Newspapers . . . books . . . the written word. Through a shy and lonely adolescence, *these are the things I turned to* in marking my way forward, reaching for the boundaries while seeking my center.

Yes, the years of my youth and young manhood leading up to April 1965 had been a "long journey" for me, but it had all played out within a radius of five miles from where I then sat before Abe Berkowitz, and the essence of that single interview now resides comfortably in my memory, as if it had occurred only a short time ago, though many of the details have faded. Except for the truncated version I told Mr. Berkowitz that day so long ago, I don't recall that I have ever recounted the story of my personal journey to anyone else. I've been too caught up since then in the "everydayness of life," as Walker Percy put it in *The Moviegoer*—my family, my career—to reflect on the course of my own life.

It doesn't seem possible that since I was first interviewed by Mr. Berkowitz almost a half-century has passed; but now, at seventy-four years of age, I have the time and perspective to tell the whole story as I best remember it. I think it's a story worth telling, not for the sake of my own ego, for I did little in those years but receive the gifts and kindness of others. No, as much as anything, this effort to tell my story is a belated expression of gratitude to those remarkable individuals in my life who made a difference in a time of troubles.

As I ruminated over how to present my story to you, the reader, I came to understand how impoverished a memory can become when untended for a lifetime. I wish I had kept a journal but never did, and, as I thought about my life's story, I found that much of it was too dim, too deeply buried to retrieve. I also found that a life in remembrance is not a linear thing like the railroad tracks close to my house that I could follow, as I often did as a child, walking the rails, step-by-careful-step, with arms outstretched for balance. No, a life remembered seems instead to be more like a series of events or high points loosely strung together like Christmas lights.

So, I've written my "story" as a series of unconnected "stories"—stories from my childhood, adolescence, and young adulthood—stories I recall of the people who made a difference in my life as I came of age in a difficult time in a tough and unforgiving city.

These stories are true in their structural elements. I've tried to place them in the proper chronological order. The dialogue is true to the spirit of the situation, but I cannot and do not claim accuracy to the letter of what was said. The truth is that my growth and maturity during my youth did not follow some sweeping arc in an altogether positive manner. I often resisted, pushed back, and, at times, regressed.

The names I've used for the customers on my newspaper routes (as well as a few others) are mostly fictitious, except for the Millers. After these many years, I simply cannot remember them all and a few I've changed for obvious reasons.

I've used the old-fashioned, at-the-time-polite terms "Negro" and "colored" to describe the African Americans who appear in these stories. I hope you will understand I have no intention to offend anyone by my choice of those terms. For integrity's sake, I'm merely using the vernacular of the time.

Unfortunately, however, I have been compelled by truth to use "that other word" on occasion, and must apologize for its presence. It struck me as dishonest to ignore the reality of the time when, among many citizens of Birmingham, such a hateful term was not taboo.

1 • The Question

Abe Berkowitz's Law Office
The Empire Building
Birmingham, Alabama, April 1965

Stepping into the elevator of the Empire Building on the corner of First Avenue North and Twentieth Street in downtown Birmingham, I asked the operator, a middle-aged colored woman, to take me to the fourteenth floor, please. She closed the brass accordion gate, turned the crank, and we jerked into motion. As we ascended, I vacillated about whether to follow through with my plan or not, thinking *Am I really doing this? Walking in to see Mr. Berkowitz, an important man? Why would he want to see me?* My resolve was so weak I decided I would ask the operator to take me back down ... but then was too embarrassed to do so.

When we reached the fourteenth floor, the elevator bounced uncertainly, and then she cranked the doors open. To my surprise and consternation, I was not in a vacant hallway where I could gather my courage, as I assumed I would be. Instead, I was looking directly into the eyes of a receptionist behind a long desk no more than ten feet in front of me. Retreat was now impossible.

I timidly stepped from the elevator into the anteroom.

"Yes, sir, may I help you?" the receptionist asked as the door clanged shut behind me.

She was a neat, composed lady of about sixty years of age, with white hair and a kindly, but suspicious, smile. I stammered, "I'm here to see Mr. Berkowitz."

"Do you have an appointment?"

"No, ma'am, I'm here to see him about a job."

"But you didn't call for an appointment?"

"No, ma'am." I studied the carpet in front of her desk, then looked to her for help. "I'm a first-year law student at Cumberland Law School, and I need a summer job."

"Yes, sir. And what is your name?"

"I'm sorry," I floundered, "my name is Chervis Isom. Do you think Mr. Berkowitz will see me?"

"I don't know," she smiled, "but I'll find out."

She lifted the telephone and dialed a couple of numbers. "Mr. Berkowitz, a young law student is here to see you about a summer job. His name is Chervis Isom. He doesn't have an appointment, but he would like to talk with you, if you have the time."

Then she smiled and placed the phone on the cradle. "Mr. Berkowitz will be glad to see you. Just have a seat over there. He'll be with you in a few minutes." She motioned me to the seating area.

I was too fidgety to sit, but I did as she said, and studied the name of his firm posted in large brass letters on the wall behind her desk—

Berkowitz, Lefkovits, Vann, Patrick & Smith

—I knew only the name "A. Berkowitz," and was surprised he had so many partners.

Rehearsing in my mind the little speech I planned to give, I wondered if my words and delivery could possibly make a good impression. Doubt on one shoulder, regret on the other. Why had it not occurred to me to call for an appointment?

After a few minutes that seemed like an hour, Mr. Berkowitz came into the reception area. He put out his hand and warmly greeted me. "I'm Abe Berkowitz. I'm glad to see you. Come on back to my office," he said in a gravelly yet mellifluous voice that spoke of cigarettes and whiskey and a long, interesting life.

I followed him down the hall and into his office. He was stylishly dressed in an expensive, dark suit with white shirt and tie, his jacket buttoned over a moderate paunch. He was perhaps sixty and about five-feet-seven-inches tall. Though I'd never seen him before, I'd expected someone much taller because in my view he was a giant of a man.

I knew of him only from his many letters to the editor of the *Birmingham News* written over the past few years as the civil rights struggle in Birmingham came to a boil. These were desperate years in Birmingham. The Supreme Court decision *Brown v. Board of Education*, which ruled segregated public schools unconstitutional, had been issued in 1954, but the white public schools in Birmingham more than ten years later had not yet admitted colored students. George Wallace had publicly obstructed every effort to integrate the school systems, culminating in his stand at the schoolhouse door at the University of Alabama in June 1963. Eugene "Bull" Connor[1] was Birmingham's public safety commissioner, clashing with Rev. Fred Shuttlesworth (and later Dr. Rev. Martin Luther King Jr. and his followers), taking every initiative to frustrate the hopes and dreams of colored people. Those events had occurred only a short time before I entered law school in the fall of 1964. It was now April 1965, about eighteen months after the fatal bombing of the Sixteenth Street Baptist Church on September 15, 1963.

By his public letters during those years, Abe Berkowitz had stood up to Bull Connor and the forces of evil. Now, here, right before me, was the man I wanted to work for.

He directed me to a chair before the largest desk I had ever seen. There were no papers on the surface except for a single file, closed and orderly. Near the file was a neat, wooden letter box with a lid, and on the front corner of the desk was a dark sandstone statue of a man in robes holding a broken sword above his head, which I took to represent some biblical prophet.

"Have a seat, young man, and tell me what I can do for you."

"Yes, sir, thank you for seeing me. I'm sorry I didn't call for an appointment."

I hesitated, took a deep breath, and began. "I'm in my first year of law school at Cumberland, and I need a summer job as a law clerk. My grades for the first semester were good, almost all As, and I think my grades this semester will be good as well.

"I'm married. My wife, Martha, is a teacher. We have a baby boy, one year old—Hugo. Martha is helping me with expenses. I'm currently working part time at Sears in men's clothing, but they won't have much work for me this summer. Even though I have a partial scholarship, I need a full-time summer job to earn enough money to pay my tuition for the next school year."

He then asked me about the law courses I had taken and the grade in each class. He asked me several other general questions about law school, my college background, and where I was from. We spoke for perhaps fifteen minutes. I was pleased that Mr. Berkowitz, a busy and important lawyer, had listened to me with interest and respect.

But then he said, "I'm really sorry, but we don't have a place for you this summer. This is a small office. We have room for only one law student, and we've already made a commitment to someone else."

The interview, it seemed, was over. Though disappointed, I thanked Mr. Berkowitz for his time and trouble. Having expected nothing, I was grateful to have been treated respectfully. I straightened myself in the chair, was about to stand—but Mr. Berkowitz continued to sit quietly at his desk, alert, focused, watching me carefully, so I remained on the edge of my chair.

A few moments of uncomfortable silence passed, and, with his dark, half-hooded eyes searching my own, I could tell he was on the verge of speaking.

"Tell me," he finally said, not unkindly, "why are you here?"

I hesitated. *What could he mean by the question?* He knew I had come to inquire about a summer job as a law clerk, and he had only a moment before told me he had hired someone else. *How could I answer a question that seemed to make absolutely no sense?*

My heart skipped a beat, my vision blurred. My mouth finally fell open to speak but nothing came out. I had come because I wanted to work for Abe Berkowitz and no one else. But I couldn't bring myself to say that. Nor could I answer his question in a simple sentence or two. He didn't have time to hear (and I would have been too embarrassed to tell him) my life's story—how I made the long, arduous journey from the place where I had started—as an anti-Semite and a racist—to the chair in which I now sat before the desk of a Jewish civil rights hero.

After a moment or two, he seemed to appreciate my discomfort. "I understand you're here looking for a summer job," he said, firmly, and then he repeated the critical question.

"I want to know why you are *here*."

2 • Throwing Rocks

The time—1943. A war year.

The place—Eleventh Avenue North and Twenty-third Street, Birmingham, Alabama, on the margin of a neighborhood called Norwood.

A tow-headed boy perhaps four years old plays on the edge of the dirt road next to the white, clapboard house he calls home. Squatting in the dust, he rolls his imaginary truck—a simple wooden spool—in the dirt and scattered gravel.

Several children play in the road near him, but he doesn't know who they are.

Colored children appear at the end of the block, down where the trains go by.

They come up the road toward him. Motionless, he stares.

Then he stands, his spool in the dirt, and rocks in his chubby fists. He and the others throw rocks at the colored children, who throw rocks back.

He doesn't know why.

3 • My First Fishing Trip

I was perhaps ten years old when we visited my father's three uncles in Lake City, Florida. Uncle John offered to take me on a fishing trip to the Suwannee River.

"The S'wannee River?" I asked. All my life I had heard Stephen Foster's great song about the S'wannee River, down where "de old folks stay."

"Yeah," he said, "it's not too far away. An easy drive. We'll go in the morning."

I wanted to hear more about the river, but he clammed up. He was a man of silence, a crusty old veteran of World War I. He was then over sixty years of age, and lean as a rail. Dressed in fresh, starched khakis, creased as sharp as the blade of a knife, he looked like the soldier he had once been. His face and neck were wrinkled and leathery and deeply flushed in color, while his forehead and temples were stark white, protected by his wide brim hat. He was an outdoor man. His blue eyes, alert as a bird's, were almost colorless from squinting into the sun.

Then the sun was gone and it was time for bed. It had been a good day, and tomorrow would soon be here—my first fishing trip.

Early the next morning, Uncle John said hardly a word to me as we packed our fishing poles and other gear and our lunches in the back seat of his car. As we drove off, I was excited. I was also apprehensive. Uncle John was my father's uncle. I hardly knew him except through family stories. There was something about the way those stories were told about the old bachelor I never understood. The grown-ups would sometimes cut off their stories with meaningful looks.

We drove to the edge of town, then stopped at an old shack and waited. I had no idea why. He had been so quiet I was afraid to ask. Then an old colored man emerged from the house, trudged to the car, opened the door and looked at me in surprise, as if to say, "Who in the world are you?!"

I looked to Uncle John for direction. He looked at the colored man. Then Uncle John cut his eyes to me.

"Hey, boy," he said, snapping his narrow head backward, almost flinging his floppy hat into the back seat where he was directing me to go. I jumped from the car and squeezed myself into the back seat with fishing rods, cane poles, nets, and other fishing stuff.

"Get in, Rollie," he said to the colored man. "My nephew, Sonny," he continued, nodding his head once again in the direction of the back seat, "he's going fishing with us." As we drove off, the two of them spoke about the fishing trip, while I sat in disbelief, thinking you would never see something like this in Birmingham. *A colored man in the front seat? Unbelievable!*

In Birmingham, I had seen colored men chauffeur whites, who sat in the back. And I had seen white people chauffeur their colored help downtown to catch the trolley. But I'd never seen white and colored sitting together. It was unheard of in those days.

I recall little of that day so long ago. Only a few indistinct images have turned up, like faded snapshots in an old cigar box.

*   *   *

A narrow, shady, one-lane sand road running through miles of piney woods.

A tall, faded two-story mansion deep in the woods, the only sign of civilization, its columns supporting a sagging portico.

Dirty kids and dogs in the yard.

From the car, watching, as Uncle John and his colored companion buy bait from a man, taking their time, and, then, upon their return, the earthy suggestion of crickets, worms, and minnows.

A narrow, deep-looking river, greenery choking in on both banks, nothing like the grandiose Suwannee River I had expected. *Where are all the old folks?*

Sitting on the bank, watching my line, the men, silent, intent on their fishing.

A fish the size of my hand on my hook, and my revulsion that the hook had popped out its eye.

Uncle John roughly yanking my fish from the hook and throwing it back. "Too little to keep," he said.

My fish floating away with the current.

* * *

I close my eyes and try to squeeze out more detail, to fill in the blanks between those silent photographs in my mind; but after all these many years the details won't come. How sad the most distinct, the most prominent memory from my first fishing trip was my puzzlement and dismay over the color of Uncle John's fishing buddy.

4 • James and the Skatiemobile

I'd been warned over and over again never to go down there, down that rocky, rutted dirt road known as Thirty-fourth Place. I never knew if my mother was afraid of the people who lived in the "quarters," as we called the handful of shacks where the colored folks lived, or was it the railroad tracks she feared, which lay beyond the dirt road that petered out and was swallowed up where the brush and the briars began? Either way, I knew I'd be in trouble if my mother learned I had ventured down that dirt road through the quarters to the tracks beyond. She just didn't understand that down those tracks lay the trestle and the creek below. What was a boy to do? It was, after all, the adventure of the tracks, the trestle, and the creek that summoned me, that called me to race with fear through the quarters.

There was nothing I'd ever known that felt so good, so exhilarating, as balancing on that railroad beam high above the water, tiptoeing, arms outstretched, flailing like a tightrope artist—focused on nothing but the rail—trying to avoid looking through the gaps between the crossties— the creek far below—planting one foot carefully before the other all the way across the narrow trestle—as narrow as the length of the cross-ties and wide enough for only the train itself.

Of course, there would be absolutely no room for a walker when the train came. On more than one occasion, with a shiver, I had experienced a train barreling toward me, coming when I least expected it. The slightest rumbling of the trestle beneath my feet set me to running as best I could on the cross-ties of the wooden structure, praying I'd reach the apron of land at the trestle's end before the train—then, just as I made it clear, there it was, snorting and hissing steam and pumping iron, vibrating the ground, and with a concussive pounding in my ears I looked up in awe at the engineer, who shrieked his whistle, waving me back, scowling, as he thundered by.

After traveling that forbidden road to the track time after time, my fear of the quarters eventually abated and then turned to curiosity. I became more observant.

The houses in the quarters were run-down, dilapidated shacks, most covered with tar paper. Our street, Seventeenth Avenue, on the other hand, was paved, and the houses were small cottages occupied mostly by blue collar workers and their families. We were all white.

I never knew anything about the colored families who lived in those shacks. They were so different from us in so many ways. I remember one Sunday we heard shrieking and wailing from the quarters that wouldn't stop. It was summertime, way before air conditioning, and all our doors and windows were open. We couldn't shut out the wailing. I asked my mother what was happening down there. She told me it must be a wake—that someone had probably died. Nobody from our block cared so far as I know. What happened down in the quarters didn't much matter to us except for the sounds, and I guess whatever happened up on our block didn't much matter to them.

But that all changed, for me at least, when I met James.

I'd seen him there in the quarters a few times when I'd run through, headed for the tracks and the creek under the trestle. I didn't know his name then. He was a year or so older than I. He was as alien to me as I suppose I must have been to him, and he had a pronounced limp that made him even more mysterious.

That's how I recognized him later, when I saw him trudging in his awkward way up the dirt road toward my street, his right foot turned outboard, dragging by a rope some kind of contraption which bumped and clattered over the gravel. Whatever I had been doing I stopped and quietly watched.

When he reached our paved road, it began to roll. It was some kind of homemade car. From the metallic sound the wheels made on the asphalt, I knew they had once been roller skates.

I really couldn't see his car very well, but I stayed there on the sidewalk, immobile, as he came alongside me and continued up the slight grade of our street. He was not smiling or frowning. He was studying something far ahead.

I was about ten years old at the time and had never owned anything with wheels. Some of the older boys had bicycles they peddled around my street, showing off. Envy was a word that had probably not yet entered my vocabulary, but I couldn't wait for the day I had something to ride. I'd never even thought about a homemade car! And here it was. On my street. I might have asked for a ride, but pulled by a boy from the quarters? No way I'd ever have a chance to ride on that car.

He didn't seem to notice me as he slowly lurched by, tugging and jerking the car behind as it darted from side to side. He held his right forearm level with the street, his hand drooping down, flopping lifelessly as he lurched along.

Polio! It had to be polio. We knew about polio and what it could do. Polio caused a boy at my church to become paralyzed and confined to a wheelchair. Polio was on my mother's mind all the time. You can't do this, you can't do that. You don't want to catch polio, now, do you? That was another reason we weren't allowed to play in the creek polluted by the industries.

By then, I found I had unconsciously moved along the sidewalk in tandem with him, but holding my distance. I wondered. *Will it work? How can he steer it? Will it go fast? How will he stop it?* The questions kept coming, but not a word passed my lips. He was not "our kind."

When he reached the end of the block, he had a lot of trouble turning the car around. Mostly, he lifted the front end by raising the rope above his head with his left hand. His right hand didn't seem to give him much help. I had the impulse to race over and help him turn the car, but I dared not. At the same time I was surprised to find myself on the sidewalk at the end of the block. So I just watched as he struggled with his one good arm.

When he got the car turned to go downhill, he awkwardly plopped down on the skittish vehicle. Once seated, the car barely moved. He bounced but nothing much happened. He got off it and held the rope. He pushed the car with his good foot and almost fell down.

For the first time, his blank face showed something. He was visibly frustrated. Then he began to pull the car, and when it was in motion, he tried to leap on. But he simply couldn't do it. He sat dejectedly on his car, motionless and staring at the pavement. I didn't say a word. He never looked at me. It was like I was invisible. I came to myself there in the street beside him. I felt sorry for him. He had tried so hard. Plus (and maybe mostly), I wanted to ride. I knew I could make it go.

I stood there in indecision. I wanted so badly to help him. In Sunday School, we were taught to help other people, to express compassion with deeds. But this was different. He was not white like me.

And he wore ragged, threadbare clothes. We were certainly not rich. I suppose at the time I was unaware of how poor we really were but my clothes were unpatched. This boy was different from me, all right. But I wanted so badly to ride, to get my turn on his car.

I somehow found my resolve, and without a word or even a look between us, I timidly placed my hands on his thin shoulders and gave him a push. The car clattered off, then began to slow. He turned his head and looked back at me. He seemed to see me for the first time. I think he must have been as surprised as I was, but his face showed nothing.

I ran up behind him then and really pushed, the heels of my hands gouging his shoulders. I ran hard, the car clattering and bumping along and lurching from side to side as he tried to guide the car by the rope with his one good hand.

When I released him, he was really going, and I wondered how he would stop it, because he was coming to the steep downhill part of our street. He took a good ride and managed to get his car stopped before he plunged down the hill. I stood there beside him as he staggered up and hauled his car around. For a flickering moment, genuine joy and triumph flashed across his face. Then he began his trudge back up the street, his face again an impassive mask. He never looked at me or acknowledged my presence.

I returned to the sidewalk and again followed him up the street. I wanted more than anything to ride that car.

When he got to the end of the block, he tugged the car around by the rope. He looked at me for a second time, his face now wary.

"Wanna ride?" he asked, his voice flat and emotionless, as if he didn't mean it. He quickly looked away. But I wanted to ride so badly. I was aware that by accepting the ride, I was breaking the rules, doing something absolutely forbidden. It never occurred to me that he might also be breaking rules laid down to him.

"I guess so," I replied awkwardly, and cautiously picked my way off the sidewalk to the car. Then, without meeting his eyes, I took the rope, and plopped onto the seat. I tried to push off with my feet, but was not making much progress. Then I felt one hand on my shoulders, the steady pressure as he pushed, and the car began to roll. Faster and faster, as he clip-clopped behind me on his bad leg. The car darted about as I tried to steer with the rope. When I finally got it stopped at about the same spot he had, I was laughing and laughing. His face showed no expression.

We said nothing as I hauled the car around and started back up the hill. He took the rope from me without a word and limped silently back up the street. I returned to the sidewalk.

We took turns riding and pushing, no words passing between us.

Then suddenly he said "I gotta go," taking the rope and turning toward the dirt road. I followed a few steps.

"What's your name?"

"James," he responded without a backward glance.

"What do you call your car?"

"It's my skatiemobile. I made it myself," he said with defiance, as if I wouldn't believe him. He looked back for only a moment, his face lacking expression.

"Bye, James," I said, and turned toward home, feeling somehow cheated.

I watched him from the sidewalk as his car left the street and lurched and clattered behind him down the dirt road to the quarters where he lived.

*   *   *

Summertime heat in the South is oppressive, can sap your strength. On such days I normally would have played in the shade of the trees along the alley as there was no shade along our street. Several of the trees along the alley were fig trees, large, mature trees that at that age we could climb into. I hated the fuzzy leaves that would sting my bare arms and legs, and the sticky, white goo that stuck to my fingers if I pulled a fig that was not quite ripe. But the discomfort was worth it, to pull the ripe figs and pop them in my mouth. Sometimes I would break the fig into two parts and marvel at the color of the pulpy fruit inside; pale red, almost the color of a crepe myrtle bloom, with small, barely visible seeds. What I really loved was gathering a sack full of figs and selling them to the mothers up and down my block. I was well aware that the figs didn't belong to me, but somehow there were so many figs in the several trees that ownership didn't seem to matter.

The shade of the fig trees and the figs themselves faded in interest for me after I rode James's homemade car. I could hardly wait for him to come back on my street. Somehow I managed to keep myself busy in the sun along the sidewalk for several days waiting for James to return with his skatiemobile. Eventually, he did come back, and it was a lot easier that time to play together with James and his car. My younger brother, Eddie, and Tommy, from down the street, even joined in.

After that one day, we waited as weeks went by. James didn't come back. So, we trekked to the railroad and the creek, but instead of sprinting through the quarters as we had always done, we slowed to a cautious stride as our eyes darted about in search for James at each tar-paper shack. We began to think James had disappeared forever.

Then one afternoon, James trudged up the dirt road and onto my street, dragging his skatiemobile behind. I was ecstatic to see him, but his face was as impassive as ever. How many black faces have I seen since then with that stony, blank expression, a study of disinterest, of detachment, proclaiming, No matter what you do to me you can't hurt me; you can't touch me.

Even though I never thought of James as a friend (more as a co-conspirator, perhaps), still I just couldn't understand why his face was always so blank, never happy or sad, just blank. I was so happy to see him. I was confused and puzzled as he approached me. He dragged the skatiemobile as if it weighed three hundred pounds, slowly and deliberately, clip-clop, clip-clop.

"Hi, James," I said. It was all I could bring myself to say because of the look on his face.

He halted in front of me.

"This is yours!" he commanded and swung his skatiemobile around his left side and thrust the rope to me.

I stepped back, uncertain what to do.

"Why? Why you givin' me your skatiemobile?" I asked in alarm.

I still had not taken the rope from his extended hand.

"'Cause it won't run on my road," he impatiently snapped at me, as if I should have known why. Then he exploded, "And cause they tol' me I cain't come up here no mo'!"

He lurched toward me and tried to shove the rope into my hands.

I retreated, throwing my open hands above my head. His outburst had frightened and confused me.

"I cain't use it no mo' so you keep it!" he pleaded, again thrusting the rope toward me.

I didn't know what to do, but I wasn't going to take the rope. It just didn't seem right. Even though he had told me, I didn't understand why he wanted to give me his skatiemobile, and I didn't know how to accept this gift from James.

Then his face began to change. His eyes opened wide, startled looking, and there, for an instant, I saw all the pain and anger and hurt and humiliation I've ever seen gathered together in one small place. James sucked in his breath, scrunched up his eyes, and his whole body seemed to clench. Then he threw down the rope, whirled, and darted toward home, clip-clopping wildly down the street, his right hand flopping.

"Wait," I called behind him. "Wait, James."

He never looked back.

I was stunned. I didn't know what to do. I knew I couldn't follow him down to the quarters where he lived. I bent and picked up the rope and pulled the car to the curb, but I was not happy the car was now mine. As

I stood there by the side of the road, uncertainly holding the rope, the words he said rang in my ears, but he was gone before I could think it through.

I understood his skatiemobile wouldn't roll on the dirt and gravel road in the quarters. That was clear. The thing I didn't understand was why he couldn't ride it on our paved street anymore. *Why? Is it because we had played together? Is it wrong for him to play with me, a white boy? Did I cause the problem by playing with him, knowing I should not? Does he think I don't want his car because he, a colored boy, had made it or because it comes from the quarters and it isn't good enough for me?* All the reasons ran round and round in my mind until they all ran together. Suddenly, I felt very ashamed.

It was hot standing there by the curb in the sun, my shirt damp with sweat. I hadn't noticed the heat until an electric-like chill swept over me, and I went weak with indecision. I had not intended to hurt his feelings. I knew I should follow James down to the quarters and thank him properly and tell him that I did want his skatiemobile—more than anything. But I didn't know which house was his.

Mostly, though, I didn't go because I was confused and I was afraid.

Later, when we rode the skatiemobile up and down our street there was little fun in it. It just wasn't the same without James. James had disappeared from my life as suddenly as he had come into it.

A couple of years later, my family moved to the other end of the neighborhood. Soon, I was caught up with my paper routes, which kept me busy until I finished high school. And then came college and marriage and law school and family and practicing law. The years raced by without a thought of James and his skatiemobile or much of anything else from my youth.

It's now been over sixty years since I last saw James. I never learned who told James he couldn't play with me and my friends on our paved street. James didn't say, and I didn't think to ask.

But now I wonder, was it my father?—or Tommy's?—or some other person on my block? Or was it perhaps his own father or mother who had warned him of the bitter facts of life for a colored boy in Birmingham?

5 • Seeing the Bigger Picture

My father and I were driving around in downtown Birmingham searching for a place to park. He was talking, as usual. And,
as usual, I was only half listening. But it didn't seem to matter to him
whether I was listening or not. He would talk to a telephone pole. And
while he chattered, my attention was on the appointment with the optician. I really didn't want to wear glasses.

"You know, Son, after the war seems like just about everybody bought
a car. Everybody who could, anyway. That's why it's so hard to find a place
to park these days. Before the war, there just weren't many cars on the
road, 'specially here in the South. Because of the Great Depression, of
course. You don't remember those days, but your mother and I sure do.
Tough years. Back then, we were so poor, up in the country, we were lucky
just to have enough to eat. Back then, seemed like only rich folks had cars.
And then, during the war—the war went on for almost five years—no
cars were made. The car plants were making jeeps and trucks and tanks
and military vehicles of all kinds."

He turned a corner, searching for an open spot. "Gotta be careful with
these streetcar tracks. Don't wanna ruin my tires. They're 'bout worn out.
But we can buy tires now. Back during the war, tires were rationed like so
much stuff."

My father was silent for a moment, busy looking around. We went
over the viaduct to the Southside. "That's why so many folks used to ride

the streetcars," he continued, "but once the war was over, it was amazing how quickly those plants started to make cars again—and poof! Just like that, folks didn't have to ride the streetcars anymore."

I thought about the streetcar that rattled around Norwood Boulevard just a block from my house. I loved the streetcar. Only a few weeks earlier I had walked with my dog down the Boulevard to Mr. Monte's store on Vanderbilt Road. Coming back, the streetcar conductor stopped and let me and my dog ride back to Thirty-fifth Street—no charge. Three years later, in 1953, ridership became so diminished our city sold the streetcars and pulled up the tracks. What a sad day for our city.

My father finally found a parking space on Second Avenue South and deftly backed his green 1941 Nash four-door sedan into place. He locked the car, and then we walked the few blocks to Second Avenue North to the Frank Nelson Building. Inside, on the second floor were the offices of Jim Clay, Optician. My heart raced as I squinted to read the marquee while awaiting the elevator.

Apparently one of my teachers had suggested that my vision might be deficient. My father had arranged for an eye examination a week or so earlier and said to me on the way to the optometrist's office, "I can't imagine you need glasses, boy. My eyes have always been perfect. And your mother's, too. No one in our family's ever needed glasses."

But when it was all over, the doctor announced that I was in fact near-sighted. I could see close up to read, he explained, but couldn't see well at a distance, and certainly couldn't see the blackboard in my classes.

I had never done well in school. My grades a few months earlier, for the fall semester of the sixth grade, were awful. I had a P for "Poor" in history, science, and arithmetic, with the rest of my school subjects marked with Ss for "Satisfactory." I had only one E for "Excellent" and that was in library. I loved the library. I loved the books, and I loved checking out the books to take home. I had read all the series of biographies in the library, the ones with orange covers. The one I liked best was about Jim Thorpe, the American Indian who had played football and went to the Olympics. And then I became hooked on boys' adventure books by Stephen W. Meador. My mother would drop me off at the Birmingham Public Library downtown, where I would read for hours. I loved to visit the main reading room and look up almost two stories high at the wondrous murals of noted figures, both literary and historical, from around the world.

I remember on one occasion I sat outside cross-legged with a book in my hands, while my brother, Eddie, and George Likis from across the street were trying to cut a small board. One held a hatchett on the wood and the other drove the hatchett with a hammer. I sat innocently by, reading as the hammering went on, until a sliver of metal flew off and hit me, puncturing an artery in my calf. Up until that time, I could be found reading anywhere and everywhere—in the backyard, in the driveway, sitting cross-legged in the dirt—but that piece of flying metal sure enough ended my outdoors reading, and the library became my favorite retreat.

As a child, I never connected my poor grades with my vision. Had I been able to read what was on the blackboard? Maybe not . . . maybe that's why I was never particularly interested in school and why I never volunteered for anything. Shy and withdrawn by nature, I kept quiet and never got into trouble. That's not the way I wanted to be. I just didn't have the self-confidence to speak up. How I envied the boys in my class who would speak up, recite in class, volunteer for parts in the school play, even sing. Envy, yes, but I also harbored a kind of contempt that I knew was wrong, but I couldn't help it. I wanted to be like those boys. To be able to perform as effortlessly as they the extra school activities that I merely watched. To be invited to parties and social activities that always seemed to skip me.

And yet I developed a kind of comfort in my isolation. At least they left me alone. Now, however, I was left wondering if they would taunt me for being "four-eyed."

*   *   *

"Hold still," the optician directed as he thrust the eye glasses against my face. He was a big man, middle-aged, with fat, meaty hands, his knuckles hairy and knotty, his elbows resting on the table between us. I didn't know what to expect as I was fitted for my first pair of glasses. I nervously gripped the arms of my chair.

The man twisted the plastic hooks over my ears, jamming the frame onto the bridge of my nose. He then yanked and shifted the frame on my face several times, as if he were fitting a harness on a horse. All the while, he and my father, who sat in a chair beside the table, carried on a conversation about football. The man withdrew his fat hands from my face to observe the fit. I watched his cold, disinterested eyes mechanically jerk from ear to brow, down to nose, to my other ear and back again, several times, never meeting my eyes. He snatched the glasses off my face, the hooks painfully dragging across my ears, and as studious as a jeweler, bent and shaped the temples, without one word to me.

My eyes were riveted on the man's fat hands as he worked on the frames in his lap—heavy, plastic, yellow-pink, with temples ending in hooks to torture my ears. I had never seen anything so hideous. I couldn't imagine the embarrassment of glasses, ugly glasses, at school.

I had begun to notice girls, and I was painfully aware I was not the type of boy the girls seemed to like. I glanced into the mirror that sat on the desk, saw a squint-eyed boy, and confirmed what I'd always known— that I wasn't handsome or cute. These ugly glasses would put an end to my hope that I'd someday be popular. And the doctor had told me I would need glasses for the rest of my life.

I looked around the office and saw racks of glasses of all sizes, shapes and colors. I would have preferred a black pair, but no one had asked me my opinion.

After a few more adjustments, the man looked at my father and said, "I believe he's all fixed up now. They fit good." Then, looking at me for the first time, he asked, "Well, young man, whatta you think?"

I glanced curiously around the small room. "Maybe things look a little clearer," I lied, but thought to myself that there wasn't that much difference.

"Well, how do they feel?" my father demanded.

I shrugged. "I don't know. I guess they feel okay."

"You better be sure, son. I'm not gonna buy another pair anytime soon." It was the same speech I heard every year when it was time to buy new shoes.

We left the optician's office and entered the dimly lit corridor. My father pressed the button for the elevator. The glasses were uncomfortable. They pinched my ears and weighed on the bridge of my nose. I looked around the hallway, not expecting any wondrous improvement. I became more dejected than ever that I would be stuck for the rest of my life with these ugly, yellow-pink frames with ear hooks, and still see no more clearly.

Then while we were waiting for the elevator, I became aware that I could in fact read the signs on the doorway. I lifted the glasses from my nose and saw the sign—

Jim Clay, Optician

—become blurred and unintelligible. I dropped the glasses back in place and the words leapt back onto the door.

As the elevator door opened, the man at the control waved us in.

"First floor," my father said, as the door clattered shut.

As we got off the elevator, I looked along the elevator lobby toward the front doorway. I could see the individual tiles in the floor. The thought struck me, maybe that's why I cut my foot. A year or so earlier I had been running barefoot in the tall grass on Norwood Boulevard not far from our home. There was a brown tree limb partially hidden in the grass near the trolley tracks, and I had leapt on it with both feet. To my surprise and horror, a brown beer bottle exploded beneath my feet. I could never make my mother understand why I had jumped on a beer bottle and cut my foot. I couldn't explain it to myself.

Now, on the sidewalk, the cars in the street seemed to be sharper in focus. I could actually tell which was a Ford, a Plymouth, a Mercury, not only from their styles, but from the names and insignia that I could now see. I noticed people along the sidewalk coming my way. It was amazing! I could see someone's face a block away!

"Well, what about it, son? Can you see better?"

"I think so," I offered, maybe afraid to acknowledge too much too soon. I looked north along Twentieth Street toward Woodrow Wilson Park five blocks away. The oaks and magnolias jumped into focus, a profusion of shades of green. I was awestruck by the vivid colors in the park, the sharp detail along the street, the cars, the people, the signage, the storefronts.

My father became impatient. "We need to go."

Standing there, focused on the park, I needed to say something, but I couldn't find the words. Finally, I managed to croak, "The park—it's so green!"

Rooted on the sidewalk, looking toward the park, I was like a country boy in Manhattan at lunch time, with people shuffling all around me. I lifted my ugly, yellow-pink glasses off my nose. The people, the cars, the signage, the storefronts, the park, all faded into the fuzzy, foggy, blurry distance, the colors washed out.

"Let's move on down the street, Sonny. We need to get on home."

My father and I then began walking south along Twentieth Street to Second Avenue. There, we waited for the traffic light to change. I could now see the First National Bank of Birmingham a block away, and the Empire Building, and the Woodward Building, all on the corner of First Avenue.

I looked up at one of the office buildings, and I could clearly see a painted sign on a window about six stories up.—

Henry Johnston
Attorney at Law
Notary Public

—I halted, continuing to look skywards in deep thought. Then it hit me, the memory of perhaps my greatest disappointment beginning to take shape. Until this very moment, I had never been able to explain—to my teacher and my running mates on the track team—why I had inexplicably stopped at a time when they all depended on me, just stopped dead in my tracks.

*   *   *

I was in the sixth grade, one of the fastest boys in my class. Miss Bonino, the "play" teacher, usually supervised kick-ball, but it was early springtime, about two months ago, and she had organized a track team. She had selected me to serve on the relay team in second position. The team practiced around the playground, day after day, racing and passing the baton, until we felt confident. We worked toward an inter-school track meet at Legion Field, the city's huge municipal football stadium.

The track meet was important to me. I had never before excelled in anything.

The big day came and we traveled to Legion Field. All the boys were dressed in white T-shirts and shorts. I was surprised to see that all the other schools were identically dressed.

*　　　*　　　*

"Come on," my father said irritably, breaking the spell of my reviving memory of the track meet. I was just beginning to imagine the very day the disastrous event had occurred.

"Let's keep going," he barked.

My father and I hustled south along Twentieth Street, until we finally crossed First Avenue South. I could now see Red Mountain in the distance, surprisingly clear and green. It seemed bigger than ever to me.

Then, I stopped in my tracks.

There he was. There on a pedestal at the top of the mountain, he stood: the magnificent statue of Vulcan, the Roman god of fire and forge. The largest cast iron statue in the world, Vulcan represented Birmingham's storied history and pride in the iron and steel industy.

"Well, son, what do you think? Can you see any better out here in the open?"

Amazed at *seeing* Vulcan in such detail for the first time, I found myself gazing intently at his right hand, extended heavenwards. *Could it possibly be?* In Vulcan's right hand was an object, an object I knew to be a neon green light, but *it reminded me of a baton, my baton!* Immediately, I understood.

"Yes, sir," I said with measured enthusiasm, "I can finally tell a Ford from a Chevrolet. And I can even read the signs and billboards."

However, I was unable to articulate to my father the true surprise I felt at what I could *actually* see for the first time.

*　　　*　　　*

My mind reeled back a few months to Miss Bonino, Legion Field, the track meet. I was looking around in awe at the size and scope of the place, at the thousands of empty seats, the football field and the track around the field. From my position standing on the track, I searched in the bleachers for other members of my team, the team from Norwood Grammar School, but all the teams looked alike to me. My relay team was called to line up with the other relay teams in the lanes marked for the race. There were eight of them, and ours was in the middle. I was in second position on the relay.

Nervously, I looked back to the first starting positions, where the boys in white were crouching, then springing off the blocks in preparation for the real thing. I couldn't tell which of the boys was Jack.

Then, the eight starting runners took their positions in their starting blocks. My heart was drumming. I felt unsure of myself, though I knew I was fast.

The gun fired. The boys sprang off their blocks and charged up their lanes toward me. I bounced with excitement, my feet drumming the cinders. Then, like the other boys in second position, I took my lead, jogging up my lane, looking back, anticipating a clean hand-off of the baton.

But as I looked back, I became confused. As the boys charged toward me, I couldn't tell which was Jack. It should have been so simple to follow the parallel lines, but they were moving so fast. I had taken the baton from Jack a hundred times, but then there was only one Jack. My mind and heart were racing even as I slowed my pace. The few people in the stands were screaming. The boys around me were shouting. My eyes frantically darted from runner to runner of those in the middle. As they got closer, I could feel the other boys in second position taking a much greater lead than I, as I uncertainly slowed to a walk, waiting for Jack to come to me.

Then suddenly Jack was there, screaming—"Lead, Lead!!" as he passed me the baton. I whirled and desperately ran in last position. I raced for all I was worth and passed the baton to my frantic teammate, feeling a deep sense of humiliation.

As I returned to my squad, Miss Bonino asked, "Why did you stop?"

My teammates were yelling the same question over and over—"Why? Why did you stop?"

"I don't know," I responded meekly, looking at the ground and wishing it would swallow me up. I honestly had no idea why I had stopped.

*   *   *

"What are you doing, boy?" my father snapped, irritated with me.

I stared at Vulcan in absolute joy for a moment longer, then lifted my new glasses, and was amazed that the horizon blanked out into a hazy, colorless fog. "What're you stopping for? Daydreaming? We need to get back home."

Without my glasses I could barely make out Vulcan as a grey lump against the sky. I dropped the frames back onto my nose, and the horizon sprang into perfect focus, as plain as the palm of my hand.

I then followed my father south along Twentieth Street to where the car was parked. I fell in behind my father and matched his rapid pace. My heart was pounding with suppressed excitement.

As we walked along, I smiled to myself, despite the ugly, yellow-pink frames, that would, I knew, elicit all kinds of unimaginable ridicule at school in the coming weeks. No, it was because of my new glasses that I now, finally, understood the reason *why*. I understood why I had botched my relay handoff, and this remarkable discovery was both liberating and frustrating at the same time.

"Well, son, I'm sure glad you think the glasses will help. But for the life of me, I just don't know why you can't see good. I've always had 20/20, and so's your mother."

6 • My Paper Route

I **pedaled up and down the block** for about ten minutes, trying to look absorbed in my own activities, while studiously ignoring the covey of boys milling about on the sidewalk, horsing around. Then the delivery truck came and the boys unloaded the huge bundles of newspapers and took them inside the building. I parked my bike on the vacant lot across the street under the big chinaberry tree, far enough away that maybe I wouldn't be noticed as I watched them.

I sat astride my bike, a big twenty-six inch JC Higgins model, black with red trim, from Sears, Roebuck, like everything else I owned. It was leaning at about a forty-five degree angle, so that my left foot reached the ground.

Now that I'd quit pedaling, I noticed how cold it was. I turned up my jacket collar and shoved my hands in my pockets. My eyes were focused, like binoculars, through the plate glass windows into that beehive of activity. I wanted more than anything to be a part of that camaraderie, something I'd never before experienced.

Then, one by one, the boys emerged, each wrestling his large satchel of newspapers. A few of the boys were not much bigger than I. They deposited their satchels in huge bicycle baskets, mounted their bicycles and rode off, struggling with their loads. The bigger boys swaggered out of the building with authority, laughing and bantering. Each threw his leg over his motorcycle, resting his satchel of newspapers on his gas tank. Then he crouched for a moment, kick started his engine, and roared off.

After a while, all the boys were gone. I pushed off with my left foot and pedaled home, thinking about my own paper route, my own source of income, a sense of responsibility, of validation. I wanted to be among the older boys.

And I wanted a motorcycle like most of the newspaper boys rode. My parents had given my brother and me bicycles for Christmas a couple of years earlier and they were great, but how much better a motorcycle would be. Sometimes, we would fasten a baseball card with a wooden clothespin on the front fork so that, as the wheel turned, the card would flutter and flap between the spokes with a vibrating sound not unlike a small motor at work. Sometimes, we used two or more cards to amplify the sound. How big we felt to fly down the street, our motors aroar!

I would have to wait. I had already discussed a paper route with my parents, and they had been emphatic. I would have to be thirteen first. So all I could do was hang around the paper branch and dream. January, I thought, only two more months until March.

I had been watching the newspaper office, what they called the "branch," for several months, since we'd moved to our present house on Twenty-seventh Street. While I was afraid to actually go in and look around, I couldn't stay away. The branch was adjacent to the corner grocery store owned by the Graffeo family. It was located across Twenty-sixth Street on Seventeenth Avenue, only a block from our house. I always looked forward to an errand to the store because it gave me the opportunity to study the newspaper branch next door. Every afternoon, the boys would congregate on the sidewalk in front of the branch. The sidewalk and curb would be obstructed by a dozen or more bikes, small motorcycles and scooters of various kinds as the boys waited for the delivery truck. What excitement! Waiting for my birthday was harder than waiting for Christmas.

At last, when I turned thirteen in March 1952, I reminded my parents of their promise to let me have my own newspaper route. Usually, I didn't like to hear my father's advice. He was always a little too quick to tell me how to act, and much too critical of my shyness and introspection. But this time, I listened with interest because I hoped it meant he was blessing my request for a newspaper route.

"Son, when you work for a man, give him his money's worth. Do the job right, like you'd want it done. You understand?"

"Yes, sir."

"You get that paper route, won't be nobody looking over your shoulder. It's up to you. You can do a fine job, one you'd be proud of, or you can do it sloppy. It's up to you. I won't be there. Just remember, you got a job to do, it's a job worth doing right."

He looked at me hard. I looked at the floor.

"Think you can handle it?"

"Yes, sir."

"Then go down there and see the man about a job."

He smiled and picked up his newspaper.

"Yes, sir." Elated, I left the room.

A few days later, I mustered the courage to enter the branch after all the boys had taken their newspapers and left. There was a storefront of glass and a glass front door. I opened the door and stepped inside. It was nothing but a bare room with six or eight large, high, rough wooden tables, lighted by several bare bulbs hanging from the ceiling. In the front corner sat a glum-looking, middle-aged man in an old swivel chair working at the ledgers on his desk.

Timidly, I edged over to the desk and waited, a small, skinny kid with glasses. At last, he noticed me, and twisted his chair to face me.

"Hey, what can I do for you, son?"

"Uh, I just wanted to see if you might have a paper route for me."

"Well, I don't know. Lemme think about it. You live around here?"

"Yes, sir, just a block or so, up thatta way," I pointed.

"What's your name?" His pencil was poised.

My heart gave a little jump. I hated my name. I had been Sonny all my life until I started school. Then I was suddenly "Chervis." No one else had a name like that. "Uh, my name is Chervis Isom—but everybody calls me Sonny."

He smiled. "Sonny it is," and wrote in his book.

At first I thought Mr. Hawley would be gruff, but I found him to be kind and helpful. He wore horn-rim glasses and his dark hair was turning gray and thinning.

"Check back with me next week, Sonny. I may have something working. I'll know by then."

For the next week, I could hardly keep my mind on my school work or do anything. When I thought about going back to see Mr. Hawley, my stomach would flip over.

At last, the day came when a week had passed. After school that day, I hurried home and somehow kept busy until I thought all the boys would have collected their papers and left the branch. Then I rode my bike to the branch, even though it was only a block from my home. I wanted Mr. Hawley to see my bike, to know I was ready. I parked my bike directly in front of the branch, leaning it against the support of the storefront so he couldn't miss it. Then I opened the door and marched in, a boy on a mission.

He watched me carefully as I approached his desk.

"Do you remember me? I talked with you last week."

"Sure do, Sonny. You're the one who wanted the paper route, right?"

"Yes, sir, you said you'd know in a week."

"Well, I do have a route that's available. About sixty papers. Think you can do it?"

"Yes, sir."

He looked at me a long time, thinking things over, then he explained to me how the system worked.

"The company is in business to sell papers, you understand. I'm going to sell you sixty papers a day. That's how big the route is. I'll count 'em out for you, but you check me, check me every day. That's important! Sometimes I lose count. Don't mean to, but it happens. If I short you and you don't catch it, then you'll be short. It'll be your loss. So check me every time! Got it?"

He didn't wait for my response.

"Now, you heard me when I said 'sell', didn't you? I'm selling and you're buying those newspapers. Once you've bought 'em, they're yours. I'll sell you all you need. The company price to you is two point three cents a copy. You sell it for a nickel. The same kind of spread on Sunday, but you sell it for a quarter. Got it?"

"Yes, sir."

"You're in business for yourself. The more you sell, the more you make. If you lose your papers or let 'em get wet, not my problem. If you need more, you hafta pay. Got it?"

"Yes, sir." My head was going in circles.

"You gotta put the paper where it'll be safe and out of the rain and wind. Put it on the porch, in the dry. Throw it out on the steps, it rains, paper's ruined. They'll call the company, want another one. The company'll call me, I'll call you. So keep 'em dry. That's the secret. Got it?"

"Yes, sir."

"Part of your job is to get new starts. That's what it's all about. Now if you can get more starts—that's a new customer—just tell me and I'll add more papers to your stack. New starts means more profit for you and the company. But you gotta stay on your own route. Don't horn in on somebody else. Got it?"

"Yes, sir."

He looked me up and down, as if he had grave doubts. "Well, whatta you think, Sonny? Can you do it?"

I heard myself say, "Yes, sir," and I flinched.

"Ok," he smiled. "I'll show you the route." He slowly rose to his feet and trudged away from his desk, a middle-aged man of average height and a little too heavy. "Put your bike in here till we get back."

Mr. Hawley locked my bike in the branch and led me to his car. The route was located about a mile from the paper branch. It covered two square blocks, Twenty-ninth and Thirtieth Streets between Eleventh and Twelfth Avenues North. Mr. Hawley explained to me that this was the oldest part of Norwood which had been developed about 1900, over fifty years earlier. The houses were now mostly weathered two-story frame homes that had once been occupied by prosperous people. Elderly people lived in many of the homes, and had been there for years. Some houses had been divided into upstairs and downstairs apartments for two families. Still others, I learned later, had been converted into boarding homes.

Mr. Hawley showed me the route book, a loose-leaf, compression binder about four inches wide and seven inches long, in which each account was contained. These represented the sixty customers I would be expected to deliver to daily and collect from every Saturday. Then I would report to Mr. Hawley each Saturday to pay for my weekly supply of newspapers.

Mr. Hawley drove me back to the paper branch. He told me about the opportunities to make a little money and the chance to learn how to handle responsibility, and how good for me the paper route would be. When we arrived, he looked me over again.

"Well, Sonny. You've seen the route. Is it what you expected? Think you can handle it?"

"Yes, sir." I tried to sound confident, but I was definitely worried about whether I could do all that was expected of me.

I found out that delivering newspapers was a little more than I had bargained for. Sixty newspapers stuffed into a canvas bag were almost more than a thirteen year old could grapple with. I bought a huge metal basket from the *News* and mounted it on the front of my bicycle to carry my load of newspapers. That seemed to work fine on most days. After stuffing the rolled papers into my bag, I dropped the bag on top of my basket as best it would fit. Most days, the stuffed bag would not fit into the basket, and would sit high on top of the basket hanging over on the sides. That, of course, made for an awkward ride as I struggled to keep all that weight in motion while striving to steer the overloaded bike clear of traffic. My problems were magnified by my limited ability to see over the elevated satchel of papers. Some days, particularly Sundays and Thursdays, the papers were over-sized and too heavy for my bicycle. If I were not actually sitting on the bike the weight of the papers in the basket would cause the back of the bicycle to swing wildly into the air. In that case, I had to keep pressure on the seat with one hand to hold it down. It was very difficult with the other hand to hold up the bike and guide it. On those days when the papers were fat, the bike would often flip over, spilling all my papers onto the ground.

In order to reach my paper route, I had to travel for a half-mile along Twenty-sixth Street, also known as U. S. Highway 31. One Thursday afternoon, I was pushing my bike up the incline of Twenty-sixth Street only a half-block from the paper branch. I was on the right side of the road, along the curb. The cars were whipping by me. The weight in the basket was threatening to flip the bike over as I attempted to push, guide and support the load with my left hand and hold the bike down with my right. In desperation, I tried to mount the bike, aware I would have to pedal hard to propel that weight up the hill. As I lifted my right hand from the seat where I had been holding down the back of the bike, it began to flip. I leaped on board and frantically pedaled. The weight in the basket leaned to the left, which I could not correct, and suddenly I was pulled into the traffic. A car hit me, knocking me to the pavement and scattering my papers along the highway. Thankfully, I was more embarrassed than hurt. Traffic stopped, allowing me to scramble around on the highway retrieving my papers. I then packed them into my canvas bag, hefted the bag onto the basket and again mounted my bike, this time successfully.

After several mishaps, I came upon the bright idea to buy a second satchel from Mr. Hawley. On those days when the newspaper was oversized, particularly on Sunday, I would pack both bags and leave one with Mr. Hawley, behind his desk (safe against the theft or practical jokes of the older boys), while I delivered the other satchel to my route. Then I would pedal back to the branch office for my other bag. Making two trips was much safer than dealing with the dangers of an overloaded bike.

As time passed by, I solved each problem as it arose and that gave me a growing confidence. But I was not blind. The older boys had it made.

Every day, they would roll their papers and pack their satchels just as I did. Then each in turn would lug his bag outside, throw it onto his gas tank, fling his leg over his cycle and kick start the engine. Then he would race his engine and blast away. Theirs were the easiest jobs in the world, I decided—delivering papers from a motorcycle.

But a bike was all I had, and so far as I could see, a bike was all I'd ever have

7 • An Awkward Moment

While I was solving the daily problems of delivering my newspapers, my social skills were lagging. Even so, I was able to fall into a pattern for my collections. After all, it was imperative that I collect my accounts. I found it was simple enough to do that. All I had to do was knock on the door, say "Collect for the *News*, please," and, of course, "Thank you." It was easy enough to respond appropriately to my customers' polite conversation with a comment such as, "Oh, yeah, it sure is hot today." But I didn't like to go much beyond that.

My father had tried. Oh, I can hear him now. "When you meet a man, don't look at your shoes, boy. Ain't nothin' down there. Look him in the eye, shake his hand. Make him think you're somebody!" But it would be a long time before I met his expectations. Meanwhile, I had to collect my accounts on my own.

I was an earnest young boy back then, back when I was barely thirteen. My parents were religious people. We were members of a downtown fundamentalist, evangelical church, where we attended three services each week. I was pounded with moral principles at church, in Sunday school and at home. In the early fifties, public school teachers didn't shrink from moral guidance either.

I was taught that one must be honest, truthful, polite, courteous, humble, loyal, energetic; and that one must work for an honest wage.

One must not be dishonest, untruthful, impolite, discourteous, arrogant, disloyal, or slothful; and one must not take that which he had not earned. Moreover, I learned that one must not commit a range of sins which I didn't yet fully understand, with names freighted with mystery, like "adultery" and "fornication."

I was taught that the world is black and white. An activity is right or wrong. It's moral or immoral. There's righteousness or there's sin. There's truth or there's falsehood. There can be no in between. These values and principles are absolute and never vary. They cannot be compromised.

So there I stood, on Mr. Frew's porch on a Saturday morning. I rang the bell. Mr. Frew answered the door.

"Collect for the *News*, please."

"Sure," Mr. Frew said, as he reached into his pocket and began fingering the coins. "What is it, forty-five cents? Is that right?" he asked.

"Yes, sir, forty-five cents is right."

"Well, all right, here it is," and he held out between thumb and forefinger three coins. I took the coins and dropped them into my pocket. "And son, you're doing a good job. Here's a little something for you." And he handed me a quarter, representing more than a fifty percent tip. I studied the coin which rested in my open palm.

It was my first tip, you understand. I had never thought about a tip, had never thought someone would give me something I had not earned. I didn't understand the concept of a tip. I never thought of my family as poor, but we never went to restaurants. I had never heard any discussion about tips. I stood motionless, staring at the coin in my open palm.

I blushed deeply, looked at the floor, shuffled my feet and searched for something to say. It should have been simple enough to say thank you and walk away.

Instead, I resolved to do the right thing as I saw it in that moment. I shoved the quarter back into Mr. Frew's hand and blurted, "I'm sorry. You keep it. You probably need it as much as I do."

Those were my exact words. I've remembered them all these long years because I wanted to call them back the moment I let them go, but was powerless to do so. The instant the words tumbled out, I knew they landed wrongly.

I glanced up as Mr. Frew's friendly, generous face collapsed with surprise and hurt. My stomach flipped over and suddenly I felt sick.

Mr. Frew paused there a moment, puzzled, hurt, gazing at me in surprise. Then he quietly closed the door without a word. I turned, in a daze, and my body clenched up. I felt shivery all over as I walked stiff-legged to my bicycle. *Why didn't I take the money? How could I ever face Mr. Frew again?* I mounted my bike, and blindly dashed away, hoping to outrun my shame.

Other awkward situations occurred during the next few years as I slowly adjusted to a world in which there seemed to be no clear and concise answer, but none that lingers with me like the look on Mr. Frew's face as he closed the door, shutting me out without a word.

*   *   *

Years later, in my freshman year of college, I would read a book about a young man cast into more complex circumstances than I could have ever imagined. Young Ensign Willie Keith was a junior officer aboard the mine-sweeper/destroyer the *U. S. S. Caine* in the Pacific Fleet in World War II. The captain made questionable decisions, some perhaps cowardly. The crew hated him. During a typhoon, the captain seemed unable or unwilling to take the actions necessary to save the ship and its crew from shipwreck. Executive officer Maryk, who had taken notes for months about the captain's erratic behavior, attempted to relieve the captain of his command. He called on Keith, as officer of the deck, to support the decision and escort the captain to his quarters. Keith was aware of the questions about the captain's fitness for duty. He then supported the executive officer, who took command and saved the ship.

Herman Wouk's Pulitzer Prize-winning novel of 1951, *The Caine Mutiny*, suggested to me that sometimes we are cast into circumstances in which the right choice is unclear. This great book was made into an exceptional movie in 1954, nominated for seven Oscars.

Maryk and Keith were charged with mutiny and court martialed. I feared the court martial proceeding would be a boring denouement to a fine book, particularly since I had convinced myself that the mutiny had been fully warranted. I was surprised to find the trial just as exciting and complex as the story itself, and gratified to learn from the verdict that my assessment of the case had been correct. And then, in the last few pages of the book, the surprise aftermath to the trial spun me like a top.

I thought of the scene at Mr. Frew's door and my awkward response to his attempt to give me a tip. I thought of his face. I thought of the surprise on his face, and realized that life is seldom, if ever, simple; we all find ourselves, at some point or the other, in uniquely difficult spots, not too unlike, I imagine, the one which I handled so ungraciously with my customer, Mr. Frew. I hoped I would never face a decision as uncertain as that faced by Willie Keith.

And I wondered if I would always live in this state of ambiguity.

8 • The Forgotten War

𝕬 few months elapsed and I began to feel comfortable with my route. I still felt inadequate when I was at the paper branch among the older boys, but much of the job had become routine to me. It was the headlines that drove me crazy, and I couldn't do anything about them except worry.

After school each day, I raced to the paper branch, where Mr. Hawley counted my newspapers into a big stack as I stood by to verify the count. I never knew Mr. Hawley to short anyone, but I had learned well to be careful in business.

I lugged my stack to an open space on one of the tables where I would "roll" them, a process of folding and rolling my newspapers, as the other boys did, into cylinders which were then tied with a lightweight cord. The tying process was quite simple. I held the end of the cord in my mouth to moisten the end, and when I had rolled the newspaper, I held it with one hand, grabbed the string with the other and snapped it around the rolled paper. The wet end would usually hold as I quickly wrapped the cord about five times around the paper. Then in a quick yank I broke the string, placing the end back in my mouth. Then, I shucked the cord down the tube about six inches causing it to bond as if tied.

Rolling my papers could have been a quick, efficient exercise. It was for all the other boys. But I learned I could spread out a newspaper and read while at the same time mechanically rolling my other papers. Oftentimes

I became so engrossed in my reading that my rolling was interrupted in mid-motion. I can see myself now holding the rolled paper in my fist, string in my mouth, my fingers poised, ready to flip the tail of the string around the paper, but motionless as I focused on the news print.

I read mostly about the Korean War which had begun a couple of years earlier, in the summer of 1950, and was raging still in the spring of 1952. My uncle, Charlie Wood, who had been a Marine in the South Pacific during World War II, was called back into service for the Korean War. That's one reason I took such an interest in it.

I still remember the fear I felt back in the summer of 1950, before I acquired my paper route, as our forces and the ROK, our South Korean allies, were pushed by the North Korean Army into the Pusan Perimeter at the south end of the Korean Peninsula and had their backs to the sea. *Will they be pushed into the sea? Will they be annihilated?* And I remember the pride I felt when General Douglas MacArthur landed his army from the sea at Inchon Harbor on September 15, 1950, behind the North Korean Army, cutting off their supply lines and then recapturing Seoul. That heroic strategy put the North Korean Army on the defensive, and while the politicians in Washington, D. C., dithered and wrung their hands, MacArthur directed the U.N. Forces (primarily Americans) to invade North Korea at the risk of drawing China into the conflict. But General MacArthur had given President Truman his assurances the Chinese would not interfere. Then, a few days later at Thanksgiving all Hell broke loose!

The Chinese Army swarmed across the Yalu River and attacked the U.N. Forces. I remember my horror when I learned our Marines were surrounded by the Chinese at the Chosin Reservoir in North Korea. As they retreated in snow and ice, there were thousands of American casualties.

The General wanted to counter-attack across the Yalu River into Manchuria and China. President Harry Truman refused that strategy. He did not want to broaden what had been called a limited police action by the United Nations for fear of becoming embroiled in a land war on the Asian continent, a war in which it was feared the Soviet Union would join with communist China. MacArthur became vocal, making statements to the press about what our policy should be, in conflict with President Truman's policies. Then, in April 1951, President Truman fired

General MacArthur from his command! Douglas MacArthur was an American hero. He was more than a man. He was a legend. Truman had done the unthinkable. It was a very controversial decision that divided the nation, and it was particularly unpopular here in the South.

Shortly after that, the U. N. Forces formed a Main Line of Resistance (MLR), and in July 1951, a year after the war started, truce talks began among the parties at a small village in the MLR called Panmunjom.

I was well aware of the War before I began delivering papers. My parents spoke of it. We had acquired our first television about that time and I watched the news with interest. We also subscribed to the newspaper and I always looked over the front page, particularly to learn news of the War.

When I became a paperboy, it seemed the main news was always about Korea. The thing that was so baffling to me was the horrifying battles and battlefield deaths that were occurring even while truce talks were pending. That just didn't make sense to me. *Why are men fighting and dying when peace talks are proceeding? Why could the fighting not wait to see if the peace talks are successful?*

As the days and months rolled by, the newspaper spoke of more truce talks at Panmunjom, along with battles at Bloody Ridge and Heartbreak Ridge. Month after month the talks continued as the battles raged. Bunker Hill. White Horse Hill. Heartbreak Ridge. T-Bone Hill. Pork Chop Hill. Old Baldy. More killing and dying, even while the negotiations at Panmunjom droned on.

It seemed to me that the front page articles about Korea would continue forever. I was well aware of the military draft and the fact that young boys were inducted into military service at eighteen. As I read each afternoon of horrifying battles in one column and truce talks in another, I worried. The War had then ground on for two years. While the Chinese and their North Korean allies fought for victory to drive the U.N. Forces and the ROK from Korea, ours was a desperate attempt to gain and hold and re-take an imaginary line in the dirt. Meanwhile, the diplomats at Panmunjom had dithered for a year with no results. *How long could this go on?*

Each day as I stood before the tall table rolling my stack of papers, those headlines were impossible to ignore. I wondered is it possible this War will still be raging in a little over four years when I reach eighteen?

Will I be inducted and sent to Korea to be killed or frozen to death like so many thousands of other young men while diplomats sip tea and posture interminably over the terms of an agenda they can never set?

By the time I turned fourteen, in March 1953, there were continuing front page articles about the Korean War. The war see-sawed back and forth along the MLR. The U.N. Forces had taken a defensive posture, since MacArthur was fired and the determination had been made not to "win" the war but merely to achieve a cease fire and maintain the status of a divided Korea. The Chinese Army continued its massive offensive in support of the North Koreans even though their diplomats pressed on with talks about a cease fire. There were often two separate articles in the paper about Korea, one about a bloody battle and another about more peace talks in Panmunjom. Sometimes, there would be a third, telling of the war in the skies over North Korea.

The Korean War was truly a "no-win" war for the United Nations forces. We had one hand tied behind our backs for the entire war after the Chinese came in. We were afraid of a final showdown, afraid of what would happen if we crossed the Yalu River into Manchuria, afraid the Soviet Union would come to the defense of China and push the war on the Korean Peninsula into a full-scale World War III.

It was clear to me that the Soviet Union could join the fighting at any time. The MiG-15 fighter jets flown by the Chinese were made in Russia. They operated from airfields in Manchuria, just across the Yalu River from North Korea, which were definitely off-limits to U. N. forces.

The United States had almost complete air superiority over Korea until the Chinese came into the War. Then the MiG-15s flown by Chinese pilots (or Soviet pilots for all we knew) gained ascendance for several reasons. The MiG-15 was superior to America's F-84 Thunderjet and in many ways could out-maneuver our F-86 Sabre. But the U.S. had superior pilots and over time regained dominance in the skies over Korea.

There were articles in the paper almost every day about spectacular dog fights in "MiG Alley," the air space over most of North Korea, abruptly ending at the Yalu River. I read about how the MiGs raced across the river into Korea, delivered strikes and then escaped back over the river to Manchuria knowing our pilots couldn't pursue. But while in open airspace over Korea, the battles were great swirling affairs, sometimes involving as many as twenty jets swooping and looping in the skies.

The articles about the air war were exhilarating, because there, in the sky, we seemed to be winning, even though we couldn't legitimately chase the enemy aircraft to their bases. The ground war, though, was another story. It seemed to me our armies had found themselves in a World War I style war, where every square foot of ground was contested. They fought to hold their positions against waves of Chinese forces that attacked again and again, causing massive casualties. The hilltops along the MLR were contested, often taken, then re-taken, in combat that resembled the trench warfare of World War I, including gruesome hand-to-hand fighting. There were hills on which thousands of men died while peace talks persisted, hills now mostly forgotten with improbable names like Pork Chop, Old Baldy, Vegas, Little Gibraltar, Eerie, and the Hook. How depressing to know our soldiers could not fight to win, but were dying only to hold a line in the dirt. What was it all about anyway?

While Korea was the hot spot on the globe where communism was threatening to overpower us by force, I was also aware from other articles in the newspaper that we were in danger of being taken over from within. Senator Joseph McCarthy was naming names of those communists inside our government, in Hollywood and in other professions. He was exposing not only those communists, but their "fellow travelers" as well. As a member of the Senate Internal Security Committee, he used his position to search for communists wherever they operated in our society. McCarthy was a big man in 1953, and it looked for a while that he would save America from communism.

As I studied the articles every day in the paper, I gradually became aware that the war in Korea was a part of a much bigger problem. Even if the war in Korea were resolved before I turned eighteen, there was no question the bigger problem, the growing Cold War, was burgeoning in numerous areas around the globe, even within our own country, and eventually war with the Soviet Union would break out, fought on an unimaginable scale. There was no way I could escape it.

It seemed to me we had made a huge mistake, that Truman had been wrong about General MacArthur. We should have taken the war to China and if the Soviet Union interfered, then we would fight them too. It just didn't make sense to bog down in a stalemate with one hand tied behind our backs, and all the while our country was being taken over from the inside by the communist conspiracy that Senator McCarthy was warning us about.

The Korean Conflict ended on July 27, 1953, after three years of desperate, bloody conflict, and two and one-half years of negotiations. The fighting ended, it's true, but there was no settlement, no agreement ending the conflict, only an agreed cease fire and the reinstatement of the boundary at the 38th Parallel, where it was marked at the end of World War II. The cease fire that came after thirty months of negotiations was a great relief to me, but I was frustrated because we had lost over 36,500 Americans killed in action, and more than half that number while negotiations at Panmunjom dragged on. I was unsettled, too, about the continuing threat by the Soviet Union and China to impose communist dominion over the entire world, either by force or by subversion. The threat loomed larger than ever, it seemed to me, as I surveyed the daily headline articles.

The Korean Conflict is today called America's "Forgotten War." We did what we had to do to halt communist aggression in Korea. Today, North Korea is probably the most repressive, backward country in the world, while South Korea is a great success story by almost any standard. Truman's strategy proved to be sound over the long term. It gave the time within which the economic systems of capitalism and communism might be tested and worked out. Almost a half century later, the Soviet Union's economic model imploded.

I now look back in wonder at the simplicity of my adolescent logic. Thank God Truman saw the bigger picture, understood that we should never embark on a full scale war on the Asian continent, and knew personally the horror of the Atom Bomb which such a war would no doubt have necessitated.

Thank God Truman pulled MacArthur back.

Thank God Senator Joseph McCarthy was finally censured after ruining so many lives.

Thank God our leaders followed a course that gave peace a chance, even as the Cold War continued to rage for half a century around the globe.

9 • Unknown Forces

When I was a child, my world consisted of my immediate neighborhood, bounded generally by Norwood School, Norwood Boulevard, Vanderbilt Road, and the railroad. Within that small area, I had all I needed: a few friends to play with, the Boulevard for open space to run, the forbidden railroad and creek for adventures, and the corner grocery store for a snack if I had a nickel. How soon I would find my small world had expanded in directions I could never have imagined.

My family moved when I was twelve across Norwood to Twenty-seventh Street, only a block from Carraway Methodist Hospital, which we called Norwood Hospital. By then, my brother, Eddie, and I had bikes and we began to explore our larger neighborhood and learned how isolated and insular Norwood really was, cut off from downtown Birmingham to the south, less than a mile away, by railroads and industries. To the east and north, it was bounded by heavy industry and railroads. To the west, our neighborhood merged into another residential neighborhood known as Druid Hills.

Norwood was also bisected by the L&N Railroad (now CSX), a double line located one block from our new home. The tracks lay between our home and Norwood School. Every morning, Eddie and I would take a shortcut across the double tracks on our way to school. We began to see a new sight from time to time that always made us pause to watch—sleek, modern diesel locomotives.

At Christmas, when I was twelve years old, I received a Brownie Hawkeye box camera. I would park myself beside the tracks, sometimes prone in the gravel for a dramatic, wheel-level shot. I'm now amazed at my lack of vision, as I waited for the diesel engines, my finger at the ready, as they slipped smoothly by, while completely ignoring the snorting, hissing, thundering steam locomotives that were, unbeknownst to me, rapidly becoming extinct.

Yes, vision, or rather, perhaps, caution and foresight, is something my brother and I could have used in those days. One morning, a train was chugging by as we waited beside the tracks to cross, anxious not to be late for school. There must have been a hundred cars. Just as the caboose passed us, we bolted across the rails, unaware another train was pounding our way on the opposite track. We screeched to a stop as it blasted by us. Had my brother and I been one second faster, we would have been directly in front of the speeding train.

A year later, my paper route opened new vistas to my imagination and examination, an ever-expanding world, and geography was only a part of it. Before my paper route, it was kids like me I noticed. Adults were merely adornments who hung about the fringes of my youthful domain. The chasm between children and adults was so great it was almost like we were of different breeds. Now, as I dealt more and more with adults, they became my focal point. Every Saturday, I knocked on their doors and collected my accounts. I soon found these men and women were as varied and different in the way they looked, the way they acted, and even in the way they treated me as the endless variety of patterns and colors of marbles I'd collected over the years, which I stored in a Roi Tan Cigar box that I slid under my bed to join my other "valuables."

For example, one such customer was Ms. Dennis. She lived in a big house on the corner of Twelfth Avenue and Thirtieth Street that had been divided into apartments. She was a tall young woman, handsome and professional. She wore tailored clothes and kept her dark brown hair in a tight, flawless French bun. Striding in high heels, a study in poise and grace, she could have been a queen. She was quickly courteous as I collected each week's account, as efficient and fatal as a mouse trap. No wasted motion. No wasted smile. I never saw her relax, not for a moment.

Years later, when I began working downtown, I saw her occasionally, chin in the air, marching regally between office buildings, a woman on a mission. I wondered then if she still lived in Norwood, on my old paper route. I wondered if she was completely bound up in business. I wondered if she were married, if she had kids. I wondered if she had ever loosened her bun, had ever let her hair fall down.

I'll never forget Mrs. Garber, who was the oldest person I'd ever seen.

"Collect for the *News*, please," I would say as she struggled to open the heavy wooden door that barricaded her within her old, run-down, two-story home.

"Oh, come in, come in," she would chirp, as I reluctantly entered a dark foyer redolent of liniment and mildew and camphor balls. She was a tiny woman, dressed in black. She would leave me standing there each week, holding my breath, as she retrieved her change purse. Mrs. Garber's world seemed so dark and ancient.

When she returned, ready for business, she locked her eyes on mine and they glided from left to right and back again, never losing their focus from mine, as her head rocked rhythmically from side to side like a metronome, as if set to music. Her arms and hands jerked uncontrollably as she cheerily asked me questions about the weather. Her fingers twitched. I watched in boyish horror and awe as she fished coins from her change purse. At last, she would extend the change to me one coin at a time and deposit each with trembling fingers onto my open palm. I mentioned her condition to my mother who said she probably had the palsy. Regardless of the diagnosis, each time I collected from Mrs. Garber, I was struck by the absolute certainty that if I were she I could surely have controlled my limbs. *Nothing!* Nothing in this world, not even the palsy, could make *me* shake like that. But I would soon learn on that very paper route that even young boys like me can be made to tremble by unknown forces.

Mrs. Ramer! Most of my customers were either old or young. There were almost no children on my first route. Mrs. Ramer was one of the young ones. She and her husband lived in a garage apartment behind a big, two-story house. I always knocked on her door with anticipation, because she was an attractive brunette, as buxom as some of the women I'd seen on TV and wondered about. My father had bought our first television about a year earlier and I was fascinated by the novelty of it, but particularly interested in the beautiful young women in strapless evening gowns who appeared on the screen. I wondered about a double question as I gazed at them: Did their breasts somehow hold up the dress—and if so, what then held up the breasts?

Sometimes Mrs. Ramer answered the door not completely dressed. For some reason I didn't then understand—I was not yet fourteen—my heart would race when I'd see her and I'd have conflicted feelings: a sense of attraction, of fascination—of mystery—and at the same time, abhorrence, an intimidation and fear that to feel such attraction was wrong, a sin, and must be repressed. The preacher had been quite explicit about the sins of the flesh and the eternal punishment that lay before those who strayed from the narrow paths.

Once, deep in the dog days of August, on a silver hot Saturday as the sun shimmered through the gray, industrial haze, I lurched to Mrs. Ramer's door. Though exhausted from the heat, I instantly perked to life. This was Mrs. Ramer I had come to see. Standing tall, I knocked, then waited, alert as a bird dog. She came to the door wearing only a bra and a long, flowing skirt. She pushed open the screen door, and her breasts undulated right before my eyes. Her shoulders glistened in the heat. Perspiration slipped from her oily throat and slowly slid between her breasts. I was a shy kid, and it was natural for me to look down instead of directly into one's face. And as I looked down, I found myself gazing, for as long as I could stand the heat, at two partially covered nipples. *Ahgh*—my breath caught in my throat. Blood pulsated in my ears. I plunged into a ringing silence. Those half-moons, as dark as ripened figs and dimpled like strawberries, peeped over her bra at me. My face flushed so red it glowed. I glanced up at Mrs. Ramer and she smiled, amused, I feared, at the color my own face had suddenly turned. She opened her change purse, found the correct change and extended her hand. Through a kind of blur, I fought to keep my mind on my job. As I reached to take the coins from her open hand my eyes rocketed back and forth from nipple to palm. I clumsily collected the coins, as my fingers quivered against the damp flesh of her palm. When at last I thanked Mrs. Ramer, my voice was trembling as well. As I turned to leave, I suddenly remembered Mrs.

Garber, how her fingers had skittered across my own palm and my certitude that *nothing* could ever make me shake like that. Embarrassed, I picked my way on rubbery legs to my next customer wondering what had happened to me.

An hour or so later, after I had completed my collections but before I returned to the *News* branch to pay Mr. Hawley, I stopped at the Norwood Pharmacy and ordered a limeade. As I sat at the counter sipping the icy drink, I examined my fingers carefully, as if I'd find some clue to what had befallen me back at Mrs. Ramer's door. They looked the same as before, not like Mrs. Garber's frail fingers. Though they were not now visibly trembling, I was surprised that somehow my fingers felt as weak as if I had climbed a thirty-foot rope without using my feet.

10 • Motorcycle Dreams

One day at the paper branch, after Mr. Hawley counted out my papers, but just before he pushed the stack across the table to me, he gave me a long, hard stare that woke me up. *Had I done something wrong?* Then he said in a low, conspiratorial voice, as if he didn't want anyone else to hear, "Sonny, you've done a pretty good job with your route, a bunch of new starts. I got a bigger route coming open in a week or so. About a hundred papers. Think you could handle that?"

"Yes, sir, I think so." I paused, then asked, "Where is it, the route?"

"Don't matter where it is. You either want it or you don't. I gotta new kid ready to take your route if you want the bigger one. Whatta ya say? Need to talk to your parents about this?"

My wheels were turning. A lot of the older boys had motorcycles to deliver their papers. I loved the idea of making more money and eventually buying a motorcycle. But I was not yet fourteen and couldn't imagine I'd be able to buy one any time soon. *Could I handle a hundred papers on my bike? And what if the new route was in a really rough area? I might have trouble collecting my accounts.* I wondered why Mr. Hawley wouldn't tell me where it was. It was only later I understood he didn't want the word to get out that a particular route was coming open—he didn't want to deal with a dozen supplicants for the position. I don't know where I got the nerve to overlook my concerns, but I heard myself say, "Uh, yes, sir, I think I can."

"You sure?" He was looking at me hard, like he wanted me to be sure I'd made the right decision, his arms cocked behind the tall stack of newspapers he leaned against, ready to push them across the table to me.

"Yes, sir."

He pushed, and I was the owner of a stack of newspapers half as high as I was myself.

I staggered away to an empty spot on a table nearby, deposited my papers and began the rolling process, thrilled at the prospect of a larger route, more money, and getting an odd rush of adrenalin from the unknown dangers I'd encounter on my new route. I wasn't sure what I was getting into, but I trusted Mr. Hawley. I had from the first day I spoke with him. He was impatient and not very pleasant sometimes. But he was always fair with me and even seemed to favor me over the older boys, maybe because some of them were disrespectful to him. They would talk about him behind his back, spreading rumors about his drinking, complained about alcohol on his breath, laughed at him for sleeping at his desk while waiting for us to roll our papers and leave.

From that day forward, whether I was in school or delivering my papers, I day-dreamed about the opportunities for more income and responsibility and the problems I'd face if I got the unidentified paper route. I thought about how much more work there would be in delivering one hundred newspapers, a much larger responsibility than the route of seventy I now serviced.

Part of the difficulty I faced was the variety of housing. Norwood was made up primarily of single-family houses set back from the sidewalk leaving a front yard of twenty to thirty feet or more. It was an old neighborhood and many of the houses dated back to 1900. All the houses were different in size and shape. Some were cottages, and some were large two-story homes. Some had spacious front porches, and some had only stoops. Some houses were level with the sidewalk, while some were elevated.

In most cases, I could pedal along the sidewalk and toss the papers onto porches. But in other areas, in order to put the papers on the porches it was necessary to park my bike and run from house to house. A bicycle has a kickstand to support it when it is parked. But if the basket is loaded with fifty pounds of newspapers, the kickstand will not support it. So,

I had to find a tree or something solid against which I could lean my loaded bike. Sometimes, that was not convenient.

On rainy days, when the rain blew across porches, I tucked the paper behind the screen door or found some other place safe from the rain. The canvas bags I bought from the *News* had a flap that gave some protection for my newspapers against the rain, but when the bag was fully packed it never quite covered them. For my part, I wore a poncho in wet weather, using the front of the poncho to cover myself and the papers. It was hard when covered by a poncho to pedal a bicycle loaded with papers and to get on and off it a hundred times. I wanted the larger route Mr. Hawley mentioned to me. I felt I was ready for the larger responsibilities. If Mr. Hawley gave it to me, wherever it was, I knew I could handle it better with a motorcycle like so many of the older boys rode.

I discussed my new opportunity with my parents, though I had already given Mr. Hawley my word. Actually, I was laying the foundation with them to get permission to buy a motorcycle. I carefully explained how much I wanted the larger route and how hard it was delivering papers from a bike and how all the older paperboys had motorcycles. My mother fretted that they were dangerous and she didn't want me to have one, but my father listened carefully and said he'd think about it. While my parents didn't tell me I could buy a motorcycle, I was surprised they didn't say no.

A couple of weeks later Mr. Hawley told me the route was mine. All of my tricks of the trade I would take with me to my new route, which I learned was on the eastern fringe of Norwood, on the backside of Norwood School, in an area referred to as the Bottoms. Unlike my previous route in an older section of Norwood, the houses on this new route were mostly small cottages. There was also a garden apartment project that posed an interesting contrast in benefits and burdens. On the one hand, how quickly I could throw my papers to the apartments. But on the other, the customers there were renters and would often move, leaving me unpaid.

There was one part of my new route that I hated, a long loop road behind Norwood School around by Village Creek. The road was at least a quarter mile long and unpaved. There were no street lights. It appeared to have been carved out of the wilderness. There were only a few houses on the dangerous looking road, and they were the kind you'd see out in the country—unpainted wooden shacks. I heard someone say the people who lived back there were outlaws.

Once when delivering my papers, some men had strung up a hog from the limb of a tree in the front yard and were butchering it in plain view of the road. I couldn't get that off my mind for months. Riding a bike on the dirt road loop with all the washed out gullies and potholes was difficult, particularly with a basket of newspapers. But it was not the hard work I dreaded. It was Sunday mornings when I'd arise at four A.M. to get my newspapers, knowing I had to pedal through that wilderness in the dark. How much more quickly I could do it on a motorcycle, I thought.

With a motorcycle, I could run around that loop so quickly I wouldn't have time to be frightened. Though at that time I had never ridden a motorcycle, I imagined it would be the answer to virtually every problem I had on my new, bigger route. With a motorcycle, I could zip from the branch office with a load, deposit it in a safe place and zip back for another. And there would be little need to park. With a motorcycle, I could leave the sidewalk and ride across front yards close to the porches in order to toss the paper from the best position.

My parents were not very sympathetic. My father didn't want to spend the money and my mother had safety concerns. But I mentioned on several occasions that I had saved almost all I had earned since I'd been delivering papers and I had over one hundred dollars. I could buy my own motorcycle, if they would permit me to do so.

I'm not certain what changed their minds, but it might have been when my mother drove me along that loop road. It was wintertime, a Sunday morning, and I had a terrible cold. It was four A.M., the wind was blowing and rain was pounding against the house. My father was out of town. My mother carried me in the car to deliver my papers. I had to dash from the car to carefully place each paper behind the screen door or in some other dry spot. She was horrified when I directed her down the dark loop road, and I still remember repeatedly jumping from the car into the cold, muddy water streaming ankle-deep down the gulley of that dirt road.

I think that did it, because soon after riding with my mother, my father told me his friend, Joe Morgan, another bus driver, had a son who wanted to sell his motorcycle. We made arrangements to see it, and traveled out to the eastern side of town and met Mr. Morgan and his son. The boy was several years older than I and had recently bought an old car and didn't need the motorcycle any longer. It was a red Harley-Davidson Model 125, powered by a small one cylinder 125cc engine that generated about three horsepower. The Harley was several years old, probably a '51 Model, though now I have forgotten that detail, and, as I recall, they wanted one hundred dollars. I quickly agreed to pay. In fact, I had the money with me. I was very excited. Until that day, I had dealt mostly in nickels and dimes. This was for me the first major transaction of my life. We made the trade and I mounted a motorcycle for the first time. I trailed my father home, overjoyed to be riding a motorcycle that would easily make fifty miles an hour.

When we reached home, my brother, Eddie, was almost as excited as I, it seemed. He was not yet twelve and was begging to ride. My father consented, so I turned it over to him after showing him how the brakes, clutch and gears worked. There were two brake levers; one to press with the right foot and one to grip on the right handlebar. The clutch was a lever on the left handlebar, while the three-speed transmission was shifted with the left foot. To accelerate, you twisted inboard the right handlebar grip. It was easy to learn to ride.

Eddie traveled two blocks, and as he circled in the street to return home, a policeman flagged him over and gave him a ticket for driving a vehicle without a license plate. I had driven across town with no tag. You can imagine how deflated Eddie was.

I found after only a few weeks I had been right—delivering papers by motorcycle was much easier than from a bicycle. But soon it was the dead of winter and I quickly learned how cold it could be traveling on a motorcycle in winter. Before, I had kept reasonably warm pedaling my bike and running between houses. Riding a motorcycle required no exercise. The engine did the work. And it moved much faster. I would come home frozen to the bone, unable to flex my fingers. After parking my Harley in the garage, I would dismount and trudge spraddle-legged toward the back door, my hands half-closed as if still gripping the handlebar. The tingling, excruciating pain in my fingers and my feet lasted for fifteen minutes or so as they thawed.

Riding a motorcycle in the winter, even with gloves, is a tough business. James Arrowood, a friend of mine, delivered his papers from a Whizzer, a bicycle with a motor mounted on the frame, driven by a belt that turned the back wheel. One afternoon, James had completed his route and was headed home. It was already dark and very cold. He reached down to adjust his carburetor and his fingers were snagged momentarily in the drive belt. James told me his hands were so frozen he hardly felt the pain. He had no idea until he reached home and removed his gloves that the last digit of two fingers was missing. His mother found them in his glove.

11 • So Lonesome I Could Cry

Late on New Year's Day 1953, I heard the news. Hank Williams had died! The great Hank Williams! *Could it be true?* I could hardly wait until the next day to get my afternoon *Birmingham News* and learn what happened. I raced to the paper branch early to pick up my papers. I sat impatiently inside on a table instead of joining in the horseplay outside on the sidewalk. I was expecting a big headline. After all, Hank Williams was an Alabama music idol and the greatest country singer/songwriter in history.[2]

My family rarely listened to music, but if the radio was on, it was tuned to a local hillbilly station. We were essentially country people trying to find our way in an urban neighborhood, and it was the country music of Hank Williams that appealed to my family, particularly his plaintive cries of frustrated love. He sang of loneliness, of not being good enough, of alienation. And I ate it up.

The truck finally arrived. I helped carry the heavy bundles inside, was the first to get my stack, and moved to a table against the wall to roll them.

But the headline was about some political junk, not Hank. Where was the story about Hank? Rolling my papers had to wait while I searched. Maybe it wasn't really true.

"What're you digging for?" one of the older paperboys inquired. "You're like a rat digging through those papers?"

"I'm looking for the article about Hank Williams. He died yesterday. You heard about it, didn't you?"

"Nah, but I don't like that old hillbilly music anyway. Don't care if he did."

Mr. Hawley spoke up. "Yeah, I heard about it too, Sonny. If you find it, show it to me. I've been looking for it too."

Mr. Hawley didn't say much more about it. The rumor was, of course, that Hank Williams was a drunk and a dope addict, and I guess Mr. Hawley didn't want to call attention to what the article might say about Hank's drinking, since he himself fought such talk. But not from me.

I finally found the story on the inside of the paper, on page nineteen, way back in the second section.

"Oh, here it is, Mr. Hawley."

He read it quietly, then handed it back to me.

I learned Hank Williams had died while sleeping in the back seat of his Cadillac somewhere in West Virginia as his driver chauffeured him to his next appearance. The article said something about an autopsy to be performed, not much more information than that.

I stood there before my stack of unrolled newspapers. I could hardly believe that Hank had died in the middle of his brilliant career. I wondered about his religious life and whether he was ready, spiritually, to face the unknown. Then I remembered one of his songs, one of my favorites, that we often heard on the radio. I could almost hear Hank's bleak country voice as he sang,

I saw the li—igh—ight.
I saw the li—igh—ight.
No more darkness,
No more ni—ight.
Now I'm so happy, no sorrow in si—ight.
Praise the Lor—ord,
I saw the light.

I was relieved to remember that uplifting song he had written, but even more relieved that I had selected a table against the wall to roll my papers. Even if he caused his own death by alcohol and drugs . . . even if he was ready for eternity . . . still he was only twenty-nine.

I was thirteen, and I wanted to cry.

12 • My Last Halloween

I **knew when I headed out I was too old** for that kind of stuff. Trick or treating was for children, not a big, strapping fourteen year old boy like me. But I didn't know what else to do on a Halloween evening.

With a dime paper mask on my face I'd bought at the drug store, I visited a few houses and gathered some candy. And then—the unexpected!

I knocked on a door and when the old man opened it, I said, "Trick or treat, please," very politely. He must have been seventy years old, tall and gaunt, and his face said it all. I didn't move as he drew himself erect and sucked in a breath, his eyes growing larger and his eyebrows arching. Then his jaw muscles tightened and his lips turned down into a scowl. I could see there would be no treat from this house. Before I could turn away, the crusty old man blasted me.

"You way too old for this, you big sonuvabitch! Get outta here!" And he slammed the door in my face. I say "my face," but the truth is I was hauling away from there well before the door banged shut.

I tossed my paper mask in a trash can and slunk down the street with my tail between my legs. Trick or treat, I pondered distastefully. Beforehand, Halloween was about treats. I'd never given any thought to the trick part, but it was now pretty clear I wouldn't be getting any more "treats" tonight—or ever again.

I ran into Buddy and we decided to see if there might be a trick out there somewhere we might get into. We were walking up the hill on Fifteenth Avenue when I noticed the street light was out at Twenty-ninth Street. The road was pitch dark from Thirtieth Street down the long hill all the way to Twenty-eighth. We dragged two full metal garbage cans into the middle of the dark street at Twenty-ninth, and we waited by the side of the road to see what would happen. In a few minutes a car came careening down that long, dark hill, screeched and then—Bam!—knocked the cans and all the garbage for a hundred feet down the hill. It was better than we could've hoped for. We looked at each other with expressions somewhere between elation and alarm. Then we raced away as fast as we could go.

A few minutes later, after we had recovered our breaths and our courage, we found ourselves on Sixteenth Avenue near Norwood School. That's where I had another bright idea. This is the way I told it at the paper branch the next afternoon.

"It was really dark last night. It was about ten o'clock and Buddy and I were across the Boulevard from the School. I had to take a leak, big time. I could have done it anywhere, of course. I mean it was dark! But I was looking for just the right place. I didn't know what the trick would be but I was looking for some opportunity and I'd been holding it back for just the right moment. And then it hit me. 'Hey! Watch this.' I jogged over to the car, unscrewed the gas cap, and began to pee right into the gas tank.

"Man, I was feeling good—the relief of just letting it go—that, and knowing I was pulling the greatest trick of the evening, both at the same time. Buddy was behind me laughing, waiting his turn.

Everyone at the paper branch was by this time smiling and laughing, and that acceptance fueled my enthusiasm. I continued with abandon.

"You know how it is when you're just getting started with a good pee—the instant relief you feel? It's hard to stop, right? Well, I'd just got it going when—you won't believe this—the lights in the car popped on and the car door exploded out. And then the biggest guy I'd ever seen sprang outta that car, fast, coming right at me. In that split instant, I saw his girlfriend, her blouse was off and her arms were crossed like this"—and, here, I crossed my arms across my chest, fingers splayed—"a look of horror on her face. And on mine too, I guess."

Now, I had their full attention and they were guffawing.

" 'What the hell . . . !' this big old boy yelled at me. Then, he lunged at me and I whirled and sprinted for my life. He was right behind me, my pecker hanging out, flapping and slapping with every flying step, like a baseball card stuck in the spokes. Man, it hurt like hell! And I couldn't stop peeing. I was pissing all over myself when I sprinted across the Boulevard toward school, fast as I could go . . . Scared the crap outta me."

They were all howling with laughter. One of the boys, snorting, managed to ask, "Did he catch you?"

"No, but he should have. Could you imagine running like that, with your pecker hanging out and peeing all over yourself? My jeans were soaked. I finally stopped about three blocks away, behind the school—caught my breath and tried to finish what I'd started. But I found I'd already finished. I don't know when the big guy turned back, but if he'd caught me, I wouldn't be standing here talking to you right now."

There was another round of laughter. Then we all turned back to rolling our papers.

It was fun while it lasted, being the center of attention as I told the story. And it was thrilling to do something wrong for a change. I knew I never would have done those tricks if the old man hadn't upset me so badly. I felt like I had to do something. Now that it was over and done and I hadn't gotten into trouble, I knew that would probably be the last time I'd ever play a trick on someone, particularly since I'd almost been caught by that big guy. That was high risk. He would've beaten me to a pulp if he'd caught me. I had no doubt that this was my last Halloween, and that was sad. But it did turn out positive in one respect. I had unexpectedly learned something in the process.

There are a great many old-fashioned words and phrases in the King James Version we studied at church that made the text seem obscure and hard to understand. One of those many phrases that had mystified me for some time had now been clarified by this trick that turned so bad on me. After that chase across the Boulevard, it had dawned on me what the scripture must have meant as it instructed the Israelites to "gird up their loins" as they prepared for battle. I hadn't understood before what the words meant or the reason why; but, yes, that term had now become quite clear to me.

13 • The Benchmark Date

May 17, 1954, is a date branded into my memory. That's the day when I thought it would all unravel.

I was barely fifteen at the time, and had carried newspapers for well over two years. Those papers carried news that I earnestly read. Mostly, I focused on disturbing articles about the Cold War, which continued to rage around the globe. But I also read about racial problems in the South that seemed to loom larger with every passing week. It's funny now how seriously I took it all back then. Or sad.

It was after that date that the radical remarks adults made about colored people found their mark with me. I was particularly struck by the things my father said. As a Greyhound bus driver, my father had a difficult job after May 17, 1954, enforcing separate seating by race, as the state law required. That date marked the beginning of a constant wave of pressure brought by colored people on our white institutions and our Southern way of life, particularly in transportation. But the states in the Deep South were determined to maintain and enforce our Jim Crow[3] laws requiring separate seating on buses, and it mattered little what interstate travelers from other sections of the country thought.

The Birmingham school system was segregated by race in those days. There were five white high schools in Birmingham: Phillips, where I attended, West End, Ensley, Ramsey, and Woodlawn—the Big Five. The colored schools were little known to us. Whether they had five or two high schools, I didn't know. The sports section of the newspapers carried long articles about the Big Five, but I rarely saw any information about the colored schools.

My neighborhood was segregated by race as well. There were only a few colored people in Norwood, and they lived in servants' houses. But there were many who lived on the margins of the neighborhood adjacent to the railroads and industries.

Except for the frustrations my father brought home from his work and articles I read in the paper, I had been largely unaffected by Birmingham's burgeoning racial issues. I lived in a segregated world. I had no contact with any colored people. All the adults I had contact with were staunch segregationists and most weren't timid about expressing their views.

What a shock I had when I picked up my afternoon newspapers on Monday, May 17, 1954. That headline blared—

COURT RULES OUT SEGREGATION IN SCHOOLS

And the article's lead reported:

> The Supreme Court today declared unanimously that race segregation in the public schools is unconstitutional, and eventually must end.

As I read on, I suddenly went cold. I actually stopped reading and made a mental note of the date. May 17, 1954. That would become a benchmark date in my life. And for others in the South, as that date became known as "Black Monday."

That was the day I realized the "Negro problem" would no longer be confined to a supper table rant. Until that date, the problem touched my life only as it impacted my father and his work. But now, the United States Supreme Court had done the unthinkable, and, in *Brown v. Board of Education*,[4] had declared unconstitutional separate-but-equal schools! I was in my freshman year at Phillips High School. I had three years left to go. I wasn't worried about myself. I'd get through this uncharted territory some way. I was worried about my little sister, Dale, who was in the second grade. *What will she do? How will this affect her?*

Frantically, I searched the paper for the rest of the article.

"Hey, dipshit! Whatcha looking for? You buildin' a nest?" one of the older guys hollered, pointing me out to the others. They all laughed.

"I'm looking for the rest of this article about the Supreme Court, that's what! And if you were so smart, you'd be looking too. 'Cause it's gonna change everything."

"Whatta you talking about?"

"You didn't read the headline? Listen to this." And I began reading the article. That got their attention. All the laughter stopped. Then came the defiance.

"They ain't makin' me go to school with no niggers!"

"They don't know who they're dealin' with. They come down here with their court order, we'll stuff it down their throats!"

"We ain't gonna take that shit!"

We all turned back to rolling our papers, but the frivolity and horse-play had disappeared, just like that. We rolled and stacked our papers and seethed with rage, then silently hoisted our loads, and even as we turned our attention to our paper routes, I knew we all wondered if and when the next shoe would fall, the unthinkable would actually occur and our world would cease to exist as we knew it.

I worried for months about where it was all headed. Things looked pretty bleak. While the war in Korea had been resolved a year earlier with a cease fire arrangement that seemed to be holding, other dangerous aspects of the Cold War continued unabated with no end in sight. At fifteen, I was only three years from all that fearful word "induction" would mean. The draft was a certainty facing all young men in America. I knew some were eager and some were reluctant. I was in the latter camp.

Bombings by the Ku Klux Klan were so common in Birmingham in those years the city was jokingly referred to as "Bombingham." That's the reason, I suppose, one day shortly after that benchmark date—May 17—I drew the cartoon in one of my classes that expressed my contempt at that time for the Court and its opinion. I can still call up that cartoon, all these years later, by closing my eyes. It was a birds-eye view of the United States Supreme Court building, huge columns in front. Nine justices flee out the back door, black robes billowing, arms thrown in the air in panic, just as the building explodes out the top.

That was my reaction to the Court's decision.

A few months later, my father took me and my brother to the Temple Theatre where we saw *Birth of a Nation*, the D. W. Griffith classic film from 1915. That story burned into my memory the horrors of the War between the States and Sherman's Campaign against civilians in his infamous March to the Sea. The film depicted the subsequent Reconstruction, when carpetbaggers and freed slaves controlled a devastated and humiliated South. The image of the hulking shadow of a huge Negro man chasing the young white woman through the woods to the cliff lived in my heart for years afterward. And, finally, the story told of the emergence of the Ku Klux Klan as it fought against the injustices of Reconstruction. The War and Reconstruction occurred less than a hundred years before and were well remembered in the South. For months I simmered over the movie and the story of my own family's history with Sherman's army.

14 • A Man of Two Minds

My earliest memories of my father were joyful. He was a lean, handsome man in his Greyhound uniform. His large, honest blue eyes were set in a round face, his cap perched jauntily on his head. Of my parents, he was the talker.

He always had a story to tell about what had happened on his latest trip. He traveled all directions out of Birmingham—to Atlanta, Chattanooga, Nashville, Tuscaloosa, Mobile, Dothan—with loads of interesting passengers. My mother was a listener, and that suited him to a T.

For all the years I lived at home, he worked the "Extra Board" for Greyhound Bus Lines. That meant his name was posted on the board in sequential order with that of other drivers who waited for their names to turn up, at which time they would receive a call to drive when a regular driver was ill or too many passengers had shown up for a particular route and a second bus was needed. He might sit at home all day ready for the call and then, when the call came, he would dash to the station to drive a bus for fifty miles or 250 miles in a direction he would then learn. He never knew when the call would come or if he would get a return trip for pay or whether he would have to "dead head" home as a passenger on another bus. Sometimes he would sleep over to become "fresh" in order to drive a bus back to Birmingham. Even after he had the seniority to rate a steady route, he remained on the Extra Board because it had the possibility of paying more money than some of the regular shorter routes. The best paying routes went to the drivers with the most seniority. Sometimes he would get a good route with regular hours, but invariably some driver with more seniority would "bump" him and he'd go back on the Extra Board.

I never thought much about the uncertainty of his work. That's the way it had always been. He never complained. He loved his job, and I'm certain he was normally an emissary of goodwill for his company.

Occasionally, though, when I was young, he would come home from a trip and tell us about some unpleasant event that had occurred. Usually it involved some colored person who got uppity and didn't want to go to the back of the bus as the law prescribed. That was a rare occurrence for a bus departing from Birmingham—everybody here understood the law and the custom and the implications that might arise from one's failure to comply.

As the driver of his bus, he was the captain of his ship, and as such, it was his job to maintain order and transport his passengers safely and courteously to their destination. He was the sole representative of law and order on his bus. He would occasionally have some incident that required an unpleasant exchange, such as someone who insisted on drinking whiskey on the bus or who otherwise became rowdy or unpleasant.

As the early fifties wore on, he could count on trouble out of Tennessee. Colored passengers would come into the Nashville or Chattanooga Bus Station from Northern or Eastern States where the seating was open. When my father assumed responsibility to bring the bus to Birmingham, it fell to him to post the sign for "Whites" and "Colored" at the appropriate location in the bus and, unfortunately, to inform the colored passengers to relocate their seating to the rear of the bus in accordance with Alabama law. Usually, upon request, they would rearrange their seating. They were aware of the law and they swallowed their pride and complied. But there were instances with increasing regularity when some colored passenger took umbrage at the suggestion. Some of them took great offense, and thereupon a struggle ensued between my father and those troublemakers, the people who deigned to sit where they pleased. During the mid-fifties, his job became almost intolerable as more and more colored people pushed the envelope, which required my father to exercise his faculties of reason and patience, then ultimately force to relocate people against their will. Sometimes he could call the police and have his own customers removed from the bus.

I remember on one occasion I came in from delivering my afternoon papers. Mother was putting our supper on the table. My dad was in the kitchen with her, moving from place to place as she worked around him. I could tell from the color of his face he wasn't happy. He had a fair complexion, but that day his face was flushed and ruddy.

"Hey, Dad. I didn't know you'd be home tonight."

"Yeah, just got in from Nashville. Glad to be home."

I washed up, and a few minutes later we all sat down to supper. My dad said the blessing as he always did when he was home.

He asked about our school days.

Then he began. "Well, I had another problem today. Another problem with another nigger." He shook his head. "I just don't understand it. It's not that complicated. They know the law when they come into the South. I can always count on a problem in Nashville."

We all looked at him. He could talk and eat at the same time when he was telling a story, but now he had stopped eating. That meant he was pretty upset.

"It didn't use to be this way, back before that Supreme Court decision. I would post the—

Colored Only

—board and they would sit behind it, just like the law says. Like they're supposed to. But it's not that way anymore. I post the board and most will go on back. But one or two wanna test it—wanna sit wherever they like. What's wrong with 'em?"

No one responded. Finally, my mother said, "What happened, Honey?"

"Well, this young buck was seated down near the front. I tried to be friendly. I smile and say, 'Hey, fellow, you're in the wrong seat. Better move on back.'"

He paused. You could see his big blue eyes begin to sparkle with anger.

"Then he said, 'This *is* my seat.'"

"So I said, still trying to be friendly, but seems like the good humor I had might have slipped away some. So I say, 'Look, son, this seat's reserved for whites. Colored in the rear. It's the law. You know that.'

"He looked me over and then he says real cool like, 'I been sitting in this seat since Cincinnati. I paid the same for my ticket as the whites. I'm not moving.'

"So I could see he meant business. But I couldn't let that go. I'm the captain of my ship. I'm the one in charge. And the law says he goes to the back. I can't just let it go. Now some drivers, they don't have the guts to get tough, but I knew what I had to do.

"So I say to him, 'Look here, boy, I'm not leaving the station with you sitting here. The law's the law. I'm in charge on this bus, and you're going to move whether you like it or not. You know what's going to happen next, don't you?'

"He sat quietly while I waited. He was staring at the back of the seat in front of him, and I could see his jaw muscles working like he was chewing on a piece of rawhide. Mine was working pretty hard, too. Looked like he was about to explode. What he didn't know was, I was about to explode too.

"Well, what's it gonna be?" I said.

"And he says, 'Look, Driver, I'm a Korean War veteran. I've fought for my country. I'm as good as anybody.'

"Well, I've gotta respect any man who fought in the war, but I've gotta follow the law, too. So I says to him, 'I'm sorry, but the law says you sit in the back. Either you move on back or when we get to the Alabama line, I'll stop the bus in the first town and call the cops. I don't believe you wanna go to jail in north Alabama.'"

My dad stopped eating and reflected for a moment. I was riveted on the story and had stopped eating as well.

"What happened next?" I asked.

"Well, he sat there for a full minute, looking off into the distance, like he might explode. Nothing moved but his jaw muscles. He looked like he could chew nails. I was all tensed up too, ready for a fight if he came at me. But then he just took a deep breath, got outta the seat, got his jacket from the rack and moved on to the back. Didn't have any more trouble outta him—but it sure did upset me. It was a good fifty miles until I could get calmed down."

He continued eating but his eyes were unfocused, staring at nothing.

We were all pretty quiet the balance of the meal. When we finished, Mother poured coffee and there was a long pause while he sipped. I was getting edgy. I could tell he was winding up for a long harangue and I wanted a way out. I said I had homework to do and excused myself from the table.

I thought about how strange it was my dad could be so tough sometimes, particularly when it came to colored people, and be such a softy at other times.

I think he was hard in those years because colored people were alien to him. Alabama is and has always been about one-third African American. But much of the hill country of Alabama is virtually all white, while many counties in South Alabama have overwhelming black majorities.

My father had no basis (other than fear of the unknown) for distrusting or disliking colored people. He grew up in a part of Alabama, the Northwest Alabama hill country, where there were no Negroes. My father told me many times that he was sixteen years old before he ever saw a Negro face to face, and that was in Russellville, the county seat, miles from his home town. Before that, he had seen colored people only from a distance as they looked out the windows of the Illinois Central trains as they sped by.

My father's background was not unique for white workers who flocked to Birmingham from the hill country of Alabama, but the history of Birmingham is unique in the South. It was established after the Civil War by industrialists who attracted black workers from the delta and plantation country of South Alabama and white workers from the Appalachian foothills of north Alabama.

George R. Leighton mentioned that history in an article published in Harper's Magazine in August 1937, seventy-five years ago, which he entitled, "Birmingham, Alabama: The City of Perpetual Promise." He began his article with this sentence:

> In a mountain wilderness, laid in a region devastated by the war and inhabited by bankrupts, a group of speculators and industrialists in 1871 founded a

city and *peopled it with two races afraid of each other*
(emphasis added). This town, without parallel anywhere, was Birmingham, Alabama.

Thousands of Alabama hill people flocked to Birmingham to work
in the steel mills, coal mines and other related industries, bringing with
them suspicion and fear of the blacks, a competing source of labor in the
growing city. The Jim Crow laws required complete segregation of the
races which insured that whites could never learn their own commonalities with blacks nor consider the possibility of combining their forces
against the power of the industrial barons.

My father, with two children, moved his family to Birmingham in the
early forties. Like thousands of other hill men, he came to Birmingham
to work in the mines or the mills. Luckily, he had driven a school bus for
a short time and that skill launched him into a career as a commercial
driver, first as a truck driver for Republic Steel, then a gasoline tanker, and
finally a long career at Greyhound Bus Lines.

As a driver for Greyhound, he may have been the face of white racism
as he enforced the Jim Crow laws on his bus. But he was not a hard man,
in spite of his attitude about race. If his mother, Frankie, were mentioned,
his big, blue eyes would mist over with tears. She died at the age of eighteen when he was two years old and he never reconciled to that loss as he
grew up without a mother. He was as sentimental and soft-hearted as he
was tough.

I remembered a story I'd heard him tell several times.

My parents married young. My father was older, at twenty-four, and
had experienced a lot of life. As the oldest child, he had been held out
of school a great deal of the time to help with the duties on the family
farm, and he also helped his father with a number of other odd jobs. He
never had the opportunity to finish high school. He had traveled around
the country by railroad freight car without any money during the Great
Depression, scrounging jobs from place to place, and he had worked tem-
porarily in Birmingham, but each time had returned to the farm.

My mother was only seventeen when he talked her into marriage. Perhaps she would not have succumbed to his charm, but her father had

died the year before, in 1936, at the depth of the Depression. Her older brother, Charlie, was in the CCC, the Civilian Conservation Corps. It had been created during the Depression to provide jobs for young men. My mother was next in line by age. Though I never heard any speculation about the matter, my grandmother did have five children to feed at that time and marrying one off might have been a blessing.

At any rate, they set up housekeeping in a shack on some land my father rented in a share-cropping arrangement. He had no money. I don't know what kind of furniture and other possessions they had at the time, but someone had given them as a wedding gift a few chickens and a rooster, something from which to begin their flock.

As my dad would tell the story, he would chuckle and a wistful look would come into his eyes. He said my mother had not been taught to cook by her mother, who was always too busy trying to get the job done to teach a daughter how to do it. My mother, shy and withdrawn, would not have thrust herself into the kitchen, demanding to learn. She must have been, at seventeen, a beauty. She was tall and thin with long black hair, an olive complexion, flashing green eyes and a thin, straight nose. She looked like English aristocracy. Learning to cook was probably the last thing on her agenda.

But then, with her father dead, and surprised to be married so soon, she found it necessary to learn.

My dad would chuckle as he told of some of the early experiments. He couldn't cook either, so they probably had some rough times. But my father was smitten with her beauty, I suppose, and cooking was not that important at the time.

They had been married a few months and had invited another couple to their home to dinner. This is the way my father would tell the story to us over the years.

*   *   *

"Honey," I said, "James and Maylene will be here in a few hours. Guess it's time you went outside and got us a chicken for supper."

Your mama looked at me in horror.

"Me?" she said. "I'm not going to kill a chicken. I've never killed a chicken. I'll do my best to cook it, but you gotta kill it!'

I looked at her like she was nuts. All the chicken killing in my family had been done by women. I'd never killed a chicken and didn't intend to now. I told her, I said, "Baby, I've never killed a chicken either. That's woman's work. You know that! Now get out there and do it!"

She looked at me with those killer green eyes, and she stomped her foot, and then she said, "I told you, I'm not doing it. If you wanna serve chicken for supper, then you get out there and do it yourself!"

Well, we were having company, and we couldn't just serve them what we'd been eating—blackeyed peas and turnip greens—so, I was pretty hot with her, but I went on out back and got my hatchet. Now, you gotta understand, we'd had these chickens for months and they were all kinda like yard dogs to me. I knew each one and its personality. Why, some of 'em I felt so close to I'd given 'em names. So I ran around and grabbed one and I'm thinkin' to myself this is just terrible. I can't do this, but how embarrassed will I be if we don't have chicken for supper. So I gritted my teeth and took the hen over to a stump, went down on my knees and held its neck on the stump. She was flopping around trying to get loose and craning her neck ever' which way. I swear, the way she looked at me, I could almost hear her asking, How can you do this to me? I trusted you.

I hesitated long moments as she craned her neck and looked me in the eyes. It was a hard thing to do. But I finally did it. I can tell you for a fact it was the first and last chicken I ever killed. Your mama cleaned it and cooked it, and, so far as I know, our company enjoyed it. But I know this! It was all I could do to choke down one bite.

And that's one more big reason we don't live in the country anymore.

*   *   *

My mother would listen to his story, smiling and clear-eyed. Each time after telling the story, my father would try to chuckle, but he would turn his head away in embarrassment, his round, blue eyes floating in tears.

15 • The Challenge and the Challenged

The months flew by and Mr. Hawley gave me a larger route of more than one hundred subscribers. In late 1954, he told me a morning *Post-Herald* route was open and asked me whether I'd like to take that job in addition to my afternoon delivery route. I said yes again, and opened myself to a myriad of new learning experiences.

Birmingham enjoyed two daily newspapers—the morning *Post-Herald* and the afternoon *News*. These newspapers were owned by different companies, but shared the same facilities—the same offices, printing presses and distribution services. Mr. Hawley was in charge of the Norwood branch for both papers.

The afternoon routes were small in number of customers and compact in service area. Most residents subscribed to the *News*. An average route would probably have been about one hundred customers, comprising five or six blocks. I learned that the *Post-Herald* routes were much larger in geographic area, because fewer people subscribed to the morning paper. I viewed that as an opportunity, but found to my chagrin that most people could afford only one newspaper.

There were roughly two hundred customers on my *Post-Herald* route, which covered all of Norwood west of the railroad, including most of the commercial district of Norwood. Physically, it was roughly ten blocks long and four blocks wide. Delivery from a bicycle would have been a time-consuming job. Luckily, I had a motorcycle.

By the time I got my morning route, my afternoon deliveries of the *Birmingham News* had become routine. but venturing into the lonely streets before daybreak was another matter. Many months would pass, and dozens of frights in the pre-dawn darkness would occur before that work, too, would become a grind. First, I had to learn to grit my teeth and carry on despite the fear.

And like the deliveries, my collections for the afternoon newspaper had fallen into a familiar pattern. I quickly found, however, that collections of some of my morning accounts would never allow me to simply "go through the motions." In fact, I would never have believed that collections from some of my morning accounts offered as many challenges as plunging alone into the darkness, although of a different character altogether. It was the mental and spiritual stress that took me by surprise.

For example, the emergency room of Norwood Hospital. Occasionally, when I would deliver the paper, it would be necessary to scurry past accident victims and try not to gaze as they lay on gurneys awaiting attention. And it was often the same on Saturday when I went by to collect. Sometimes, the nurses would be too busy to bother with me and I'd have to return at a more convenient time. I didn't mind the inconvenience. It was the drag on my spirits from seeing hurt and injured people and worried relatives that got me. It never failed to put me in a pall.

But that was mild compared to collection at the Brown-Service Funeral Home. On Saturday, the business office was closed. I was forced to go to the back side of the building, to the service entrance, to collect. That's where a hearse was often parked. Usually no one would answer my knock, and I would reluctantly open the door and go into the service area where the bodies were taken. There were gurneys parked about. Whether they were loaded with bodies or not, I didn't want to know. I hoped only that someone would hear me before I lost my nerve. I wanted my money and I wanted out. Never before had I thought about life and death, but as I nervously waited in the service area of the funeral home, and even as I went about the balance of my collections, you can be certain I was musing about mortality.

On Saturday mornings, I would also call on the Cerebral Palsy Center on Twenty-fifth and Eleventh where I would struggle in my attempts to understand what a young boy about my age named Johnny was saying to me. I saw Johnny almost every Saturday as I collected my accounts. I was learning about life, about the truths I'd never learn in school. I'd never before thought about the things I thought about each week as I left with my money. Johnny would never ride a motorcycle or have a normal life. *Why is Johnny the way he is, while I am healthy?* I couldn't believe it was something he had done to be punished that way. *Why would God do that to Johnny?* The unfairness of it hit me squarely in the face each Saturday. Somehow the message I got at church about sin and punishment and righteousness and reward seemed totally misplaced. All that business about God having a plan for our lives lost all its meaning as Johnny struggled on Saturday mornings to communicate with me—and I struggled with God for an answer.

I remember one Saturday morning as I came to a stop on the sidewalk in front of the Center, I could see Johnny through the glass door. I knocked down the kickstand of my motorcycle, taking my time. Normally, I galloped or loped to my customers, anxious to make my collection and move on to the next one. But not here. Seeing Johnny through the door, waiting for me, always slowed me down. I sucked in a great breath and turned the knob.

"Hi, Johnny." It was about all I could bring myself to say each week.

Johnny twisted in his chair, making unintelligible sounds and reaching his skeletal and twisted arms toward me. I couldn't understand a word he tried to form. The vestibule was empty but for the two of us. Johnny gestured in every conceivable way to make me understand. Finally, his nurse arrived to pay me.

"I hope Johnny's not bothering you, is he? He's such a sweet boy, but he can be a pest sometimes." She gave me and Johnny a big smile, all the while patting Johnny's shoulder in a reassuring way.

As she paid me, Johnny kept at it, making guttural noises and almost twisting from the wheelchair.

The nurse smiled again as she paid me, and pointed to my motorcycle. "Johnny wants to know how fast it'll go."

"Oh, I guess about seventy," I told the nurse as I stuffed the coins in my pocket. "I don't get out on the highway very often."

It was only a few moments later as I straddled my cycle about to kick start the engine that it hit me and an electric shiver of shame washed over me. I made myself wave goodbye to Johnny who watched from his chair as I eased out into the street. I should have told Johnny how fast it would go, not his nurse. He was the one who wanted to know.

*   *   *

I suppose it was because I always considered myself inadequate for almost every occasion, never had the confidence to believe I could achieve anything, always felt isolated and alone, that I thought of myself as an underdog. I envied, yet despised, over-achievers and the cocky, arrogant kids in my school, but identified with other misfits.

Bill was a giant of a boy at my grammar school, a large-boned, hulking boy who loped with one leg and dragged the other. When he spoke, his words were indistinct and spittle dribbled from his mouth. He was a gentle giant with whom no one would play. He was teased unmercifully by the boys. Sometimes the boys would gang up on him and wrestle him to the ground. Occasionally, Bill would become enraged, grab one of the boys with his huge hands, and leave him sniveling on the ground. But mostly, Bill endured. Bill was not exactly a friend of mine, but I felt great empathy for him. I watched with a sense of dread and anger and guilt. I never had the courage to face down the bullies who beat and humiliated him. But I would talk to Bill. It was the least I could do.

Bill's family was poor. He once told me the only thing he enjoyed in life was practicing piano at the First Methodist Church in downtown Birmingham. They allowed him to come after school where he practiced alone. Oftentimes, as I was delivering my papers after school, Bill would be trudging down Twelfth Avenue toward downtown, less than a mile away, and I assumed he was headed for the church to practice.

Bill was crippled and ugly and awkward, and I've always assumed he was not very smart. He had no friends except perhaps for me, if I could have been called a friend. I was the only one, to my knowledge, who would talk with him, if not defend him I never knew if he went to the church to play the piano or to enjoy the solitary solace that a church might throw, like a blanket, over someone whose life had been frozen by society.

Later, after we had left school behind, Bill's only jobs, so far as I know, were at restaurants. When I would take my family out to dinner, we might run into Bill at a café where he bussed tables. That never lasted long. He told me he was always afraid of being fired. He was so awkward he couldn't keep from breaking things as he cleared the dishes.

I never heard Bill play and never knew whether he had any musical talent. His fingers were so large and he was so awkward in all his movements, it doesn't seem possible he had any talent. And yet I wonder . . . .

It's been years now since I last saw Bill. I don't know what has become of him. God bless the members of the First Methodist Church of Birmingham for providing a sanctuary through all those years of solitude for that sad underdog of society.

*   *   *

I've often thought, as I look back on my teenage years, how strange it was that my sympathies, my heart, went out to Johnny and Bill and other individuals who had been cast aside by society and never had a fair chance at life, yet I wholeheartedly believed in separation of the races and holding the colored race in its place in society, notwithstanding the fact that anyone could see that they were truly America's underdogs. What strange things are we human beings. We are blessed with rational minds, yet our minds somehow permit us to hold positions that are radically inconsistent, even to empathize with one who is rejected by society, and at the same time, to scorn an entire class even more rudely rejected. Is that perhaps the explanation? We may condemn and reject and turn our backs on an entire race of humanity, but once it takes on a human face, once we've come to know the person, his values, his hopes and dreams; once we've come to respect him and his culture; perhaps then we'll form a new attitude; and perhaps that is the hope for humanity.

16 • The Man of the Hour

J liked him from the start. He carried the look of authority, of courage and wisdom. His single-syllable name blazed with raw power—Ace, Ace Carter. He was the man of the hour, come to lead us from the ditch in which we'd found ourselves.

Even as he stood on the dais with several other men, there was no question in my mind who among them we'd come to hear. They all were so ordinary they faded into insignificance—except for him.

Tall and burly, he was almost bear-like in his muscularity as he hovered over the others. And dark. I thought he looked like an Indian, strong and silent. His straight black hair shone under the lights as his black, mysterious eyes studied the crowd before him. Unlike the others, there was no small talk about him. He patiently bided his time.

We had come to attend a rally for the White Citizens Council in Birmingham. And Asa E. "Ace" Carter[5] would be the featured speaker. He was already known from his radio program as a fiery speaker for the Southern cause.

I was only fifteen at the time and had little interest in speeches. When my father asked me to go with him to hear Mr. Carter, I was pretty wishy-washy about it. I'm not certain I'd ever heard a speech before, other than the sermons I'd mostly ignored on Sundays. My mind usually wandered, whether the preacher droned softly or bellowed his warnings. I really didn't want to sit through a lot of boring speeches. And another reason I was reluctant to go was my morning paper route which Mr. Hawley had turned over to me a few months earlier. I didn't need to be out late because I was up at four A.M. each morning to deliver my route of over two hundred *Post-Herald* newspapers.

But then, on the other hand, I'd been greatly upset about that Supreme Court decision that would put coloreds in our schools. I wanted to do something about it, but didn't know what.

It was clear from the articles in the newspapers and the word on the street that the South would rise up yet again at this Yankee oppression. We would never accept that decree without a fight. We believed that integration of our schools couldn't be forced in the face of "massive resistance" of the Southern people. I had read in the newspapers that the marshaling of that massive resistance would begin with the organization of White Citizens Councils in every city and community across the South.

Already, the Ku Klux Klan had become more and more active across the South in a campaign to "keep them in their place," but the business community and ordinary citizens would not follow the lead of that ragtag bunch of thugs. The Citizens Council then would be an organization formed among business and political leaders and joined by the mass of respectable citizens. This was to be a vehicle to raise money and provide legal and political opposition to the integration of our schools.

At last, they got organized and sat down. I have no memory of any of the proceedings prior to his speech, but eventually he was called on. I was all attention as he slowly rose from his chair and loped to the podium. He then seized the sides of the podium and for a long moment studied the crowd, as if sizing us up. Then he began.

> Ladies and gentlemen, I want to thank you for asking me to come before you this evening. It's an honor to do so in furtherance of this noble cause we're all so concerned about.[6]

I was surprised. His speech pattern was not some anonymous, midwestern TV voice nor the syrupy, deep-South drawl of easy living. It was the familiar, folksy hill country accent I'd grown up with and known all my life. He'd sold me in a dozen words a bill of goods, long before I knew the goods he was selling. He seemed like my relative, my neighbor, someone I could trust. I sat up straight and listened.

> Now I know y'all have heard of Karl Marx. He was famous for writing *The Communist Manifesto, Das Kapital* and other works. He was called the father of communism.

> Now Karl Marx said that the victory of communism would be assured if the people could be convinced that the cause of communism was inevitable. In other words, if the people became convinced that it was coming anyway and there's nothing you can do to stop it, then the people give up. You know, you hear people talking like that most every day when you mention the left-wing take-over of this country and the integration of colored kids with our children—the injustices that are growing every day—you hear people say, well, it's coming anyway. There's not anything we can do about it. You've heard that I'm sure.

> In fact, you hear it all the time.

Oh no, I thought, as he began his speech. He sounded like a preacher or what I thought a professor might sound like. I thought about my preacher and wondered if I'd soon be nodding off. But then, as he mentioned "Grandpa," he picked up the pace, and I soon found myself wide-awake.

> Well, now, Grandpa, he was different.

> When he got in hot water, and he got in hot water right frequently having all the natural enemies of a mountain man, like revenuers and politicians and such. I remember he'd take out a plug of Brown Mule Chewing Tobacco and cut off a chew with the sharpest knife I ever saw. He was

always testin' the blade of that knife by jerking a hair out of
his head and holding the hair by just one end and whippin'
the knife around to cut the hair in two. But he'd take out
his knife and thumb-open the blade, all with one hand.
Mountain men, you know, all have a way of doin' this by
weakenin' the spring so they can thumb the blade out using just one hand. Grandpa performed all this in a non-
hurried, nonchalant manner and appeared to be thinking
right hard about something else all the time. Then he'd
turn to me and Buck who was sittin' on the pine needles
watchin' him. Buck was a red bone hound and a fine red
bone, one of the finest I ever saw. Real smart too. In fact,
smarter than a lot of people I know. Well, anyway, Grandpa would look at me and Buck real hard and say, "Well,
let's just take stock of our situation."

Well me and Buck, we didn't exactly know what the situation was at the moment, whether it had to do with rev-
enuers or politicians Grandpa was having trouble with at
the time, or a recounting of injustices that the stinkin' Yankees had done at some time or another, but we was mighty
proud to be included in the situation and we was all-fired
anxious to get slap-dab in the middle of it and know what
it was all about.

Well, Grandpa would take stock of the whole situation
and then he'd start figuring out ways to come out on top.

By this time, I was following his every word, even though I was baffled.
All this stuff about "Grandpa" and the "dog." *What does it mean?* I could
see he was leading up to his topic, but I just couldn't guess where he was
taking us.

You see your grandpa and mine come from a breed of men
who never doubted they'd come out on top. Any victory

the opposition ever won over them they regarded as just a temporary victory. They knew they were gonna win because they had the will to win. That's where the old saying came from—where there's a will, there's a way. That was always said in hopeless lookin' situations. Well, they had the will and they knew they were gonna win. It was just a matter of figurin' out how to do it. Every time the opposition whipped 'em or beat 'em down, it was just temporary, and they'd chalk that up as another score they had to settle when they went out.

He sounded like a preacher, the way the words hit me, but for once I was wide awake. Polite applause interrupted his cadence.

This will they had came from a deep conviction and a deep love for their civilization, their way of living. It was a will no enemy could defeat. Oh, yes. The enemies of our civilization could win victories. They could even get on top and dominate everything where it looked like it was all over but the shoutin'. But our people come from a stubborn breed that knows we're not gonna give up!

The audience clapped and hollered. Mr. Carter waited, his eyes slowly moving around the room, but his face was immobile, showing no emotion. I was surprised at how hard I was listening to this speech, not wanting to miss a word.

You never heard our great-grandfolks say there is nothing we can do about it. You know, when the War between the States ended, the South was a desolate land. Sherman—oh, you remember that name, how could you ever forget?—how his army marched across the South burning and pillaging and raping. Crops were burned in the field. Cribs of corn burned. Mules and horses and hogs were slaughtered and burned. Cowpeas uprooted, peanuts, any-

thing that was edible, heaped into piles and burned. And
there was no seed, no fertilizer, no way to start over. The
people were starving. The number of men in the South was
greatly depleted—they'd been killed in the war—and there
was a great scarcity of horses and mules. Into this desolate,
burned, stripped and crippled land came the carpetbaggers
and politicians, backed up by military dictatorship.
They called it—Reconstruction!

Reconstruction! That word snatched my breath. Horrendous visions
from *Birth of a Nation* rolled before my eyes, and the urgency of Carter's
message grabbed me by the throat. It must have grabbed a lot of others.
There had been applause before, but now the audience was thunderous.

It was a beaten, hopeless and terrible land. But it had an
ingredient in it that no politician and no military dictator could conquer. It had a rock-hard stubborn people. A
people with a will that says you just don't die.

Now across this desolate land rode the proud victors. They
rode up to the dogtrot houses and the shotgun shacks and
the once proud but then dilapidated big houses. They rode
up with a piece of paper that they were confident that these
beaten people would sign. A written agreement. It was an
agreement that these beaten folks would accept the rule
that was now over them, that they would integrate, that
they would declare themselves wards of the conquerors
and at the bottom of the paper there was a provision that
if they signed this agreement, they were allowed to draw
food and clothing and stores from any federal installation.
They'd be allowed to eat, to hold up their heads. And you
know what? They refused to sign. Almost to a man and a
woman across this great Southland, they refused to sign.
They had a stubborn will. All that was needed was to figure
a way.

There weren't many mules and horses available and many was a time your great-grandpa and mine hitched themselves to plows and drug the plows inch by inch and foot by foot, their backs bent and their heads straining forward almost to the ground. And your great-grandmother and mine guided those plows through the new ground roots and around the stumps. Many times they were barefooted. They borrowed the seeds of Indian corn, the thin red ear that don't need much cultivation. They'd grind this corn and make grits of a morning. That's all they had for breakfast. And that's why grits are now served in every café in the Southland. They went into the woods. They cut poke salad. They made meal and coffee out of acorns. They stewed roots into soup. They learned what to do with sassafras for a tonic with skunk cabbage. That's right. They fought. They loved freedom—freedom from central government. And they were determined to have it too. The civilization—our civilization—hung by a mighty thin thread on the brink of savagery. But it was a stubborn thread. They saved the book, the Bible, the prayer, the organic law of freedom. They knew what they wanted, and from a desolate, prostrate position, they fought their way up to the knees. And from their knees, they got back on their feet. Well, they won a war after a war had been lost. Oh, yes, sir, they did.

Sometime when you've got nothing else to do, you take the young'uns to the state capital in Montgomery, Alabama, and you walk through the front door and there on the wall you'll see a plaque that was placed there by the Daughters of the Confederacy. And it commemorates the year that they finally won their victory—1874. A long time after the War between the States was over. Some politicians'd like to take it down—it embarrasses them—but don't you let 'em do it. It doesn't say much, but it's a reminder to your sons and daughters that these folks who won, these great-grandfolks of ours, loved freedom above all material comforts the government could provide. They loved their race, their kind, their kin, their blood, their breed, their stock. This is our heritage, yours and mine, and our children's. These are people of our blood and our stock. These are our people who could spit in the face of poverty and starvation, set their jaw against iron might and tyranny and come out on top for the freedom, the civilization, the race they determined to save.

That's why the South is number one. Oh, I know the politicians talk about us being last in this and that, but we're not—not in what counts. If you count love of freedom, spirit of liberty, love of God and willingness to fight for it, those are the things that count anyway. Those are the everlasting values that determine men's souls. That's why we're number one. And that's why the liberal and that's why the communist hates the South with a bitter hatred. Be proud of that hatred, ladies and gentlemen.

Grandpa always said be proud of your friends, but you be prouder of your enemies and make the right kind of enemies and then you'll stand for something. The South stands for something. This is a heritage that belongs to every schoolboy and every schoolgirl. It's the heritage of the Southland.

And I reckon that's why, even though I don't particularly cotton to grits, I'll always order 'em for breakfast in a café. Because the liberal and the ignorant laugh and don't know what they mean, and maybe it ain't much, but still I eat 'em, renewing a kind of a covenant with those ragged great-grandparents of ours. It's a covenant that must be renewed—now—in these days that face us—the times that are with us and to which we must remain faithful—in the eternal struggle for the freedom of our children.

This is the time, friends—our time. The Citizen Councils are our last chance to save our children from degradation, atheism, mongrelization, and communistic dictatorship.

On behalf of the Citizens Councils, we hereby serve notice that we shall take our stand firmly to fight for segregation and our race, to stand up for Jesus, our rock of strength and comfort. We need you to join together with us now as we again take up the cause for which our grandparents fought so long and hard. Get in line, folks. Get out your billfolds. Put you name on the line. Make yourself count. We've got a fight ahead and we need every one of you. Thank you, and God Bless.

I was mesmerized. I was on fire. I would have followed him anywhere. And so would everyone in the room.

*   *   *

Later, I realized I should have pinched myself to stay awake during all those sermons I'd day-dreamed through at my church as a young boy. Had I been alert to the message of those sermons, perhaps I would have gained enough insight to wonder how joining the White Citizens Council to fight for segregation of the races was actually in line with standing up for Jesus.

But then, on deeper reflection, I came to the conclusion that in truth I could have listened closely, Sunday after Sunday, and I would never have heard a single sermon about brotherly love or anything that touched on the subject of love between all humans. A sermon like that would have sealed the fate of our preacher, and he would have been sent packing by the congregation that hired him . . . and at whose pleasure he served.

17 • Fever

I slept fitfully that night. We had no air conditioning back then, in the summer of 1955. The windows were open, but there was no breeze and the torpid air lay on me like a blanket. When the clock began clamoring, I was too tired to face the morning.

I slapped the alarm into silence and sat on the side of my bed. Four o'clock in the morning! I knew better than to lie down—I'd probably doze off and who knows when I'd awake. I had newspapers to deliver, over three hundred of them between both my routes, and Sunday papers were huge.

As I slumped there on the side of the bed, my lips suddenly felt hot and feverish. I sprang in panic from my bed. As I replayed yesterday's big event, a wave of embarrassment swept over me and I flushed to the top of my head. I rushed to the bathroom and splashed cold water over my face.

Then I quickly dressed, went outside, coasted my Harley down the driveway into the road, and faced the day, my lips burning like fire.

The previous day had been a Saturday, the day I collected my accounts. It was usually no big deal. I'd go from house to house, "Collect for the *Post-Herald*, please," make a few pleasant remarks about the weather, make change, and keep moving.

It was a particularly warm Saturday, about eleven A.M., when I entered the big frame house on Eleventh Avenue North between Twenty-third and Twenty-fourth Streets. I didn't knock at the front door because the house had been divided into apartments, like so many of those fine old houses in my neighborhood. In fact, the earliest memories of my childhood were framed in and about an old two-story house on the corner right next door. That house was adjacent to Twenty-third Street, a dirt road on the edge of a neighborhood called "Norwood," no more than a half-mile north from the center of town. My family had lived downstairs, while another family occupied the rooms at the top of the big mahogany staircase I was forbidden to climb. It was there, in the house next door, that my very first memories had been formed, and I was reminiscing about those memories as I began to climb up the old staircase to collect from my new customer.

At the top of the staircase I turned left and approached a heavy mahogany bedroom door above which a metallic C was tacked to the lintel. This was the apartment of Miss Talley, a new customer who had called in her subscription to the newspaper. I had not met her before. I had made an account sheet for her and placed it in the proper order in my route book.

I paused at Miss Talley's door, concerned that I make a good impression on my new customer, I raked my fingers through my hair, straightened up, took a deep breath and knocked.

"Who's there?"

"Collect for the *Post-Herald*, please."

As the door slowly opened, fingers wrapped the edge, and the deep red nail polish grabbed my attention. Then her face appeared. Her hair was red, and she was young and pretty. And just below her face her bare shoulder slid into view and jolted me to attention. My heart gave a little leap. She saw that I was harmless and opened the door just enough for me to enter.

"Well, don't just stand there, son. Come on in here!" she commanded in a friendly voice. "Or are you *afra-i-i-i-id* of me?" she teased, laughing. My mother sometimes called me Son, but there was nothing motherly in the way Miss Talley said the word. The way she breathed it out carried grown-up overtones for which I was not prepared.

I may have choked out an okay, but that's about all I could utter as I studied the threshold and budged into her room.

The door closed. I looked up and my mouth must have fallen open. Neither she nor her roommate wore any clothes, except for panties and skimpy bras. The roommate, a peroxide blond, sat on the side of the bed. The room was warm as were all rooms in the Alabama summer heat, and their skin glistened with perspiration. It must have been the look on my face that caused them to fall into peals of laughter, bending and slapping their knees. I tried not to stare, but all I could see were breasts struggling to pop out of bras that didn't seem adequate for their purpose.

They must have known I'd never seen anything like that before. I stood there like a fool, drawn up inside myself, struggling not to stare at those objects I'd been dreaming I'd one day see. I was desperate to learn more about girls, though I was fully aware this was not the time or place. What I really wanted was to collect my money and get out.

Miss Talley, standing beside me, reached around my shoulders and pulled me tight into her left breast. I clutched my route book with both hands. When I knocked on the door, my finger marked Miss Talley's account, but now I lost my place and pulled the book to my chest. Pulling me close, crushing my right upper arm and shoulder into her left breast, she put her lips to my ear and whispered seductively, "Now son, what is it you really want from me?" I don't know if the blonde heard what she said, but she collapsed on the bed in laughter.

"I just want to collect for the paper please," I croaked.

As she pulled me to her, I somehow kept my feet planted, even though I was about ten degrees off the perpendicular, completely off balance, clutching my route book to my chest.

I also struggled not to look at her breasts. I'd look at the floor, then out the window, then glance at the blonde, then sneak another quick look as I again riveted my attention on the floor. It was all so improbable. I'd been obsessed with the female breast for the past couple of years, but had really gained no better understanding of them than I had when I first became interested. And there they were, right in front of me! And I'm acting like a fool!

*   *   *

My family had finally bought a television a few years earlier and had watched the talent shows, in black and white. There was one show on which Dagmar regularly appeared. Dagmar was a large, voluptuous Scandinavian woman with platinum hair. She wore evening gowns that exposed the top side of her enormous breasts which extended, unsupported, like a mantel from her chest. She always read from a script as if she were not very bright, and supported her arm across her breasts as she read from her script. At first I'd thought that breasts might be supported by a bone structure. How else could they extend perpendicular from the body with no visible means of support?

But then I remembered the time I'd been standing in a long line in the lunchroom about a year ago and a girl I didn't know was in line behind me. The line surged back, but the girl didn't react quickly enough and I collided with her. I turned to say, "I'm sorry," and glanced down at her chest. I was fixated! One breast was a perfectly proportioned convexity. The other breast was the same shape and size, though inverted. I couldn't help it. I stared in wonder at her identical breasts, the one convex, the other concave. It was a fascinating incongruity. Because I held my gaze so long, she looked down at her own breast, threw her arms across her chest, collapsed into tears and raced from the lunchroom. I now held evidence there was no bone structure involved—but were they filled with air? I never saw her again.

The nature of the female breast then was to me one of the great mysteries of life. Now, here I was, face to face with the real thing. I could have solved the mystery right here and now. She probably wouldn't care if I did. But all I could do was stare at the floor.

*   *   *

"Son, look at me," she said, pinching my chin between her thumb and forefinger and lifting my face to eye level. She was smiling, having a great time, and it seemed the blonde across the room had never ceased laughing. My face felt as flushed as if I'd been tending a fire.

"You can't just stare at my boobs. Oh, no, son. You can't do that."

I looked back down at the floor, sneaking another look on the way. She snapped my head up again.

"Now look, son. You're trying to collect money from me. But if you look at this," and she released my chin and cupped her right breast, hefting it about for emphasis, "you'll want to squeeze it, won't you? And then, if you squeeze it, son, you know what?" She threw back her head and laughed. Then she looked me in the eye and pinched my cheek. "Then I'll be collecting from you!"

Miss Talley was smiling, very satisfied with herself, still holding me tight with her left arm and pinching my cheek. Then the blonde suggested, "Hey, Thelma, maybe he'll work it out with you in trade." They shrieked with laughter.

Work it out in trade? That got my attention. Even though I was as thoroughly inexperienced an adolescent as could have been found in Birmingham in 1955, I thought I understood what was meant by that term. *Could it be?* I wondered. *Could these pretty women be . . . prostitutes?*

The question was unsettling, particularly given my situation. But it was certainly possible. Why, wasn't it only a few months before, at about five o'clock in the morning, when I had witnessed the police marching four or five pretty young women in handcuffs away from a house on my paper route? And several men, too! They were all packed into a paddy wagon. Yes, I knew about those kinds of people.

And across the street from this very house, on the corner, was Mary's Place, another of my customers. Mary's Place was a beer joint. When I would go in to collect on Saturday afternoons, there usually would be shady-looking older women in the booths drinking beer. Sometimes one or more of them would tease me with suggestive comments. I had wondered if they might be prostitutes.

But Miss Talley? She was still holding me tight, completely off balance. *Could it be? No! She's way too pretty and too young for that. But if she is, then what kind of sin am I committing to let a prostitute hug me?*

My temples were pounding like my chest. My discomfort was compounded by the teaching of my church. While I managed to day-dream through a lot of what the preacher said, he came through loud and clear about fornication, which he said was among the worst of the sins, and the sin of lust was as bad as fornication itself. The flames of hell lapped at my legs, even as I struggled with myself not to gaze at those things that were a compelling mystery. But lust itself was not my problem. My real desire was to escape.

Maybe they got bored with teasing me. All I know is I was standing there pulled off center into her breast and struggling to stay vertical and not stare, and feeling the flames of hell at work. She again took my chin between her thumb and forefinger and lifted my face. I thought she would tease me again. But this time she was not smiling. Her lips were parted and she looked very serious. She placed her left hand on the back of my head and with her right hand slowly removed my glasses. Then she pulled my face to hers. Our lips came together, and she kissed me. If the blonde laughed I didn't hear it. I didn't hear anything. Her tongue stroked my lips, circling and strong, then forced its way into my mouth. She held me tightly and after a moment I ceased to struggle. My first kiss. I didn't know what to do or expect. I should have explored her body with my hands. Instead, I clutched my route book in a death grip with both hands. How long did she kiss me? I don't know. It may have been only thirty seconds. But I think it was much longer.

Then she released me and pushed me away. My legs went wobbly, and in that moment I fumbled my route book. It fell to the floor, as if in slow motion. And there was nothing I could do to stop it.

The corner of the book struck the hardwood floor and exploded! The account sheets sprang from the book and fanned across the floor like a deck of cards, as inexorably as a train of dominos. As the end of the train slipped beneath the bed, I exclaimed excitedly. "Now see what you've made me do!"

They screamed with laughter as I dived to the floor and scrambled on my hands and knees. I scooped up my account sheets in a flash, clutching them all in a heap to my chest, and clambered to my feet. Miss Talley had mercifully opened the door for me to my great relief. She handed me my glasses as I escaped out her door.

Their laughter rang in my ears as I stumbled down the stairs, account sheets clutched to my chest. The echo of those stupid words followed me out of the house. I paused on the front porch long enough to cram the sheets into my route book so I wouldn't lose them. I would have put them in order, but I couldn't wait to escape. I had to go somewhere and lick my wounds. I was embarrassed and felt rubbery. My singed lips sizzled as if she had slathered them with Tabasco. I wondered, then, does kissing cause your lips to burn? I didn't know. But I do know for three days afterwards, my lips constantly burned, and I felt hot and flushed, like I had a fever. I was distracted and worried a lot about what it meant. *Have I contracted some disease?* Afterwards, for a month or so, whenever I thought of her kiss, which was every day, every hour, my lips would sizzle again, and I'd feel feverish.

The thrill of her kiss gradually diminished as time passed by. Eventually, many months later, my lips ceased to burn when I thought of her. But to be truthful, thinking of it now, over fifty years later, I'm sad to say that my first kiss was the most intense, most memorable kiss of all.

You may want to know, did I go back and collect my money. Did I screw up my courage and return to Apartment C to "work it out in trade"? The truth is, I'm ashamed to say.

(On second thought, what's the harm in the truth after more than fifty years? No, I never returned to Apartment C.)

I was embarrassed for months afterward each time I thought about Miss Talley, that first kiss and the silly words I uttered. That singular event may have retarded my social development for a year or more. If I had been apprehensive of girls before, now I was positively cowed. But leaving aside the embarrassment and intimidation resulting from that event, and on a more objective note, I do value the symmetry of the time and place of that event: that ten years after having left the house of my earliest childhood memories, my first adult-type memory was created in the very house next door.

18 • Summer Camp

My mother took the call that Monday, the morning Eddie went missing. She was frantic. I thought he'd be all right. My little brother was too level-headed to do something foolhardy.

My mother had wanted Eddie to attend summer church camp. Neither of us had ever been to camp. I was too old at sixteen, and he was marginal at fourteen.

He didn't want to go for several reasons that he would verbalize only if put on the spot. Otherwise, he didn't say much about anything. Eddie was taciturn, a strong and silent warrior.

For one thing, he didn't want to go because we attended an urban church instead of a neighborhood church, and the kids we knew there were only casual acquaintances, not neighborhood friends. But the main reason was his newspaper routes. These were daily obligations, and he took them quite as seriously as I took mine. My mother pressed me to learn his routes and deliver his papers for a week. That wouldn't be so hard to do, would it? And it's summer time. What else do you have to do? So I agreed.

My parents drove him to camp on a Sunday afternoon, somewhere in Talladega County near Cheaha Mountain, seventy or eighty miles from Birmingham. Next day, Monday morning, I delivered his papers as well as mine.

At fourteen, Eddie had been delivering papers for two years. Our parents had relaxed a little over my paper route and that led the way for him to get his first afternoon route when he was barely twelve. Then, at fourteen he got a morning route. What a relief. He was super-responsible. With him in charge of the clock, I would usually snooze for a few more minutes while he pestered me to get up.

Our routine was the same. We'd arise at 4:00 A.M., deliver our papers, arrive back home around 6:30 A.M. I remember how Mother would have the kitchen toasty warm on school days when Eddie and I arrived and our breakfast would soon be ready. She always made us a full breakfast of eggs, bacon, biscuits and coffee. Coffee, you might ask, for young boys? How else would we be able to sit through classes, alert and ready? We always drank our coffee black, without sugar, just as our father did. He was a bus driver, and that's the way he took his, snatching a cup at every rest stop along his route.

Our mother must have thought we were quite a sight back then, as we hustled into her kitchen after delivering papers in the dead of winter. We had no winter gear in the deep South. But it often got cold, sometimes down to zero, and we had a lot of snow back then. We'd wear two pairs of jeans, two pairs of socks, several shirts, a heavy jacket, gloves and black engineer boots. On our heads we wore canvas pilot's helmets with earflaps that we'd bought at the Army-Navy Surplus Store. We had no scarves so we'd use hand towels around our necks if it was cold enough for that.

I remember parking my motorcycle in the garage, unable to open my hands, frozen into half-fists, as though still griping the handlebars. I'd shuffle spraddle-legged to the house and hold my hands above the flames over the eye of the stove. I still remember the intense tingling pain as the feeling returned to my hands and feet, and how that black coffee warmed my stomach. Eddie and I were addicted.

But this was summer time, and there was chaos in my mother's kitchen. I didn't understand the telephone call. *Why would Eddie go missing? Where could he be?* Our mother's piercing green eyes would freeze my blood when she was angry. But she was not angry now; she was pacing the floor and wringing her hands. She was alone in her worry. My father was on the road, taking a busload of passengers somewhere. There was no way for her to contact him. And I, who had confidence in Eddie's ability to handle himself, was not overly concerned.

Mother said they told her not to worry, that the County Sheriff had been alerted and the Highway Patrol as well. "He'll turn up soon," they assured her. I told her the same, and added that Eddie knew how to take care of himself.

For an hour that passed like a day, she paced in silence, from the kitchen to the front door and back again. Each time she reached the front door, she opened it and looked up and down the road. Then she would sit down and put her face in her hands for a moment, then bounce up again to pace.

We were in the kitchen when we heard the front door open without a knock. Mother and I dashed to the living room just as Eddie walked in carrying his small satchel. He was as nonchalant as if he were returning from a visit to the bathroom. Mother shrieked. Eddie stopped in his tracks as she bolted toward him. She threw her arms around him, hugging him and at the same time screaming at him for leaving camp.

Eddie simply stood there, bag in hand, a quizzical frown on his face, waiting for the fury to subside. Finally, she released him.

"How did you get home?" she demanded

"Hitchhiked."

"Why did you leave?" she asked, standing there helpless.

"Well, it was like this. I woke up early, went over to the galley. A bunch of ladies were drinking coffee, getting ready to make breakfast. I asked for a cup of coffee. They all looked down their noses at me. One of them told me the coffee was for adults—not children. So I went back to the cabin, packed my duds and left."

"You didn't tell them you were leaving?" she asked incredulously.

"No, ma'am. Just left. Walked down the trail to a county road, then followed the road. Somebody picked me up and dropped me at the highway. And from there I hitchhiked home. And I ain't going back."

Then she cried some more, but Eddie never went to camp again.

19 • The Carpetbaggers

After almost three years on the job, I'd found that delivering newspapers was easy. And collecting my accounts was a snap. I would say "Collect for the *News*, please" or "Collect for the *Post-Herald*, please," depending on which route it was, and that was it. I responded politely to all the questions that might crop up but kept it short so I could make my collections quickly on my very valuable Saturday mornings. Plus, I wanted to avoid the more difficult task of actually talking to people.

It was soliciting new accounts that was the hardest part of my job. There, conversation would be required.

Anxiety was my partner on these new starts. I would slowly shuffle to the front door, my arm cocked, ready to knock, telling myself it was good to add another customer. Mr. Hawley had been pressing me to increase my morning subscriptions. And I'd make more money.

I had seen the moving van the past Saturday parked in front of the old empty wooden two-story square house on Twenty-fourth Street and knew that a family was moving in. Most families wanted a newspaper delivered to their home. They could choose the morning *Post-Herald* or the afternoon *News*. In my neighborhood, almost no one took both papers. Most families subscribed to the afternoon newspaper, but my afternoon route was in another section of Norwood. It was the morning *Post-Herald* I delivered on this route. I took a deep breath and tentatively pecked the door several times, half desperate to make a sale and half hoping no one would answer.

I rapped again on the screen door, this time more firmly. The weather was unusually warm and humid for a day in November, so the main door was standing open. I heard movement from the back of the house and braced myself to deal with the new people.

She came from somewhere in the back of the house and crossed the living room. I could see her dimly through the screen as she limped toward me, a thin woman leaning on a single crutch under her left arm. She pushed the screen door open, extended the crutch through the doorway, planted it on the porch and deftly followed it out, closing the door behind her. I retreated a step or two, sharing the space with her. The brilliance of the deep autumn morning set her face aglow. I was stunned. She was beautiful. Her face was framed by strawberry blond hair. Her eyes were blue, a blue I'd never seen before. I had grown up on the city sidewalks and had never seen a cornflower, but cornflower blue came to my mind. She was maybe twenty-five years old. There was something about her face, a gentleness, a vulnerability, a peach-fuzz softness, that reminded me of Ingrid Bergman.

"Good morning," she said with good cheer, "What may I do for you?" *Her accent? She's not from around here.*

"Good morning," I stammered. Embarrassed, my eyes jerked from her face to the floor. "I'm from the newspaper, the *Post-Herald*. Just wanna know do y'all wanna take the paper? It's forty-five cents a week. I'll deliver it to your door every morning, collect on Saturday." I lifted my face and ventured a look into her eyes.

"Well, I'm sure we will." She turned, opened the screen and called, "Vern, can you come to the door?" She turned back and smiled. I looked at the floor. I knew my sales pitch had been awkward, spilling out so quickly.

I wondered if she might be from Sweden, like Ingrid Bergman.

I was something of a fan of Ms. Bergman. I had seen her in a couple of movies and liked her more than any of the other actresses. I was aware of the bad publicity surrounding her over the last several years. She had left her husband and had moved to Italy to live with an Italian filmmaker. There had been a big scandal. I had seen pictures of Ingrid Bergman in the paper and in magazines so many times. And, of course, I had forgiven her all her indiscretions; because her face was so pretty, so innocent, so vulnerable, it simply couldn't have been her fault.

Then I heard footsteps, and looked back through the screen as the door opened. A big man stepped over the threshold onto the porch. He was tall and big boned, but thin, an easy smile on his face. Following him out on the porch were two little boys, each looking at me curiously. He reached out his hand. My father had told me a thousand times, "When a man offers you his hand, stand tall, look him in the eyes and give him a firm grip."

I took his hand, trying hard to meet my father's expectations.

"Hi. I'm Vern Miller. This is my wife, Helen. What can we do for you?"

The strange accent. *Where are they from? What are they doing here?*

At that instant, I lost the battle to stand tall, look this man in the eyes and grip his hand, so I cast my eyes from Mr. Miller's face to the floor and made my pitch again.

"Oh," I stammered. "I'm just trying to get y'all to take the paper from me. I bring it to you every morning, throw it on your porch. An' I collect on Saturday. Forty-five cents a week."

During the long pause, something came over me and I blurted, "Where y'all from?"

Mr. Miller was looking down at me, his smile friendly and easy. He had a gap between his big front teeth that reminded me of Uncle Miltie, Milton Berle.

"We've just moved here from Little Rock—we were there for several years—but we're from up north. I'm from Minnesota and Helen's from South Dakota. But, hey, that newspaper sounds like a bargain. When can you start us off?" he responded.

"I can begin tomorrow morning, the Sunday paper."

Minnesota? South Dakota, that's way up north. As alien to me as Tibet.

"Well, okay, then. Let's get started—tomorrow morning it is. So, what's your name?"

"Sonny."

"Well, Sonny, it's nice to meet you." Mr. Miller looked down at his boys, who were fidgeting around as boys will do. "This is Richard," he said, pointing to the boy who was about six years old, "and this one," he continued, capping the boy's head with his big hand, "is Randy. Boys, say hello to Sonny." Richard spoke, while Randy clamped tighter around his dad's leg.

"Do you live around here?" Mrs. Miller then asked, friendly and interested.

"Yes, ma'am. Up by Norwood Hospital." I pointed to the north. "About six blocks up thataway. On Twenty-seventh Street."

"Does your paper route cover a lot of the neighborhood?"

"Yes, ma'am. It runs from down past the commercial area on Twelfth Avenue," pointing south, "all the way to Twenty-first Avenue, almost to the railroad up thataway," turning and pointing north.

Mr. Miller asked, "Well, Sonny, tell us, what's it like around here? I mean this neighborhood. We've just moved in. I'll bet you know everybody all around here and what's going on."

I stood mute, looking confused.

Mrs. Miller smiled and said, "Now look, Vern, Sonny's a busy boy. He's got his collections this morning. He doesn't have time to chat with us all day."

Then she turned back to me and smiled. "But Sonny," she said, "next Saturday when you collect, I'll have a lemonade for you and you can tell us all about yourself."

Her demeanor was so genuine, I blinked back the tears.

"Yes, ma'am."

I thanked them and left the porch. As I turned and trudged away to the house next door, I felt grotesquely awkward, my legs spraddled with the weight of hundreds of coins bulging in my pockets. Even as I was elated at getting a new start, I was embarrassed to present such a picture to Mrs. Miller.

All that morning, I replayed the short encounter with the Millers from up north. I knew my map, though I'd never been anywhere. I knew the location of all the states and the names of all the capital cities. Minnesota was as far north as you could go before entering Canada and South Dakota was almost next to Canada. That meant, of course, that they were Yankees—that their views were probably very different from Southerners. It was the federal government, and the Yankees, who were again putting pressure on us here in the South to change our way of doing things, to treat the coloreds different. It was commonly known in the South that Yankees regarded us as backward and slow.

I felt some comfort knowing I'd never again have to do more than simply collect from the Millers and move on to the next customer. I resolved to be all business with the Yankee intruders, those carpetbaggers, the next Saturday. On the other hand, as I pursued my collections for the rest of the day, every time I knocked on a door I thought how nice it would be to see Mrs. Miller's face.

Okay, I began to think, so they are from up north. So what? They'll probably be good customers, and they might not be like the other Northerners trying to destroy our Southern way of life. They certainly seemed all right, based on the short visit I had with them. They were friendly, that's for sure.

I continued my collections, and found my thoughts returning over and over to the Millers. I flip-flopped. It was clear to me that they had given me no time to throw up my defenses. I should have been all business, alert and aloof. No need to be rude of course—just cool and detached. After all, even Yankees need their newspapers.

I completed my collections and returned to the branch and paid Mr. Hawley for my newspapers that week. Then, he counted out my copies of the *Birmingham News* for delivery that afternoon. I dutifully rolled the newspapers and tied them with string, stuffed them into my canvas bag, slung the bag onto the gas tank of my Harley, and raced off to deliver them, determined to push those carpetbaggers from my mind.

When I completed my route that afternoon, I stopped by Miller Drugs and ordered a limeade. As I sipped it, cooling off from my work, I wandered over to the magazine rack. Customers were discouraged from loitering around the magazine rack, but I saw no one looking in my direction. I picked up *Time* and absently thumbed through it, trying to look business-like. Meanwhile, I surveyed the covers of the picture magazines—*Life*, *Look*, the *Saturday Evening Post,* and *Collier's*. Surely, one of them would have it—a photograph of Ingrid Bergman. All I needed was a glance.

20 • The Confirmation

Saturday morning. Collection day. A deep autumn day. My kind of day. Although it was now November, winter had not yet arrived. I plunged down the road on my Harley, a fine mist peppering my face, a brisk wind chilling the air, falling leaves swirling in my path.

I had a pocket full of change, my route book and the challenge I had been thinking about for the last week—the Millers. The Millers from the far north. I felt a mission to find out what they were up to, why they'd come down South.

When I arrived at their block on Twenty-fourth Street, I parked my Harley on the sidewalk in front of their home, and walked to the corner of Thirteenth Avenue to begin my collections. It was my intention to work my way down the block, skip their house and complete the block before returning to their home for my last collection.

At last I found myself standing on the sidewalk in front of the Millers' home, pondering whether to collect quietly and leave or to ask the hard questions on my mind. I flipped my route book to the page inscribed "Vernon and Helen Miller." *What if she doesn't remember me?* She had asked me to tell her about myself, something no adult had done for as long as I'd delivered papers. She wanted me to tell her all about the neighborhood. But what if she had forgotten it? After all, I was only a paper boy.

Finally, I mounted the porch and knocked on the door, but I'd changed my mind. I would keep my mouth shut, collect the account and keep moving. She probably wouldn't remember me anyway.

Mrs. Miller answered the door and smiled.

"Collect for the *Post-Herald*, please."

"Oh, hi, Sonny. Come in here out of the weather. How've you been?"

"Just fine, thank you." I stepped inside. She had remembered me!

"Take your jacket off. Sit down here for a minute and rest. I'll get you a hot chocolate. Would you like that?"

"Yes, ma'am."

Just then her boys came running into the room trying to get their mother's attention.

"Boys, I'll be with you in a moment. Let's go back to the kitchen where your father is. I'm talking to Sonny right now. They galloped from the room and she followed.

Then she returned, bringing me a cup of chocolate and sat down in a chair opposite me.

"Well, Sonny, since you'll be delivering our newspaper and coming by to collect each week, you need to tell me about yourself. Tell me about where you live, and your family and where you go to school."

"Yes, ma'am. I live up near the hospital," pointing toward the north. "I'm a junior at Phillips," pointing to the south. "I have a brother and a sister and my mom and dad." I took a deep breath, clamped my lips shut and looked to her for approval.

"Well, that was quick!" She clapped her hands and laughed. Then, smiling, she asked "Are you the oldest?"

"Yes, ma'am. My brother, Eddie, is two years younger. He's in school at Norwood. He delivers papers, too. My sister, Dale, she's eight years old. She goes to MacArthur School."

"And your father? What does he do?"

"He drives a Greyhound Bus."

"Do you like school? What's your favorite subject?"

"No, ma'am. I don't much like school. I like to deliver papers—make money."

"Well, I'm surprised at that! But you must stay in school."

"Yes, ma'am. That's what my father says. He tells me all the time."

After a few more pleasantries, I just couldn't stand it any more, and had to know whether these northerners would fit in. I had to know how they felt about the most important issue facing me and my family and the people of the South.

I read all about the *Brown* decision in the paper and I'd been going to meetings of the White Citizens Council. I was worried. I knew that people here in the South, the white people, would never accept mixing the races. I feared there could even be another war between the South and North over the issue. Ace Carter was saying at the White Citizen Council meetings that we had lost one war and might lose the next, but we wouldn't take it lying down.

I sucked in my breath and took the plunge.

"What do y'all think, Mrs. Miller, about that Supreme Court decision that says niggers get to go to school with whites?"

Her eyebrows arched. Her round blue eyes got rounder and bluer, but they were no longer friendly. She sat up straighter and sucked in her breath.

"Young man, you're not to use that word in my house! Do you understand?"

Incredibly, her soft, round face had become hard and angular right before my eyes.

I was as incredulous as she. *What did I say that was so bad? The word "nigger"... was that it? What's so bad about that?*

"Well, it's just the way we talk down here," I suggested quietly, my palms turned up for mercy. "I didn't mean anything by it," I pleaded with Mrs. Miller.

There was silence. I was looking at the floor. I was aware that most polite people in my neighborhood used the term "colored people" or the word "Negro," although it usually rolled off the Southern tongue as "Nigra." After a few moments, I looked at her. She didn't seem happy. I guessed it was time to say I'm sorry.

"Mrs. Miller, I'm sorry I used that word."

"It's not the way we talk, and it's not the way we'll ever talk. You're never to use that word in my home again."

I dropped my eyes. "Yes, ma'am."

I sat quietly, not knowing what to do or say next.

"Why in the world did you ask me such a question, out of the blue like that?"

"Well, y'all are from up north. I just been wondering if y'all feel the same way we do, here in the South, about the . . . uh . . . the colored question."

"What colored question?"

"Uh, well, you know. Whether coloreds and whites ought to go to school together. The Supreme Court said separate schools won't work anymore. So I wonder what y'all think."

Her face was still not friendly, as she thought about the question.

"This is what I think, Sonny. The Court got it right. The South has got to change. Colored people are American citizens too. They should have the same rights as whites. I know you probably think separate but equal works, but it doesn't."

Her voice was firm. She sat quietly for a moment, letting the point sink in. Then her face eased into a warm, friendly smile. "You'll find that people of all kinds are more alike than they are different. The colored people you think are so different from you are really not so different at all." And she smiled again, even more reassuringly.

I was listening carefully, as she dropped her voice into a lower register. It was like she was telling me a secret just between the two of us.

"Have you ever wondered what their hopes and dreams are about? I mean the colored people. Well, I'll tell you. Their hopes and dreams are the same as ours. They want a fair chance at life. They want to bring their children into a better world than they had. That's really all any of us want. I'll bet it's what your own parents want."

I wanted to disagree with what she said, even though the last part at least I knew to be true. I'd heard my parents say words like that before. I remember my father telling me he hoped I'd never have to face the things he'd faced, trying to get by in the Great Depression with the limited education he had.

"Yes, ma'am."

That was about all I could utter. I couldn't argue with her for two reasons. The first was because I was still stunned at the reaction I had caused.

And second because her face was now soft and friendly again, and I didn't want to see that other face.

I thanked her for the collection and for talking with me. I slipped my jacket on and reached for the door, thinking that in the future my collection would be quick and efficient, that I'd never have a chance for another visit, that I'd never be invited back inside. I thought about saying, once again, that I was sorry.

"Thanks for stopping by, Sonny. I'll look forward to seeing you next Saturday."

Then she smiled and said, "Study hard this weekend and make good grades next week. Your studies are much more important than this paper route, you know."

"Yes, ma'am," I lied. I returned to my collections elated that I would have another visit with Mrs. Miller.

I cranked my Harley and eased into Twenty-fourth Street. I was only barely aware of the frigid drizzle peppering my face, clouding my glasses. How could I feel so good when I had just confirmed that Mrs. Miller's views were exactly the opposite of mine? Thankfully, I had all week to think it through. I could hardly wait till next Saturday.

21 • Ancient History

Isat at the kitchen table sipping my coffee. There was no rush. It was Saturday morning and too early for collections.

"Did you have any problems this morning?" my mother asked.

"No, ma'am," Eddie said. If he had a problem he wouldn't have mentioned it. That's the way he was.

"Well, it sure was cold and drizzly," I responded, then turned to my brother. "You don't know how lucky you are, Eddie. My glasses were fogged over all morning. Sometimes, I couldn't see anything. And you know it's impossible to clean your glasses when your clothes are all wet."

"Aw, it couldn't be that bad," he smirked.

"Yeah, you try wearing glasses and riding a motorcycle in the rain." Maybe I was a little too loud.

"Now, boys, don't bicker. You'll both be back out there in the weather in a few minutes, collecting your accounts. Why don't you boys have a pleasant morning while you can?"

"Yes, ma'am," I said. I felt like I needed to say something else, but the only thing on my mind was Mrs. Miller. I wondered if she would invite me in this morning or was she done with me.

"I've got a new customer on my morning route. They're from up north. Miller's their name."

"Oh, really? Why'd they come here?" my mother asked. We didn't get a lot of people moving here from other parts of the country in those days.

"Mr. Miller got a job here."

"Oh. Do you like them?"

"Yeah, they're real nice—even if they are Yankees."

The conversation moved on to other things, mostly between my little sister, Dale, and my mother. Then my mother turned to me.

"Sonny, please quit drumming your knees up and down. You're vibrating the table all over the floor."

"Yes, ma'am." I held both knees still with my hands. I was impatient to get on with my collections. But it was not the money that caused me to be edgy.

Several hours later Mrs. Miller answered my knock. I stood at attention holding my breath, as taut as a tight balloon, wondering if she would waste her time with me today. She smiled and asked me to come in out of the weather. Relief flooded through me like released air.

"Sit down. Rest for a few minutes."

"Yes, ma'am. Thank you."

Then she brought my money and a glass of water.

"I've been thinking," she smiled, "about our last visit. Tell me, why in the world do you feel so strongly about colored kids going to school with whites. Where I grew up, and in other parts of America, that's not unusual."

"Yeah, but you just don't understand. Here in the South, the races have always been separated. That's the way it's always been, and it's the way it needs to stay. There'll be trouble—lots of trouble—if the races are mixed."

"But that's so unfair. It's just not right." She paused. "It's got to change, you know."

"Yeah, that's what Mr. Carter says. He says that's the big argument of the federal government—that it's going to change and there's nothing we can do to stop it. But he says there is something we can do. We can resist it—fight back—just like the white people did during Reconstruction after the War."

"The Reconstruction? That's ancient history, Sonny. Almost a hundred years. What do you know about that? About the War?"

"Well, down here, we remember. About the War. And about how after the South was whipped, the federal government sent colored soldiers and put them over the white folks. That's how it was explained in that movie, *Birth of a Nation*. And that's how Mr. Carter explains it.

"Who is Mr. Carter?"

"He's the head of the White Citizens Council. I've heard him speak several times."

"Well, I don't think it was all that simple. Reconstruction was primarily about rebuilding the South after the War, not further destroying it."

"I've never studied it, Mrs. Miller, but I know what I've heard. And I've heard that the federal government would have put the colored over the whites here in the South if the whites hadn't fought back."

"What about your own family? Were they involved in the War?"

"Yes, ma'am. My great, great-grandfather was drafted into the Confederate Army. He was a private. He was captured in Virginia and sent to a prison camp in Delaware. He died there."

"Oh, that's terrible. What about his family?"

"Well, this is the story I heard. He had a wife and two little children. They had a farm in South Carolina. After he was captured, maybe about a year later, Sherman's men came through and burned the farm—the house and barn and all the crops—and killed all the animals. My great-great-grandmother and the children hid in the woods."

"What a horrible story! No wonder your family remembers that. So your great-great-grandmother had to raise the children without a husband?"

"Yes, ma'am. Except she died that winter trying to build back the house. Then the kids were orphans."

"Oh, my God. How unbelievable." She looked thoughtful for a few moments. "The Civil War was horrible. How can people do those things to each other?"

"Yes, ma'am. So when the federal government pushes us around, like they're doing right now, it reminds us of what they did to us before."

There was a long, quiet spell while she reflected. I studied my hands. My nails and cuticles were ragged. Printer's ink and grease from my Harley were imbedded in my fingers and under the nails. I saw that she too was looking at my hands, though I'm not sure she noticed them. Her eyes were far away. I quickly tucked my hands between my thighs and looked out the window.

"Thank you for telling me that story, Sonny. It helps me better understand you and other Southern people. Not being from here, it's hard for us to understand these attitudes. But that helps. It really does."

"Yes, ma'am. Thanks for listening."

We stood and walked to the door. As I opened the door, she placed her hand on my arm.

"I know you feel strongly, but I want you to know what I think about colored people—they're no different from you and me. They want the same things from life as white people—a fair chance. That's all really. And this situation with the schools? It's not going to be nearly as bad as you think. You just wait and see."

She smiled, and for a moment—just for a moment—I thought she might be right.

22 • Terror in the Night

Months had passed, and the memory of Miss Talley's kiss could still set my lips and face on fire. Though I knew she had just been playing with me, it was the only such experience I had to remember, and it was branded into my imagination. I tried, however, not to remember.

I grew up in a time and place where sex was taboo—a subject to be suppressed. My preacher seemed to be speaking to me alone as he hammered on that scripture about lust in one's heart. As a sixteen-year-old, almost seventeen, I was certainly familiar with sexual urges, but innocent of any significant knowledge of sex.

Because of something I'd seen one moonless night, I wondered if it was possible for the sexual urge to actually take control of a man's mind.

It was early morning, well before dawn. As I left my house to deliver my newspapers, I slumped half-asleep on my motorcycle. Suddenly, on the corner under a street light was a man not more than ten feet from where I passed, gazing up into the street light, oblivious to the world and me, and doing in public what everyone knew to be wrong, even in private. I snapped wide awake, horrified by the sight. But he completely ignored me, though my motorcycle engine rumbled as I passed him, turning the corner.

That event troubled me for months. I wondered if the man I'd seen was normal in the day time but changed somehow at night. I wondered if he was a vampire, or some kind of Jekyll-Hyde character.

Later, several paperboys and I were in the branch early one morning rolling our papers when suddenly he was there, that strange man, outside the storefront window. His left hand was high over his head, splayed flat against the window, his eyes locked on the bare light bulb hanging from the ceiling above us, a horrific public spectacle. There we were, there in plain view, but his flat black eyes saw nothing but the bright light. We yelled for Mr. Hawley, who had been napping. He grabbed a stick or something, but by then the guy had disappeared up the street.

At first no one said anything—we just looked at each other with wide eyes. Someone asked Mr. Hawley why a man would do such a thing, but he had no explanation other than "Aw, he's just crazy." Since I'd seen him before, I wondered if there might be some connection to the light, like the moon for a werewolf. Were the street light and the bare bulb's light substitutes for the moon on a moonless night? I didn't bring up my speculation to the other boys, but I thought he was some kind of sex maniac. We all concluded he was crazy, as Mr. Hawley had said. That seemed to be the best explanation.

Then, a month or so later, I was delivering my morning papers on Twenty-eighth Street, a dark dead-end road along the railroad. I tossed a few papers and then slowed my motorcycle as I began my turnaround at the end of the road where the woods began. A headlight on a motorcycle throws a narrow shaft of light, illuminating only a portion of the road directly in front, creating the appearance of a tunnel. The contrast is powerful, and the sides of the road seem to lie hidden in unearthly darkness. Coming almost to a halt about a hundred feet from the end of the road, I slowly brought my Harley around. As the bolt of light arced across the woods, suddenly, an arm's length from me, something burst from the shadows into the beam. Bam! An explosion of light from my Harley mushroomed against a man's mid-section. A horrifyingly ugly appendage, lurid in the light. A stubbled face, underlit from the beam below. Stark contours and cavernous shadows. Shaded eyes, locked on the headlamp, vacant and dead, as if from another world. The crazy guy!

I whirled to the left as he grabbed my shoulder with his left hand. In one frantic motion, I bolted from my Harley, shoved it against him, shed my heavy bag of newspapers, scrambled to my customer's house, and banged on his front door. "Mr. Bates, Mr. Bates!" From the porch, I watched in horror, my heart pounding in my throat as I waited at the door, afraid the crazy man would follow me onto the porch.

My Harley lay idling, its back wheel turning in the air, its front wheel wedged upward, headlight illuminating the man and the trees behind him. There, in the spotlight, he gazed, fixated, into the lamp, my jacket hanging from his left hand, his right hand at work. When the porch light suddenly snapped on, the man bolted from his trance, shook his head, and abruptly disappeared down a trail through the woods. Mr. Bates remained on the porch as I nervously retrieved my scattered papers, stuffed them in my canvas bag, mounted my motorcycle, and hurriedly escaped. It was only later that I missed my jacket.

Finally, a few weeks later, I decided to tell my father what I had seen. Maybe he would have an answer. He listened with interest, anger and frustration rising in his eyes. But he offered me no explanation for what could possibly cause someone to act like that. Instead, he sprang from his chair, motioned for me to stay put and strode to his bedroom. When he came back a moment later, I stood up to meet him. He was pounding his right fist into his open left palm. He then opened his fist and removed a metal object.

"Here," he said. "Put your fingers through these."

I slipped my fingers into the four rings, these gripped the bar in my fist as he had done and admired the heft and feel of it.

"These are brass knuckles," he said, caressing the metal in my fist as if conferring a blessing on me. "I've had 'em a long time. They've come in handy for me more'n a few times."

I examined the heavy metal exterior of the rings protecting my knuckles and wondered with awe what that might do to the crazy guy's face.

"You take those knucks with you every morning," he said. "Anybody messes with you, give 'em a taste of that. I guarantee you, they won't mess with you again."

I pounded my fist into my open palm. "Thanks, Dad."

I carried those knucks in my pocket every day after that though I never saw the crazy guy again. Still, those brass knuckles provided me with a new sense of confidence, a feeling of security against the unexpected dangers of the dark, against the madness that a full moon might cause.

But I knew there must be another side to sex—innocent, sweet and loving—and I thought of Mrs. Miller. That was hopeless, of course, so I made myself think about the rest of that mysterious and baffling, flirting and giggling, subset of humanity called girls. And whenever I thought about girls, I remembered Miss Talley and the "kiss," and my face would flush and my lips burn. I wondered if my dad knew something to give me confidence on that front. Was there a remedy he knew of as simple as a pair of knucks to help a boy deal with this other kind of terror? But I could never bring myself to ask. It was way too personal. And what was the point anyway? There was no immediate reason to raise that question. Girls mostly just ignored me. But to tell the truth, I could have used some help with Miss. Talley. I was leaving her a paper every morning and still had not gathered the gumption to knock on her door and collect.

23 • A Divisive Force

I came to myself lying on my back, looking up into the pre-dawn sky. I sat upright and was surprised to find myself seated on an asphalt road on the side of a hill. My head pounded. *Where am I?* Then I began to remember. I had been delivering my papers. I struggled to my feet. Standing on a sharp incline, gazing down the hill, I fought to keep my footing as the earth tilted and rolled. Slowly, my mind cleared. I recognized the place. Fourteenth Avenue, a few houses down the hill from Twenty-third Street.

Standing in place, I shook my head and tried to reconstruct the morning. I turned and looked up the hill. I had turned down Fourteenth Avenue—I remembered that—and had tossed a paper at that house. The rolled paper perched on the edge of the porch. And—well, that's all I could remember.

I looked around. *Where're my papers? Where's my Harley?*

I searched behind some shrubs along the sidewalk and in front of a parked car. They were nowhere to be found. My confusion threatened to roll over into panic. I stood quietly for a moment and closed my eyes. *Settle down,* I told myself. *They're here somewhere—just relax and think.* I opened my eyes and slowly turned in a circle. They were nowhere to be seen. Then I noticed behind me and up the hill a few steps a car was parked perpendicular to the curb. The street was so steep, people often parked their cars crossways to the hill.

In desperation, I darted up the hill. *My Harley!* It was on the uphill side of the parked car along with my satchel and scattered newspapers. I gazed in wonder, but after some deliberation it became apparent to me that I had run into the side of the car and had sailed over the top, landing on my back on the other side. There was no other alternative.

I lifted my motorcycle upright. The front wheel was jammed against the frame! The front fork which held the axle of my wheel was bent so badly the wheel wouldn't turn. I had struck the car at the center post with my rubber tire. There was no apparent damage to the car. So I turned my attention back to my own predicament.

What do I do now?

I couldn't leave my motorcycle here in the street and I couldn't possibly get it home. It wouldn't roll.

Where can I take it where it'll be safe until I can deal with it? I've gotta park it some place safe. Then I've gotta finish my route. Going to school seemed an unimportant afterthought.

I tried again to push the cycle but the front wheel was locked against the frame and wouldn't turn. *Who can I trust?* I could probably have trusted any of my customers along Fourteenth Avenue to look after my bike, but I just didn't know them well enough to ask, and, besides, it was five o'clock in the morning.

I looked down the hill to Twenty-fourth Street, less than a block away. The Millers lived on Twenty-fourth Street, just around the corner. I'd go there.

I collected my newspapers, some of which had gone underneath the car. My head was pounding when I finished bending and creeping under the car to get them all together. I then stuffed the newspapers into my bag and hid it behind a bush as best I could.

I turned back to my Harley. *How could I have done such a stupid thing? It was clear I'd gone to sleep at the switch. This was going to cost me a bundle.*

I wrestled my motorcycle down to the Millers' home and left it in their yard next to the front porch where I hoped it would be safe. Even though it was too early to ask their permission, I felt they wouldn't mind my leaving it there. Then I ran home, got my bicycle, retrieved my newspapers and finished delivering my route. I was late getting home. As I walked in the back door, my mother met me.

"Sonny, what happened? You've never been this late before. We've all eaten breakfast, but here," she turned to the oven, "I kept yours warm." She turned away from me before I had a chance to explain and started a second pot of coffee.

I paused by the stove to warm my hands. The fragrance of coffee billowed around me. The morning had been frantic and I was exhausted, but now my heart was slowing down. I held my hands over the stove and absent-mindedly watched the bubble glass top of the old percolator as the water boiled up from the bottom of the pot, then rolled and bubbled around the glass top before percolating down through the coffee grounds. *Sssssh blu blu blub—sssssh blu blu blub*, the pot sang. The water darkened from an amber to a deep shade of brown as I watched. I was mesmerized by the smell, the sound, the vision of coffee percolating in the pot. By the time the coffee was made and my hands were warm, I felt almost catatonic. I sat down at the table, too tired to eat. *How can I sit in school all day? Thank God for the coffee!*

My mother laid my breakfast on the table and looked at me expectantly as I slumped at the table.

"Well? What happened?"

I picked up the hot cup of coffee, warming my hands, then took a sip.

"What happened, Mama, was I had a wreck on my motorcycle and it won't run. I had to finish my route on my bike. That took a lot of time to run home, get my bike and finish."

She looked startled. "Are you okay? You look fine, but you're sure you're not hurt?"

"Oh, no, ma'am. I'm fine. But my Harley's gonna need some work. I'll need Dad to help me get it to the shop. It won't roll." I looked up from my plate where I'd been digging into my scrambled eggs. "Do you think he'll be here Saturday?"

"I'm not sure. Being on the Extra Board like he is—he never knows when they'll need him. But you know if he's here he'll be glad to help you."

I gulped my breakfast down, got dressed and raced for school.

I sat in classes all day but my mind was somewhere else. *What did the Millers think when they saw my motorcycle in their front yard? Will they want me to move it immediately? Will it be safe there? Will somebody come along and steal it? How will I move it to the Harley shop on Southside? It won't roll and Daddy doesn't have a truck. What will it cost to fix? If I can't afford to fix it, can I go back to delivering all my papers, morning and afternoon, on a bicycle? When will my head stop hurting?*

The questions kept rattling around all day. When school was out, I raced home—Phillips High was only a mile from my house—got my bicycle and delivered my afternoon papers. Then I went by the Millers' home about five o'clock to check on my Harley. I was relieved to see it was exactly where I had parked it and appeared to be just as I had left it in the early morning. I knocked on the door.

"Oh, hi, Sonny." Mrs. Miller and her boys came out on the porch and they all directed their attention to the motorcycle. "We've been wondering all day what happened. Looks like you had a problem this morning."

"Yes, Ma'am. I had a little accident."

Quickly, she turned back. There was concern in her eyes and on her face. "Oh, no. Are you hurt? Did you see a doctor? Are you feeling okay?"

Suddenly, I felt huge and grown up. I straightened my back. "Oh, I'm fine, Mrs. Miller. It didn't hurt hardly at all. But my bike won't roll so I parked it here. I hoped you wouldn't mind. I couldn't get it home."

Then she turned to the door, opened it, and yelled, "Vern, come out here. I want you to hear this."

In a moment, Mr. Miller opened the door and popped onto the porch, all agrin as Mrs. Miller and I studied my motorcycle. He laughed aloud. "Well, I'm glad to see you didn't break any bones."

That loosened me up, I guess, and I tried to laugh some too, but I was still mighty worried over my plight and what it would cost.

Mrs. Miller was serious like me, her face full of concern, and at the same time she seemed a little irritated with Mr. Miller.

"Vern, be serious! He could have been killed."

"Yeah, but he wasn't," he grinned. Then he looked serious for a moment. "So what happened anyway? We've wondered about it all day."

One side of me wanted to tell the story as a tragedy, to get more of Mrs. Miller's sympathy. But I couldn't do that with Mr. Miller standing there grinning. So maybe, I thought, it would be better told as a comedy, though I wasn't really feeling the humor.

"Well," I said, "I'm really not sure. All I know is, I was coming down the hill," pointing up the hill, "there on Fourteenth, tossing my papers, and the next thing, I'm picking myself up off the pavement. Couldn't find my motorcycle anywhere for a while, raced all around, frantic, like a squirrel looking for his acorn. I finally found it on the other side of a parked car. All I can figure is, I was watching where my paper would land instead of where I was going. I must have run into the side of a car—don't know how I did that—and then I sailed over the top of the car," I gestured with my hand in a big arc over my head. "And landed on my back. BOOM!" I clapped my hands once. "Just like that."

Mr. Miller threw back his head and laughed, laughed so loud it caused even me to laugh too, and I was not known for my sense of humor.

Then he turned serious. "So, what will you do? Fix this one? Replace the fork? Can you buy a part like that?"

"The fork is bent. I don't see how they can fix it. I'm sure I'll have to buy a new one. Don't know what it'll cost. Don't know how I'll get this thing to the shop. It won't roll and my Dad doesn't have a truck. I'll think of something, I guess, but can I leave it here till Saturday? I'll have time then to figure out how I'll get it to the Harley shop on Southside."

"Yeah, sure." Then he focused on the motorcycle. "Here, let me help you, we'll lift it up on the porch. It'll be safer here and out of the rain too."

Mr. Miller and I lifted it onto the porch. Then he wrapped his long arms around himself, patting briskly.

"Hey, it's cold out here. Let's go inside." He began to herd the boys toward the front door.

I didn't think he was including me. I hesitated. He gave me a gentle push.

"Now that's something. Sailed right over the car! Ha!"

I was beginning to see the comedy in it, even though I was getting stiff and sore, but my head was not aching as much as it had all day. His laughter was infectious. I was grinning, maybe even beginning to find a little pride in my misfortune.

"How was school today?" Mrs. Miller asked. "I hope this accident didn't distract you too badly?"

"Oh, no ma'am," I lied. "It was just fine."

I knew it was time for me to go, but I didn't want to leave their company. They always made me feel grown up. We didn't see eye to eye on the race question—that was clear. I wanted to find something that would establish a commonality, something we could agree on.

"Last weekend, I went to a meeting and heard a speech by Ace Carter. Do you know that name?" I directed my question to her, not him.

"You've mentioned him before," she said. "What did he talk about?"

"He's trying to teach the people about the dangers of communism. He thinks there's a lot of ways the communists are using to beat us—here in our own country."

"Oh, really? What, for example, are they doing?" she asked politely, though she didn't look terribly interested.

"Mr. Carter said that we're letting more and more immigrants come to our country—Russians and Jews and Catholics—people not like us. He says our immigration policy is a Trojan Horse and if we're not careful they will take us over without firing a shot. Besides, you just can't expect an immigrant to support our country against his own."

I waited. They looked surprised, even shocked. Even now after all these years, I shudder at how divisive the very mention of Ace Carter can be.

Mr. Miller stood up, laughed, and said, "Hey, that's way too serious for me. I can't handle all that serious stuff. Now, Helen, she likes serious talk. Maybe she'll talk to you. "

He left the room.

I looked at Mrs. Miller expectantly.

"You're full of surprises, young man." She paused, gathering her thoughts, a serious look on her face.

"First of all, I don't agree with you. Immigrants *do* make good citizens. I'm sure you and your family were immigrants somewhere up the line. You don't look like a native American. Second, Vern and I *are* immigrants. My father still speaks Norwegian. Vern's family is German. And the next point I want to make," and she looked at me hard so I wouldn't miss the point, "immigrants *are* loyal. It's only been a little over ten years since Vern was in Belgium with the United States 8th Armored Division in the Battle of the Bulge. You do know who was on the other side, don't you?"

I ducked my head. I was not missing the point. I had an image of Mr. Miller fighting his own kin.

"Yes, ma'am. They were the Germans." I didn't look up. I couldn't. I was too ashamed at what I had said to even say I was sorry. But my embarrassment was only beginning.

"You should also know we're Catholics."

I suddenly went weak. I was too mortified to utter a sound. I had done it again.

Then she said kindly, "You just can't believe everything you hear, Sonny. You've got to figure it out for yourself."

"Yes, ma'am."

She stood up.

Quietly, I said, "Thank you for letting me park my motor here for a few days." Then I headed for the door.

I'm sure from now on it'll be a quick collection, no conversation. How could I have done it again?

My morning had begun with a dumb mistake that was bound to cost me a bundle of money. Now, the day was ending with another blunder, a thousand times as bad. I should never have mentioned Ace Carter in the first place. That blunder I feared had really put a chill in our relationship.

As I walked out the door, she smiled. "Work hard at school this week and we'll look forward to seeing you next Saturday."

I mounted my bike, waved, and pedaled off into the darkening dusk.

Mrs. Miller, ever patient, had smiled, and that made all the difference.

24 • More Than Ordinary

As I collected my route that morning, I looked forward to telling Mrs. Miller my side of the story. I could already see her sympathetic face. After collecting about fifty of my accounts, I finally reached her house. I knocked and when she opened the door, I greeted her with a grim visage.

"Good morning, Mrs. Miller. Collect for the *News*, please."

"Oh, good morning, Sonny. Come in here where it's warm. Here, let me close this door. It's freezing out there. Why, seems like it's as cold here as back home in South Dakota where I grew up. Let's get you warmed up."

She led me to the kitchen table where Mr. Miller was reading a book and drinking coffee. I laid my route book on the table and tucked my gloves in my jacket pockets.

"Now, sit down right here. Would you like some coffee?"

"Yes, ma'am. Thank you." I dutifully sat down.

"You look a little upset this morning, Sonny," Mrs. Miller said as she bustled about her stove. "What's wrong? Got a problem?" She smiled warmly, looking sympathetic, as I knew she would.

"No—Well, I don't know . . . .," my voice trailed off. A long pause. I looked at my hands, which were now beginning to warm up. I wondered if she had seen the printer's ink under my nails. I rubbed my hands together and then tucked them into my jacket pockets. I felt doubly embarrassed, first about my dirty hands but more so because I was desperate to confide in her. She always seemed to understand, even when she disagreed with me. She was never judgmental. Maybe that's why I trusted her.

"Well, just a little problem—with my father. He never seems to understand . . . ."

I let it hang there for a moment, thinking she might ask about the problem. I suspected she would take my father's side. I even hoped she would, since it was clear my father would never approve my plan. If she took his side, I would feel a lot better about conceding. If she took my side, which I figured was about as likely as me going to the moon, well, I knew that just wasn't in the cards.

"What's it all about, Sonny? But only if you want to talk about it."

I glanced over at Mr. Miller. He was reading a book and didn't seem to have any interest in what my problem might be. So I twisted in my chair toward her and said quietly, so as not to bother him, "Well, I got me this plan—this plan to make some money. You know, I've got a morning paper route and an afternoon route. Altogether, I've got over three hundred customers. I'm working really hard, and I'm making a lot of money. I make about a dollar a customer a month. That's three hundred dollars a month!" I cast a look to her for approval, but she was waiting expectantly for the plan. "I'll be seventeen soon. I told my parents I wanna quit school."

Her eyes widened. She pulled in a deep breath.

"You know, down here in Alabama, you can quit school at sixteen. Anyway, I told them I'll get more paper routes. Then I'll get me a car so I can deliver them better and faster and I'll make a lot more money." I then looked into her face expectantly. I didn't tell my parents and I didn't tell her what I really wanted more than anything else was the car—if I had a car, maybe girls would notice me.

My classmate, Jimmy Osborn, was a paperboy like me. He'd delivered papers for several years from a motorcycle, but he had recently bought a car—a new 1956 Ford black-and-yellow Fairlane Sunliner convertible. And he was lording it over us at the paper branch like he was the King of England. He now delivered his papers with the top down. It seemed so effortless. And, as you might expect, he had a girlfriend, too.

I had kept this information to myself. I didn't tell my father or Mrs. Miller about that car, but that convertible, with me at the wheel, cruised through my daydreams like a pesky fly zipping back and back while I sat in my classes. A car like that was the answer to all my hopes and dreams.

"I'm horrified, Sonny," she said, "just horrified that you'd even consider quitting school. That doesn't make any sense at all." She leaned closer to me. "What'd your parents say?"

Mr. Miller was now paying attention. He put his bookmark in place and closed his book.

"My Mother started crying. My Dad, well, he looked like he was gonna hit me. His eyes—he's got these big, round blue eyes—it was like red flashes of lightening exploding out of his eyes. He was furious. I could tell he was busting to hit me, but he didn't. He told me, 'Boy, whatever silly idea you've got, just forget it. I didn't have a chance to finish school. But you're going to finish. And that's not all. You're going to college. You're not quitting your schooling.'"

Mr. Miller never seemed to take a lot of interest in all my serious discussions with his wife. He was always pleasant and funny and I liked to be with him, but he always let Mrs. Miller handle the heavy discussions. On this one, though, he seemed particularly interested. He looked me in the eyes, but there was no frivolity this time.

"Tell me about your father." His eyes pinned me down. "Why didn't he finish school?"

"He grew up on a farm. He was the oldest. His daddy made him drop out of school to work on the farm. I've heard him tell about it so many times—never being able to go to school 'cause he had to work." I said it like I never wanted to hear it again.

"Has he told you why school's important?"

"He says education is the ticket to a better job. He says it's the key to a better life. He wants me to be the first in our family to go to college. But I just don't have much interest in that. I wanna make money."

"Your father is right, you know. Education is the key."

"But I really don't like school. I like to work, to make money. That's what I wanna do."

I made my case the best way I could, but I sensed I was off the track, and I really didn't have much faith in it anymore. I suppose what I really wanted now was for them to persuade me to stay in school, so my decision would be voluntary—not a knuckling under to my dad.

Mr. Miller looked thoughtful, his eyes drifting away. I could feel a lecture coming on.

"Some people have vision, Sonny. Others don't. Your father had limited opportunities, but he's got tremendous vision."

I guess I had a puzzled look on my face.

"Do you not know what vision is? It means your father has foresight. He understands what's important. He has imagination and wisdom. I bet you've heard the scripture—I think it's in Proverbs—'Where there is no vision, the people perish.' That's familiar to you, isn't it?"

"Uh, yes, sir. I think so."

He paused, took a sip of coffee, his eyes never letting me go. Then he nailed me. "Do you have any vision?"

I sat quietly, looking into my empty cup and rolling it between my hands. There were no answers in the cup. I didn't know what to say.

"Tell me about your grades," he asked. "What subjects do you like?"

Now that was really embarrassing. It was easy to say I didn't like school, but it was a lot harder to get down to specifics about my grades.

"Uh, well, I haven't done too good. Mostly Cs, I guess." I couldn't tell him the truth about how bad my grades really had been.

He looked thoughtful for a moment. Then he asked, "Do you think you're smart enough to make good grades if you tried?"

I shrugged and gazed at my own palms, as if I might find the answer there. I'd never before thought about it. So far as I could remember, none of my teachers had ever told me I was smart or dumb, so I must be ordinary. "I don't know," I stammered.

He looked over at Mrs. Miller. "You know, Helen, I'd like to do a study of public schools and find out how students' grades correlate with their IQs. Here's a kid who's reasonably bright, we don't know how bright, but bright enough. And he's making Cs—nothing more—because he's not interested. If he tried, he might be making As and Bs. But he doesn't try. How many are there like him? How many geniuses are sitting there in school making Cs because they don't know they're bright? Do you think it's the schools down here—or the culture—or what? Back home, seems like schools got more out of us."

"I checked, Vern. Phillips High School is a good school. It has been for years. It's a shame he's not doing better. But the funny thing is," and she looked at me and smiled, "we know he works hard and is as responsible and industrious as anyone we've met. I think he's just focused on his work."

I didn't know whether she meant it, but I knew she was trying to make me feel better.

Then she turned to me. "You know," she said, "delivering papers is a part-time job. Your full-time job is school. If you focused on your studies the same way you focus on your paper route—with the same energy and enthusiasm—why, you'd be making all As."

"Yes, ma'am." I really wasn't enjoying our discussion anymore. I was ready to go see my next customer. I got my gloves out of my jacket pockets.

"We've talked about books," he said. "I know you're a good reader. You've told me about the books you're reading. Readers are usually pretty smart. Readers usually make good grades."

I'd never expected this turn of events. *Why didn't I make good grades?* I'd never really thought about it. But he was right. I did like books. We had discussed books on several occasions. They were always trying to get me to read better books, but I refused to do that. I was satisfied with the pocket book westerns and mysteries my dad brought home that people left on his bus. I loved Max Brand, but I thought Zane Grey was the finest western writer I'd ever read. My favorite books, though, were Mickey Spillane's potboilers—*I, the Jury; Vengeance is Mine!; Kiss Me, Deadly.* They were great. I'd read all seven of his books. Mr. Miller had told me he liked them, too, but didn't think they were the kinds of books my teachers would approve.

"I don't know. Guess I'm just not interested. I'm a lot more interested in my paper routes than school. I study just enough to pass, that's all."

"What's your highest ambition?" he asked.

I flinched. "I don't know." Now I was really getting embarrassed.

"Do you mean you've never thought about it?"

"Yes, sir. I haven't thought much about what I want to be. I guess I'm so busy with my paper routes I just haven't thought about it."

"Well, you're running a small business here on your paper route. Would you want to be a businessman?"

"I don't know. Daddy wants me to be a pharmacist, like Dr. Black up at Norwood Pharmacy." I pointed north toward the hospital. "He says pharmacists make good money and work inside where it's warm. And they call you Doctor, even if you're not. He says that's a lot of respect. But I don't wanna be a pharmacist."

"Well, what have you thought about?"

"I've been thinking about the newspaper, I guess. I work for the newspaper. Maybe I'd like to be a printer, you know, work on the printing presses that make the newspapers. I think that's what I'd like to do." And in truth, I had thought about printing. My friend James' father worked on the printing presses at the paper. But then, I'd seen his father and didn't like him. He never even said hello to me, just kept working on his homebrew beer. James told me all he does besides going to work is make his beer and drink it. That had put a damper on wanting to work on the presses.

He chewed on my comment about becoming a printer, then said, "Well, I guess most anybody could learn to run a press. You're not thinking high enough. If you like the newspaper business, then why not be a reporter? What about that?"

"You mean a writer?" I asked incredulously. "Someone who writes stuff to put in the papers?"

"Sure."

"Well, I don't know. I've never known anybody who's written anything except for Mr. Carter—Ace Carter. You've heard me talk about him. Now, he's written tons of stuff. He even writes a monthly magazine called *The Southerner*. I've told y'all about that. I'm gonna bring y'all a copy."

"Yeah, Sonny. And I've told you before I know all about Mr. Carter I want to know from the newspapers. He's nothing but a Klansman in a business suit." There was a long pause. I knew how they felt about Mr. Carter. They thought he was a rabble-rouser, always trying to stir up the race problems we have here in the South.

"Do you have any idea what I do? How I make my living?"

"Don't you work for that company that puts out the *Farmer's Almanac*?"

"No, but close. It's called *Progressive Farmer*. We put out a magazine for farmers. I'm in the editorial department. I help with the articles for the magazine." He sipped his coffee, looking like he was thinking about something way off. Then he smiled.

"I never thought about being an editor or writer when I was your age either. But I learned early that education is important. It's a competitive world out there and you've got to prepare yourself. That's the main thing. It doesn't matter that you don't know what you want to do. Most of us don't know. I surely didn't. What's important is to get prepared. Then you can do whatever comes along. And something good'll come along, if you're prepared."

Then he sprang from his chair, stretching his long arms above his head, as if to end his lecture.

"Yes, sir," I said without enthusiasm, as I stood and pulled my gloves on.

Mrs. Miller told me to study hard this week. She patted me on the arm, telling me with her eyes that I counted for something.

As I left their house, I wondered why I had brought up the subject in the first place. Wish I'd kept my big mouth shut. Two things were certain, though. I would not be dropping out of school, and I would not be buying a car. Then it occurred to me that without a car no girl would ever be interested in me—that too was a certainty. As I walked to the house next door to collect, I pondered my dilemma.

I was glad to learn Mr. Miller was a writer. I loved books more than anything besides my paper route. I knew, of course, that only very bright people could write books and articles for the newspaper. It had never occurred to me to consider writing something other people would want to read. But Mr. Miller suggested I might be a reporter. And Mrs. Miller said I should be making all As.

For the first time in my life, I wondered if I might be something more than ordinary.

25 • Mary's Place

Mary's Place was the den of evils I'd been warned about throughout my life. The preacher spoke of the dangers of alcohol, and the path of iniquity down which drinking would lead one to his doom. He and my Sunday School teachers told of broken marriages and abandoned children, all caused by this scourge on society. I heard sermons on the subject of social drinking, and learned that a social drinker, even if he had only one small drink, was worse than the binge drinker because his behavior was an endorsement and approval of booze and might cause someone else to stumble and fall. The Christian message I heard over and over revolved around a series of activities that were off limits. Drinking was the worst, because it led to all the others.

I grew up in a home of teetotalers. Not once did I see a can of beer, or a bottle of whisky or wine in our home. Well, let me correct that: my father kept a bottle of gin at our home, but only for "medicinal purposes." Every time I had a sore throat, I could count on his remedy, a piping hot lemonade laced with gin. I hated his medicine then, but I do think it actually helped me feel better.

My parents soundly condemned anyone who consumed alcohol, my mother more loudly than my father. I never saw him take a drink until the reception following my daughter's wedding. It was plain to see my father enjoyed the champagne, and plain to see my mother's chagrin.

I was as innocent and naïve as a young boy could have been and soon discovered on Saturday afternoons that Mary's world was as fascinating as mine was barren. I could usually count on some adventure each Saturday when I entered Mary's Place to collect my account. As an adolescent, my ambitions and yearnings were often limited and misdirected. In Mary's Place, I learned that some peoples' dreams had actually expired.

Mary's Place was located on the margin of my route, on the corner of Eleventh Avenue North and Twenty-third Street, directly across the street from the two-story house in which my family lived before I was school age. Mary D'Amico was the owner and one of my favorite customers. She was a short, robust, olive-skinned woman with plenty of energy, enthusiasm, and a sharp tongue.

Sometimes when I collected, Mary would give me a Grapico, a locally made grape soda. I'd sit at the bar, resting and sipping my soda, listening to the jukebox and watching her patrons. When somebody dropped a quarter into the jukebox, it lit up like a circus. The records would spin and the music sounded as good as the Grapico tasted.

Almost every song they played was by Hank Williams. He had died several years earlier, on January 1, 1953, at twenty-nine years of age, a genius by anyone's measure. Even though I had discovered rock 'n' roll, I continued to love Hank's music best. The thumping music and the lyrics of rock'n'roll answered some emotional need I had, probably the need to break away from my father and mother who hated Elvis Presley and the other rock'n'rollers. It gave me a chance to express my growing sense of rebellion. But it was country music that spoke to me of loneliness, of lost hopes and dreams. Hank Williams was the king of country, and through his music I could understand, at least in part, why some folks were content to park on a bar stool for an afternoon. I can hear Hank now:

> Hear that lonesome whippoorwill,
> He sounds too blue to fly.
> The midnight train is whining low,
> I'm so lonesome I could cry.

I've never seen a night so long
When time goes crawling by.
The moon just went behind a cloud
To hide its face and cry.

Hank Williams connected with me. It was naïve, I know, but in my juvenile imagination, I thought I understood the loneliness and desperation, the despair, the ennui of men and women clutching long-neck beers, thought I could see into the same darkness where their eyes stared for empty hours. Many of these people in Mary's were displaced hill people, like us, and I guessed they were just struggling to find their place. Like us. Like me.

Oftentimes, sitting in a booth across from my barstool, there would be some tough looking, middle-aged women drinking beer and talking. Sometimes they would tease me. Mary knew their rough talk embarrassed me, and tough as she was, she often stepped in and told them to leave me alone. Over time, I came to learn that many of these women I encountered at Mary's Place were "ladies of the night."

Early one afternoon after collecting my account at Mary's, I sipped my soda, listening to Hank Williams. A couple—a man and woman in their late thirties or early forties—sat in absolute silence, in the same booth, across from each other. They never made eye contact, never spoke. And with them was a young boy, maybe seven or eight years old, who sat quietly in his own isolation. They never looked at him, never said anything to him. They didn't move, except to raise their beers.

I could not take my eyes off them. Perhaps I saw in them an image of what my own marriage might someday turn out to be. Or, maybe I saw something of my own history at play in that booth. In most social situations, I was silent and watchful and painfully lonely. It was not a great leap to hit fast-forward and see myself sitting in that booth, nursing a beer, thinking my own thoughts while my wife and little boy waited.

A few years later, when I was in college, I read John Steinbeck's *The Winter of Our Discontent*. There, the protagonist utters these pathetic words to his wife of twenty years, which at the time almost took my breath, and which I've always remembered:

"Does anyone ever know even the outer fringe of another?
What are you like in there? Mary—do you hear me? Who are you
in there?"

As I read those words fifty years ago, the image of that couple from
Mary's Place dropped onto the page in front of my befogged eyes. That
scene in Mary's Place has followed me all these years and has become a
metaphor to me for the times I feel I'm in a world that's short on meaning
and long on loneliness.

There on my barstool at Mary's Place I watched that small family—no,
three separate people, each terribly isolated—getting a real world view of
ideas I would later meet in college, as I read Kafka, Hesse, Bellow, Salin-
ger, Walker Percy, Thomas Wolfe, and many others who wrote of being
"lost in the cosmos."

I was getting a lesson in the need to develop relationships. I began to
see for the first time I needed to get out of my shell. So today, when I've
run out of things to talk about with my wife, that image of the couple
from Mary's Place slides back into focus. I redouble my efforts to come
up with something to say. Anything to keep the bridges open. I count my
lessons from Mary's Place worth those I learned in college.

Once, when I was in college several years after I'd given up my paper
route, I told my friend, Clarke, who I thought to have come from an aris-
tocratic background, about my favorite drinking place. In truth, I had no
favorite drinking place. I'd never even had a beer until I was in college.
I had been back to Mary's Place for a beer, but only a couple of times. I
certainly was no regular. I guess I wanted to impress Clarke with what I
thought was the radical difference in our backgrounds. He challenged me
to take him there.

When he got in my car, I regretted I didn't tell him to wear jeans.
The people who went to Mary's wore work clothes. Clarke, dressed in
plaid Bermuda shorts, looked like he was going to a frat party. *Uh, oh,* I
thought, *this is going to be embarrassing.*

When we entered Mary's Place, it was hopping, and the juke box was blaring out some hillbilly song. Everything stopped but the music. Mary froze, her arm extended with a beer. All eyes were on us, just as I feared.

"There's an empty booth right over there." I pointed and quickly loped that way, hoping to hide. Clarke slowly followed behind me, seemingly oblivious to the stares, as he took it all in.

I suddenly remembered the drunk colored guy who danced into Mary's one late afternoon, eyes half-closed, snapping his fingers and jiving like mad. He had danced half-way across the concrete floor when a couple of white guys stood. As they looked ominously at him, he suddenly realized he had stumbled into a white bar. In his drunken state, he panicked, fell over backwards, and scrambled out onto the sidewalk on his hands and knees. Everyone guffawed, finding great fun in the scene. I too was amused at the time, but I also felt sorry for the man who had simply made a wrong turn.

I was afraid Clarke and I were about to get a good taste of blue collar behavior from Mary's patrons, but their laughter was mild and seemed good-natured enough as we slipped into a booth against the wall, where I hoped Clarke's knees and his Bermudas would fade into the darkness. He was clueless, didn't know his shorts were as out of place as a turban. He looked around some more, then said, "Hey, Man, this is a real joint, isn't it?"

As we sipped our beer, I watched as a woman in the booth directly behind Clarke turned to get on her knees and then looked over the partition, straight down at Clarke's head. I wondered what she was up to, as she smiled in a gentle way. Clarke was busy looking around and had no idea of her presence. Then she reached over the partition and tousled Clarke's wavy, blond hair, smiling and cooing at him as if he were a new-found baby. Clarke was stunned, and I was laughing like crazy. Mary came from behind the counter and told the woman to "behave yourself or get out."

My friend sat there, his eyes wide in disbelief. I was having a great time at his expense. Then two old women got into a terrible fight, moved into the middle of the floor, shouting, cursing, and crying as they tore and scratched each other. Again, out from behind the counter came Mary, with a broom, and swept them out her front door. "Out, out! Take it outside." Every customer, man and woman, including Clarke and me, moved outside onto the sidewalk, long-neck beers in hand. Only Mary was left inside. We formed a circle around the two women, who had begun tearing the clothes from each other. That's the kind of place it was.

Clarke mentions Mary's Place to me every time I see him. We joke around about what fun it was, how we'd like to do it again. But, of course, there's no going back. That landmark from our youth is long gone now, like the house of my early childhood across the street . . . and everything else for blocks around. It's all now, as I write this, a vast urban wasteland, demolished by the Civic Center for future expansion. I have grown a lot over the years . . . as a matter of fact it seems I have grown more than the Civic Center.

Regardless of the size and scope of the dimensions the Civic Center may one day reach, it could never compete on the same scale as the expansion of my own sensibilities as I sat there on that barstool in Mary's Place, observing for the first time in my life the real world in which I lived.

26 • Our Greatest General

hen I knocked on the door, Mr. Miller answered. "Why, good morning, Sonny. Come on in. I'll get your money. Have a seat."

Mrs. Miller came into the kitchen where I was sitting. She looked at me and at my wet rain coat.

"Here, let me take that coat. I know you must be cold. I'll fix you some hot chocolate. Would you like that?"

"Yes, ma'am," I responded gratefully. She bustled about the kitchen, got the milk heating and said she had some chores to attend to. That was disappointing to me because I had much rather talk to her than Mr. Miller. He was kind and funny but he usually wouldn't get serious, and I had serious stuff to talk about. I took the plunge with him anyway since she was busy.

"Mrs. Miller told me you were in the Army back during the Second World War."

"Yeah, that's right. A little over ten years ago. Sometimes it seems so long ago and other times it feels like yesterday."

"We won that war, but we didn't win the war in Korea, did we?"

"Well, no, we didn't. But it wasn't really a war like World War II. It was supposed to be an action by the UN to drive the North Koreans out of South Korea, but it got outta hand. The Chinese came in to help the North Koreans. It turned out to be a very nasty war for several years before a ceasefire was finally reached."

We were pensive for a moment, and then I posed the question I'd been thinking about. Even though General Douglas MacArthur had faded away from the public eye, like he said in his speech old soldiers do, I still wondered from time to time how the Korean War might have turned out if he hadn't been fired.

"Mr. Miller, do you think Truman should have fired General MacArthur?"

He raised his eyebrows and smiled.

I could tell that he didn't want to get into it.

"There's just no way, Mr. Miller," I suggested with some enthusiasm, "no way that firing General MacArthur was a good thing. After the Chinese came pouring into Korea, Truman fired him! Then after that we were fighting the Chinese with one hand tied behind our backs. What kind of a war is that? Why, I've been told if Truman had just let him go, MacArthur and our Army would have gone through China like a dose of salts."

Mr. Miller smiled sadly and slowly shook his head.

"No kidding, right there in Korea, we had a chance to beat communism once and for all, but Truman didn't have the guts for it. That's what people here think. And everybody knows we've got to fight Russia someday. We should've gotten it over with right then and there."

I was geared up for a real discussion that Saturday morning. The rain was falling steadily, and I had no desire to get back out in it. I was comfortable and warm. Mrs. Miller had handed me the hot chocolate and left me to fend for myself with her husband. I was eager to probe just how liberal these Yankees really were. Or maybe I just wanted someone to talk to, somebody I trusted who, nonetheless, had strange notions about some things.

"Well, what do you think, Mr. Miller? Don't you really think Truman made a horrible mistake firing our greatest general?"

"Aw, Sonny, you know there are two sides to every question," he offered, clearly not interested in the topic or the prospects for hot debate on Saturday morning.

"But what do you think?" I insisted.

Mr. Miller yawned, stretched his long arms in the air. "This is too serious for me on a Saturday morning," he chuckled. "Go talk to Helen.

She'll talk to you about anything."

I pushed back, "But I want to know what *you* think."

Mr. Miller sighed as if he wanted no part in the discussion, and then leaned forward and caught me with his eyes.

"This is what I think. If President Truman had let MacArthur continue across the Yalu River into China, that might have led to another World War. And then unbelievable world-wide suffering would have occurred, maybe even on a scale larger than World War II. And we might not have won! Think about that!" Then he pulled in a deep breath and slowly let it out, relaxing back in his chair. It must have been the look on my face, the big question mark that accompanied my widened eyes and slackened jaw. He continued in a confidential voice.

"Did you know that after the war—World War II—we pretty much demobilized our army? Do you know what that means? It means we let most all of our army and navy go home. They were discharged. We weren't ready for another war in 1950. We had to call up the reserves. But regardless of that, we should never let ourselves be drawn into a land war in Asia—it's too big, too many people." He gave me a wan smile and then continued, "The President understood all those dangers. I think he made the right decision. Now, Korea is still divided, but at least it's at peace. Don't you think that's better than more war?"

I was completely undeterred. "But communism is an evil force in the world. And they wanna rule the whole world," I responded. "We can't let that happen. Our system—capitalism—is the way it oughta be—and we gotta defend it," I said with emotion, parroting talk I'd heard from adults.

I guess I had pushed Mr. Miller too hard. He sat up in his chair, the pleasant expression on his face gone.

"Why?" he said, exasperated with me. "What's so wrong about communism? What's your background? Your father doesn't own some big company, does he?"

"No, sir." He had my full attention. I sat bolt upright and waited, holding my breath.

"Under our system, seems like the rich get richer and the poor get poorer. What's so great about that system?" He paused, looking me in the eye for an answer. I was speechless. I had never heard anyone question our system. I was frozen in place and the expression on my face must have been one of incredulity.

"Now, understand, I'm not a communist. I believe in our system. But capitalism has its problems too." I could tell he wanted to stop, but he'd come too far, so he took a deep breath and reluctantly plowed on. "Look," he said, "we've got a good system, but it's because we have laws that restrict the big companies. If it weren't for laws, the rich would corner the market on everything until they owned it all. Maybe one percent of the people would own everything in the world including all of us. Maybe we'd be slaves. We wouldn't be able to advance no matter how hard we work—no matter how smart we are. And why should only the smart get ahead? Maybe society has an obligation to look after those less able to compete. That's what socialism is all about." He paused to let his comments sink in. He could see that I was squirming in my seat, confused. Then he continued quietly:

"I know the communists have removed God and religion from the process, and that's a problem." He paused again, like he really didn't want to say any more. But then he added: "Christianity in the early years was a lot more like communism than capitalism. Did you know that?"

I opened my mouth to answer but nothing came out. I could hardly believe what Mr. Miller was saying. I thought all of America, except for some foreigners who lived up north, agreed that communism was absolutely, irredeemably evil. And that Christianity gave a hundred percent support to our capitalistic system.

Mr. Miller took a deep breath. He looked like he wanted to stop, but then, in a kind and patient manner, asked, "Your father is a bus driver, right?"

"Yes, sir." It was all I could do to answer.

"Is he a member of the union?"

"Yes, sir." I took a deep breath and squeezed out, "He says he's a strong union man."

"Well, you do understand, don't you, that the unions are a direct threat to capitalism. The unions sprang up because capitalism takes advantage of the workers unless the workers organize. A union can bargain by threatening to withdraw labor. One man alone can't do that. Only the combined force of many men, the entire work force, can achieve a balance with capital. So socialism is simply taking the union model and pushing to the extreme where the workers rule and not the rich."

Mr. Miller paused, then asked me:

"Would that not be a better system for you and your family than a system in which the rich exploit the poor, since you are among the poor?"

I offered no answer. I was hardly breathing. My brain was whirling.

"All I'm saying is this: No one has a monopoly on the truth. The truth is a complicated thing. Don't ever push for a premature fight."

Mr. Miller let it lay for a minute. I sat there as rigid as a fence post. He could see I was upset.

"Believe me, you don't want to go to war over those issues. They are basic economic issues and over time we'll see which model will prevail in the marketplace. Meanwhile, watch closely, read and learn. Think these things through. That's all I'm trying to say. Don't be a pawn in some larger game you can't yet understand, okay?"

"Yes, sir," I responded without enthusiasm, my head going in circles. I had begun to slump.

"It's only been a few years ago that there were no laws against child labor. Did you know that children ten years old were working in horrible conditions, and it took years to pass the child labor laws because capitalists didn't want to lose the benefit of cheap labor?"

"No, sir."

He stopped then, laughing and spreading his big hands in surrender. "Now I don't want you leaving here thinking I'm a communist. I'm not. I believe in our system. But there's usually two sides to every question – that's the point I'm trying to make. I'm sorry I got all worked up over this. Next time, ask me an easier question."

With that, he dismissed me. I called goodbye to Mrs. Miller as I put on my raincoat. I bolted from the Miller's porch into the rain and to the house next door. I knocked on the door and when it opened I said absent-mindedly, "Collect for the *Post-Herald*, please." My customer could have paid me in clacker[7] for all I would have noticed. My mind was jumbled, my brain trying to sort the heretical new ideas Mr. Miller had scattered in my head.

27 • Taciturnity

The phone rang as I came in the door from school.

"Better get down here as soon as you can!" Mr. Hawley told me. "Your brother's been in a wreck, right here in front of the store. They've taken him up to the hospital."

My heart stuttered. My dad was at work and my mom wasn't home. I dropped my books and dashed for the garage, jumped on my Harley, kick-started it and raced the block and a half to the intersection at Seventeenth and Highway 31. The traffic light was against me. The traffic crept by. An old truck with a high-staked bed was headed north but parked in the southbound lane over by the curb in front of Johnny Graffeo's store. It had run into a parked truck. People milled around it. A police car was there. Clearly, an accident had occurred.

The light changed. I darted across, paused to see Eddie's Harley crushed between the trucks. *He couldn't have survived*, I thought in a panic.

I revved my engine and blasted past the branch and the covey of boys without so much as a wave. I was on a mission.

My conscience began to ache as I considered he might be dead. I thought about the incident a few months earlier and glanced down at the gas tank on my new Harley—bruised, scratched and dented on one side. I had been so proud of my new motorcycle. I'd had it only a few months—had traded my other one, damaged from running into the side of the car—and now this one was damaged too. Eddie should have been more careful with my new motorcycle, but now my conscience ate at me as I ruminated on my nasty attitude toward my little brother following that accident.

I rarely rode my motorcycle to school. If I did, I worried all day about whether someone was meddling with it as it sat parked in front of Phillips High in plain view of hundreds of students. I could visualize some guy tampering with the carburetor or damaging it in some way. Usually, I caught the bus or walked the one mile from my home to Phillips.

One day, Eddie was running late. I had already left for school. In order to save time, he rode my new Harley, the color of pumpkin orange. It didn't have a scratch on it. Somehow, he had a wreck on the way to school, and he and the Harley took a long slide on the asphalt.

I didn't know of the accident until I saw him in the hallway between classes. Both arms were abraded from his wrist to his elbow and were literally oozing blood. He had sat through classes all morning in pain, blotting and cleaning himself in the restroom between classes. I stared in amazement.

"What happened to you?"

"Had a little accident on the way to school," he answered, as if it were an everyday occurrence.

"You need to go home and get Mother to clean the dirt and grease outta your arms. That's a mess. How'd you do it?"

"I took a spill . . . on your Harley."

"What! Where is it?"

"Out front."

I dashed out to the front sidewalk, where the various motorcycles and scooters were parked. No! There my new motorcycle sat, replete with abrasions and bruises and dents. I was furious.

Later that day, a teacher saw his arms and sent him to the office for treatment. He told me later they poured alcohol in the abrasions and scrubbed then clean with a cotton compress. He didn't embellish, as if the pain were inconsequential

That's the way he was. As stoic as a soldier. I shouted and fumed and pouted over the damages, and probably gave him a couple of hard punches, but that too seemed to make no impression on him. It didn't make sense. I knew he was as conscientious as I but he didn't seem to carry the same emotional freight I did. He kept a close check on his emotions while everyone around me knew what I was thinking.

Regrets about the way I had acted toward him—my own brother—had chewed me up by the time I'd dashed the two blocks to the Norwood Hospital Emergency Room.

I shut off the engine and bolted through the doors to the nurse's station. I dropped off a newspaper there every morning so they knew me, even in my panic and consternation.

"Where's Eddie—my brother?"

"He's in room one, right there," and she pointed.

I imagined he'd be lying on a gurney with doctors and nurses around, all working frantically to save his life. Or worse, he'd be on the gurney, alone in the treatment room, and covered from head to toe.

I paused before the curtain—expecting the worst—regrets and prayers twisting around in my head.

I jerked the curtain open. He was alone. No doctors or nurses. To my amazement, he was not horizontal. He stood vertical underneath the examination lights, naked, illuminated, and shining against an otherwise darkened room, like an object in a museum.

David, I thought. He looked like the statue of David, there under the lights, tall, alert, and ready. I'd seen a picture of Michelango's David in a text book (or somewhere), and it had darted across my mind as I looked at him, nude and unembarrassed.

His face registered a look of recognition more than surprise. His legs were slightly apart, loose and alert, as if ready to stride out of the room. But he didn't move or even flinch.

"What are you doing here?" he asked, as if he were some seasoned tourist saying, What a surprise to run into you here in London like this.

"What am I doing here? I heard you'd been killed. That's what." I looked around at the curtains, and back. "Where're the nurses?"

"Oh, they'll be here in a minute. They went out to get some stuff to put on this," and he twisted his arms toward me. The raw abrasions down both arms were bloody. There were abrasions along one hip and leg. He must have been in pain, though he didn't show it.

"They told me to get undressed." He shrugged. "All the way," he explained in apology.

I looked again. What a sight. My brother, nude under the lights—calm, unconcerned, nonchalant—as if he were at home in the bedroom we shared, about to get dressed to go deliver his morning newspapers—absolutely nude—except for the black engineer boots on his feet and his greasy, black, Harley Davidson captain's cap clamped onto his flattop. I almost laughed at the incongruity.

"What about Brother?" he asked.

"Whatta you mean?"

"Brother Price. He was with me. Riding behind me."

"I don't know."

We learned later that Brother had been taken to the hospital in an ambulance. He had been knocked off the motorcycle onto the pavement a distance away. He'd suffered a fractured skull.

We also learned that the truck driver failed to stop at the traffic light because his brakes failed.

Eddie told me later that the truck knocked him onto the pavement and then, as it passed over him, he grabbed something behind the bumper and held on as he watched the front left tire turn inches from his face—then the crash. The truck had rolled onto his boot as it came to a stop. The paperboys had pushed the truck off him and pulled him from underneath. He had a sprained ankle. His engineer boots had saved a crushed foot. It was all as simple as that, he said.

If it had been me, I would have embellished the story with death grips and terror and grievous injury. I'd have told everyone about my accident with all the gritty details. But then, we were different, he and I.

I think I liked him the better.

28 • School on Saturday

Saturday morning. I'd been up since four A.M. I looked at my watch. Ten thirty. I'd been at it all morning, first delivering papers, then collecting. I should have been tired by now, but I felt good. Mrs. Miller's house was in the next block, and I could hardly wait.

Most Saturdays, she would take some time with me—ten or twenty minutes. I guess you might say she was trying to understand what drove my radical views. For some reason I couldn't understand, except that I liked the Millers so much, I felt a driving need to teach them about the Southern way of life. I was like a religious fanatic out to convert the unbeliever.

Even though I was well aware I'd said some dumb things before and was still embarrassed about them, I was ready to try again as I marched onto the Miller's porch and knocked at the door. Mrs. Miller opened the door and smiled.

"Collect for the *Post-Herald*, Mrs. Miller. Hope you're doing well today."

"Oh, hi, Sonny. Come in and sit down. I'll be right with you."

I was thrilled she invited me in. I hoped that meant she would have a few minutes to visit with me. Two minutes later, she returned with my money and sat down. "Well, tell me about your week. Did you do well at school?"

"Yes ma'am. Everything was good. Nothing special, but okay," I said and shrugged.

"What was the best thing that happened this week?"

I thought about that for a moment. "Well, I went to a meeting of the Citizens Council and heard a speech by Ace Carter. I think I've told you about him."

"You mentioned him, yes. What was his speech about?"

The look on her face told me all I needed to know about what she thought of Ace Carter, but I couldn't help it. I plunged ahead with my description of his talk.

"Well, he talked about the communist conspiracy to take over our country. He said all this race business here in the South is a part of the conspiracy, that the communists want to stir up a race war in America— that's what all this race business is really all about."

She had a skeptical, distasteful look on her face, as if she couldn't believe that I had bought into his ideas.

"Then he said the Jews are a part of that conspiracy. And he mentioned a school up in Tennessee—the Highlander Folk School[8]—which he said is a training ground for communists. He said," and I raised my hands and eyebrows for emphasis because this was information I knew she wouldn't know, "that Rosa Parks was an example—you know, that colored woman in Montgomery who wouldn't move to the back of the bus. Well, she went to that communist school and learned how to, uh, break the laws she didn't agree with, like moving to the back of the bus."

"And did you believe all that?"

"Well, yes, ma'am. Mr. Carter's a smart man, well educated. He sure had everybody all fired up. People were shouting and hollering and stomping their feet. I think we all believed him."

She shook her head, a sad look on her face. "Why in the world are you so interested in that? You're what? Seventeen years old now?" I nodded. "You ought to be interested in having fun. It's not healthy to be so pessimistic at your age."

Then she looked me in the eye and smiled. "If you ask me, I don't believe there is any conspiracy. Colored people just want to be treated fairly. And Rosa Parks? She paid her money like all the passengers. She just didn't want to go to the back of the bus. Neither would you. That's got nothing to do with communism. Your Mr. Carter is getting you all worked up over some half-baked idea. He may be smart, but he is selling lies, and you need to learn to see through that stuff."

I didn't have an answer at that moment, but I was thinking about what my answer would be. How could a smart, educated man like Mr. Carter make speeches about ideas he didn't believe? Or worse, how could he sell ideas he knew weren't true? I'd been following Ace Carter for over a year and believed everything he said. I thought he was the leader who would carry us through the racial turmoil and protect our Southern way of life. I knew Mrs. Miller didn't agree with any idea he had, and all her previous comments I had taken with a pinch of salt. After all, she was from up north and just hadn't got acclimated to our way of thinking. But somehow what she said this time was so simple, so straight-forward, it caught me flatfooted. 'She just didn't want to go to the back of the bus. Neither would you.' It was true. I wouldn't want to pay my money and then be told I had to go to the back, as if I weren't good enough to sit in the front. Would that really make someone a communist?

Then she smiled. "And the Jews in this county? That's a lot of hogwash, Sonny. They don't want communism either. I'm new in town, but I've been here long enough to know that Norwood has a lot of different ethnic groups. There are Italians and Greeks all over the neighborhood. I'll bet you have Jewish customers too, don't you?"

I thought for a moment.

"I do have one Jewish family I know of. Maybe more. But at least one."

"Well? Do you think they're communists? Do they look like the kind of people who'd want to overthrow the government?"

"No ma'am. They're real nice. They have a son, Stanley, who's younger than me, but I like him a lot. We used to play together sometimes before I got my paper routes."

"So, now what do you think."

"Well, I like Stanley and his family."

"If that's the case, then do you think you should repeat the nonsense that Carter man told you about Jews? You know that kind of generality is just not true, don't you?"

I knew she was right, but it was embarrassing to admit it. I took a deep breath. "Yes, ma'am, I guess you're right."

"Good. I'm glad you agree. Now let me tell you what happened to me a few weeks ago. One of my neighbors—I won't say who, she might be one of your customers—was visiting with me. She told me that since I was new in town I should know which of the department stores to shop at and which to avoid. I was curious and asked her why I wouldn't want to shop at those stores she named. They were Pizitz and Loveman's and several others. 'Because,' she said, 'they're all owned by Jews and we don't shop there.' I told her that I had shopped with Jews all my life, that I didn't appreciate her advice and that I'd shop where I pleased."

Mrs. Miller laughed. "I'm sure she won't be back to see me. At least, I hope she won't."

Then she shot out of her chair. "I'm sorry if I sound like an old school teacher. It's Saturday—no school today—so let's not be so serious."

She smiled, and I guess I did too. I always felt better after talking with her. She had a way of making complicated things seem so simple.

"All this business about conspiracies, they're for old men to worry about." Her smile was reassuring. "Not you. Enjoy life while you can."

She ushered me out the door and on my way. I went about my collections but I kept thinking about her face—how pretty and warm and soft and sympathetic it could be—and how hard it must have turned when she told her neighbor off. I had seen her face turn angry once. I never wanted to see her face that way again. And I thought about what she had just said—'It's Saturday—no school today.' Yet somehow, every time I left her house, I felt like she'd taken me to school.

29 • The Mob

I picked myself off the floor and shook my head. The mob surged against the ring. There should have been a clamor, but it was muffled and far away. My head was stuffed with cotton. My ears rang.

Walter jogged up and gripped my arm.

"You okay? You got away from me."

"I think so." I touched my face, then looked at the blood on my fingers.

A few people attempted to climb into the ring. A policeman inside the ring brandished his billy stick, threatening to beat them back, while the guy in the mask stalked around the ring. Everything was hazy.

"Let's get you to the restroom, clean you up. We sure don't need to get arrested."

I touched my temple. "My glasses."

In a moment, Walter spied my glasses on the floor and brought them to me.

I checked them out as we headed to the restroom, then put them in my pocket.

The restroom was empty to my relief. I looked at myself in the mirror over the bank of lavatories. What a mess. Blood all over my nose and mouth, dripping off my chin onto my shirt.

"What happened?" I asked as I turned the cold water tap. Walter handed me a fist of paper towels, and I went to work to stop the flow of blood and to clean myself up.

"What happened? You don't remember? He knocked you on your ass."

"Who did?

He looked at me in the mirror like I was crazy.

"The policeman! You ran right by him screaming 'I'll kill him.' You don't remember?"

I pushed a wet compress against my mouth and nose and studied myself in the mirror. *What policeman? I hadn't seen a policeman.* I shook my head slowly, in disbelief. "All I saw was a blue flash, and the next thing I know I'm looking up into the lights."

"You really don't remember? Ray was taking a pounding. He was lying on the canvas, blood all over his head. The other guy was jumping up and down on him. The crowd was really worked up. It was a mob."

"Yeah, I remember all that. The guy in the mask strutting around."

"The crowd sitting around the ring jumped up screaming and shouting, pushed toward the ring. You shot out of your seat too, like a rocket. You remember that, don't you? Then you raced across the floor toward the ring."

I began to dread what came next, and looked from Walter to myself in the mirror.

"You grabbed a folding chair on the run and swung it over your head. You ran right by the policeman. That's when he hit you."

"I didn't see him."

"That's hard to believe. He was running to the ring, his billy club in one hand, his flashlight in the other. A big guy, all in blue. You almost ran over him. How could you not see him?"

I shrugged. The bleeding had stopped. I was beginning to remember the folding chair and ducked my head in embarrassment.

"Better take that shirt off. If you go out there with blood all over it, the police will wanna talk to you."

I thought about the brass knuckles in my pocket and knew I didn't want to see the police. They would snatch me up like a chicken on a June bug.

I took off my shirt and dropped it in the trash. The blood probably wouldn't wash out anyway. Maybe my mother wouldn't miss it.

"Let's get outta here, go home. I've seen all of this I wanna see," I said, holding a wet compress to my mouth.

We shot up the hallway and out the front door onto Eighth Avenue, where the Boutwell Auditorium marquee lit up the sidewalk—

Monday Night Wrestling

—We went almost every Monday night during that summer when school was out. But next Monday night? Maybe not. I'd have to think about it.

We walked toward Twenty-sixth Street, several blocks east. Maybe the Route 23 bus to North Birmingham would come along and we could ride. Otherwise, we'd just walk home, a mile away.

Walter Henderson was my buddy. We were the same age, in the same class. We both lived in Norwood. His father, like mine, was a bus driver. And he, too, had a paper route. We liked to go to Monday Night Wrestling. We had a lot in common.

The wrestling matches were good, healthy fun. There, we could see a contest between good, represented by clean cut, muscle-bound young men like Ray Stevens and Tarzan White, and evil, in the body of giants in lurid costumes with masks and underhanded tricks. That world was a lot simpler than the one we actually lived in. It was a good escape.

Walter and I loped down the sidewalk toward home. We passed Ed Salem's Drive-In. At nine thirty on Monday night only a few cars remained, but the music thumped as we marched by.

"You know, Sonny, what happened back there—that's not like you. You know it's all a show—we've talked about it. It's just a game."

"I always thought so. But tonight Ray was really hurt. His scalp was split and he was unconscious. I could see it from where we sat. And that guy in the mask—I wanted to kill him. Everybody did."

Walter said nothing.

We walked in silence for a block.

"I told you about the crazy guy, right? The one who stares at streetlamps on moonless nights?"

Walter snatched my shoulder. "Yeah, the one who tried to grab you," he chuckled. "I'd have kicked his butt."

"Yeah, well, if you'd seen his zombie eyes, you'd been hauling ass, too."

We walked some more. Then I said, "I've been thinking about it. The crazy guy acted like he was in another world, like he had no control over himself. Well, I did something tonight I had no control over. And I'm having trouble remembering it. Whatta you think it means."

"I don't think it means you're crazy. You're not some kind of sex maniac like the crazy guy."

To tell the truth, I didn't think I'd turn out like the crazy guy. That's not what worried me. I was concerned about how Ace Carter would rile me up with his speeches at the White Citizens Council meetings. By the time we left those meetings I was bursting with patriotic rage. I didn't want to get all worked up at one of those meetings and go off and do something I'd be ashamed of or that would get me put in jail. But now I knew just how easily self-control could be lost. And that scared me to death.

*   *   *

A few years later, when in college, I read the novel *The Oxbow Incident* by Walter Van Tilburg Clark. It was set in Nevada in 1885 and involved cattle rustling and a reported murder. The sheriff was out of town. A posse was formed to find the guilty parties. The protagonist, Art Croft, was among them. When the posse found three men along the way, they jumped to the conclusion of guilt. The posse became a mob, and Art was swept along with the mindless decision to hang them. The posse proudly arrived back in town to find the true guilty parties arrested and in jail. The story provides an insight into the malleability of men in the presence of a charismatic leader, and illustrates how easily emotions may over-ride our reason. The story describes the descent of individuals into a mindless mob, and the individual regret that follows. Thank God I learned my lesson in a harmless way.

30 • The Professor

The sun had set and the sky in the east had turned dusky by the time I finished my afternoon paper route. I hustled home, tired and hungry. I wanted my supper and quiet company before beginning my homework. I had a lot of answers to learn before bedtime. Little did I know that all I'd have by then were questions.

I passed through the kitchen. Supper was almost done, and mother was bustling around the kitchen.

"Your dad got in a while ago. He's in the living room reading the paper."

I was not surprised he was home. His schedule was so unpredictable I never knew when he'd be home. I headed that way.

"Hey, Dad, I didn't know you'd be home for supper."

"Yeah, just got in a few minutes ago, Sonny. Took a load down to Dothan yesterday. Had to deadhead back today."

He grinned and folded the paper. "How'd your day go? Everything go your way?"

"Oh, yes, sir. I had a good day. Hope you did."

"A good trip." He nodded his head, reopened the paper, and repeated with emphasis, "A good trip."

That sure is strange, I thought. These past few months, since the ICC[9] stuck its nose in our business here in the South, seems like he has problems on all his trips and all those problems land right on our kitchen table. But maybe not tonight. I sure hoped he'd have a good story to tell. Like the old days. I didn't need to hear about any problems. I had to study for a history test tomorrow.

A few minutes later, we all sat down at the table, bowed our heads and my father said the blessing. He seemed to be in a rare, fine mood. Then, as we served our plates, he began his story.

"They called me yesterday morning to double on a trip down to Dothan. So, I left Birmingham with maybe ten people. The other bus was full and had already left ahead of me. Got down to Montgomery and lost several passengers, but there was a small crowd waiting to board—eight or ten folks I guess. I punched their tickets and they all boarded. One of 'em was this colored guy. A nice looking older man. Ram-rod straight, like a soldier." He paused, looked thoughtful for a moment. "You know, most Nigras don't dress so well, but this guy—he looked like a million bucks. White shirt, tie, good looking suit. And his shoes shined like a gold tooth."

Oh, no, I thought, as my body tensed up. Here we go again.

"I punched his ticket and he bounced up those steps, right quick-like, but out of the corner of my eye I noticed he didn't go on down the aisle to the back like he should've."

My dad could eat and talk at the same time, but now he had stopped eating and was intent on describing this colored guy.

"Must have been about fifty years old. Had this thin little mustache across his lip, and a goatee. They were both going pretty gray. His hair was cropped off short and was gray too.

"Well, I finished loading bags for my new passengers. Then I hopped on the bus, and yanked the door shut. I announced we were leaving Montgomery, headed to Dothan. As I looked back, I couldn't help noticing him sitting there in the front seat. He had his jacket all buttoned up. He was sitting up there very erect, like he thought he was somebody.

"Uh, oh, I thought. I got me a big shot here. He's gonna cause me trouble down the line. But no, he sat quietly, a little smile on his face. I hesitated. My first instinct was to tell him to move on back. I could have done that. He'd just got on and wasn't going over the state line.

"But, you know, it's not as simple as it used to be, back before the ICC.

I'd put that board up and they'd have to sit behind it. Didn't matter where they came from or where they were going. Whites in the front, colored in the back. That was the law. That's the way it always was. And I had the full authority to enforce it."

My stomach knotted up. I was waiting for the shoe to fall—something must have happened, or he wouldn't be telling this story. I just couldn't figure out why he didn't seem upset like he usually was.

"But now," he continued, "it's gotten so complicated. The ICC handed down this decree—like they're God or something. Said now we can't tell people where to sit if they're going from one state to another—don't matter what Alabama law says. They're called *interstate* passengers. Y'all remember back in January when the big boss posted an order on the bulletin board telling us drivers we gotta do what the ICC says? Well, he gave in, just like that"—he snapped his fingers—"without a fight! But then his little directive[10] says we should encourage the *non-interstate* riders to seat themselves the way the law says, so long as we don't then try to enforce it. Afraid they'll lose business I guess, if they give in altogether. Now, ain't that something? They leave it for us drivers to figure out."

His face reddened and he became agitated as he spoke of the Company's betrayal of its drivers. And of course, I tightened up all over too, as I always did when he raved over the latest incident.

"Well, y'all know how hard this has been for me. I just can't stand for niggers to sit up front and mix with whites. And it drives me crazy to leave the station with little old ladies standing in the aisle because they won't sit with the colored. I used to be in charge—the captain of my ship—I'd tell 'em where to sit and everything was easy. But now, there's nothing I can do about it. My blood pressure goes sky high when that happens. I feel so powerless."

He slumped a little, and stared into his plate. Then he looked up and said to us kids very seriously, "I'm embarrassed about it, but your mom knows—I've been called into the big office a couple of times because I've separated 'em anyway. I just couldn't help it. That last time, I thought they were gonna fire me. Probably would've, but for the union. Anyway, I had all that on my mind when I saw he'd dropped down on the front row.

"Oh, it would have been easy for me to run him to the back—his ticket clearly showed he bought it in Montgomery and he was just going to Dothan. He was clearly not an interstate passenger. No ICC business there. Because he wasn't going over a state line, Alabama law was what counted. But then, my own Company had told me all I could really do was ask him to move back—I couldn't tell him.

"I guess I was just exhausted from it all. And he looked important enough he might make a big stink for me if I pushed him too hard. Besides, at his age, he wasn't some young buck trying to sit with a white woman. So I decided just to let it go. I had enough troubles to deal with. I sure didn't need to be hauled back in the office for another lecture.

"I couldn't help it though. It galled me that he sat right up front like that. I gritted my teeth, got behind the wheel and took off. I tried to concentrate on the traffic and getting out of town onto 231, but him sitting up there almost in my lap was kind of eating at me.

"Then, about the time we got out on the highway, he says to me, out of the blue, he says, 'Mr. Isom?'—He could see my name plate posted up there." My dad lifted his arm and pointed over his head to an imaginary name plate. "'I hope I pronounced your name correctly,'" he says.

"Well, he said that about as clearly as any white man could. It was an educated voice.

"Before I could catch myself, I said, 'Yes, sir, you got it right.' Now that upset me a little bit—I'm always courteous to my passengers, but that might have been the first time I ever said 'sir' to a colored man." He paused and chewed his lower lip for a moment. "But it seemed natural and I guess it just popped out before I could grab it back.

"He asked me if I thought we'd get to Dothan on time since we'd left Montgomery behind schedule. I told him I thought we would—that we had so few passengers we'd have less stops to make. We should catch up, and be there on time. He thanked me and sat quietly watching the landscape go by.

"I didn't wanna talk to him, but I really wanted to know where he lived and worked to act and dress like that. So in a little bit, I cut my eye back at him and said, 'Where you from? Not from around here, are you?'

"'Oh, yes, sir,' he says. 'I'm headed home to Dothan to see my mother. But I live in Tuskegee. That's where I work. I'm a professor at the college—Tuskegee Institute.'

"We talked awhile and I learned he had three degrees in higher education. He'd been to college somewhere up north. I forget where. The guy was smart. I was really surprised. And the more he talked, the more I listened. Then I talked too. It was amazing how smart he was. I didn't know . . . ." There was a long pause. Dad didn't finish his thought. He had stopped eating, and we had, too. We were watching him as he stared into space for a moment.

I began to relax. He was like he'd been in past years, talking, telling stories, entertaining. I thought about George Washington Carver, the Negro scientist who had taught at Tuskegee Institute and had invented all the uses for peanuts, including peanut butter, one of my favorite foods. I had read his biography several years before.

"The strange thing was," and he began shoveling his supper in, "we kept up that conversation the whole trip. We talked about politics and religion and—I don't know what all."

As my dad was relating his conversation with the professor, my mind would at times wander to my conversations with Mrs. Miller. She had told me there were colored people who were just as smart and cultured as some white people but I had never quite believed her. I'd never come in contact with any colored people to actually talk to, even though Birmingham was at least one-third colored. We had separate schools, and there were no colored people who lived on my paper routes.

Finally, it seemed that Dad had finished his story; he sat quietly for a few moments, his fork in mid-air, looking out the window. I wondered if this was the first conversation of any substance he had ever had with a colored man. After a few moments, he resumed eating, but with less enthusiasm. Clearly, he was mulling something over.

At last, he looked up, laid his knife and fork down, placed his open hands on the table, and looked us up and down, about to say something important.

We waited.

"But you know," he said with emphasis, as if this would be a lesson we should remember, "I don't care how many degrees that professor's got— he could have twenty degrees—and it wouldn't make any difference. Not at all. He still wouldn't be as good as we are."

Then he fell back to his food. No one said a word, but that didn't measure the depth of what I was thinking. I wondered if my dad was concerned we might think he had gushed over the professor and was just trying to bring it all back into perspective.

That statement was particularly confusing to me because my dad had always talked about the importance of education. He believed education was the vehicle that could carry us children out of our present position and give us greater opportunities in life. He spoke of it often, and from my earliest days I remember at our house it was assumed that somehow, though we had limited financial resources, we kids would go to college. Even if he didn't have the money to send three children to college, he made it imperative at our house that somehow it would get done.

No one challenged my dad's statement. I wondered why my mother never asked the hard questions. As for me, I learned long ago not to challenge my father. So I too sat quietly, ruminating on the professor and my dad's final assessment.

By the time Mom served dessert, my dad had launched into another story, but I couldn't follow it. My head was going in circles. If education was the key to bettering ourselves, as my dad believed—he'd said so my whole life—and the professor had gotten a full education and become a professor, then was he not as good as us? If not, why? That question was really the heart of the matter. This was the perfect example of what Mrs. Miller had been drumming into my head for months—that you have to judge each person by his own character—not by the color of his skin.

My dad was in such a good mood I wanted to stay and listen to the new story he had begun, but I had my history studies. Besides, I was now preoccupied with the professor and wanted to think it through.

I excused myself from the table and went to the bedroom I shared with Eddie. The professor followed me, even as I tried to focus on my studies.

By the next morning, I'd put a lot of thought into it. Our whole way of life in the South was based on white folks being superior to colored. We had separate schools. We lived in separate neighborhoods. Even the Democratic Party which governed Alabama had on its emblem the statement "White Supremacy." I had never truly questioned the order of things, even as Mrs. Miller hammered me about it. But suddenly the professor had cast that order in a whole new light.

When I reached the paper branch, the truck had not yet brought our papers. Mr. Hawley slumped at his desk, ignoring the boys' horseplay going on around him. I went to his desk.

"Mr. Hawley, lemme ask you a question. If a colored man gets a college degree, would that make him as good as a white?"

He looked perplexed. "I don't know. It's a hard question. Sure seems like it ought to—don't seem right otherwise. But I don't think it would here in Birmingham. What do you think?"

"I don't know." I dropped it there, but I couldn't quit thinking about it.

This was almost as disturbing to me as the other thing that was eating away at me. My church. They taught that the Bible was the infallible word of God—that it was all literally true—and that if you didn't believe that was the case, you were lost for eternity.

I couldn't help it. I couldn't suppress the questions that came sliding into my head even as I clenched my eyes to squeeze them out. Like God creating the world in seven days or Jonah swallowed up by the whale. But lately I'd been disturbed by the story about the Devil tempting Jesus. My Sunday school teacher never mentioned the divinity of Jesus with that story, but I knew that Jesus was part human and part God. As I heard about the various temptations, I wondered how Jesus, as God, could have been tempted like I might have been. *How could God be tempted?* The guilt I felt because I couldn't shut out that question was overwhelming. Although I never said a word, not to my teacher nor my parents nor anyone about this and other such questions, I carried the twin burdens of doubt and guilt with me wherever I went.

I now understand the difficulty in wrestling with issues of faith and science and doubt. I've learned that the resolution of those questions is not purely rational and may involve complex family and denominational pressures as well as cultural attitudes, all of which define who we are individually as well as a people.

And so I think it was here in the South with the race question. I could see Mrs. Miller's point that treating the entire Negro people as a monolithic group inferior to whites was not right, but I had no one to discuss it with and even if I had, I probably would have kept my doubts to myself.

All around me, people seemed comfortable in their certitude, whether in religion or culture. It seemed to me that only I was yoked to doubt. I held Mrs. Miller's words close to my heart each day, never letting on to her that her words were beginning to hit the mark, afraid to admit even to myself that she was drilling deep holes in the dike of my faith, upending my confidence in the Southern way of life. And so I put up a solid defensive front each Saturday as I collected for the newspaper, afraid to let her know her ideas were percolating—afraid the consequence would be tantamount to losing my faith.

31 • Another Communist Plot

Early Sunday morning. Too tired to move. Eddie tried again to wake me. In a moment I blanked out again.

"Get up! Get up! You'll be late," he nagged. He was super conscientious. Finally, he gave me a solid punch on my shoulder, then he closed the door. I heard it click shut, and rolled over. When he gave up on me, I knew it was time to go.

Much later, I learned to my chagrin that a wife doesn't have nearly the patience of a brother.

I stumbled in to the paper branch to find a listless bunch. No one ever really expressed it very well. Even those who had made fun of Mr. Hawley seemed to miss him now—now that he had been gone for a week. But as for me, I was stunned. Mr. Hawley had become a mentor to me, someone I trusted. I couldn't believe he was gone. He was with us one day, like always. And the next he was gone. Mr. Nasser had opened the branch that morning and told us he would be with us for a few months until a new branch manager could be found. We asked, of course, but he feigned ignorance. We paperboys quietly speculated among ourselves what had happened. We were sure Mr. Hawley had not been transferred to another branch or died or become ill; they would have told us that. So we concluded he had been fired—probably for drinking on the job. If that was the case, they probably wouldn't have told us anything.

Things would never be the same at the paper branch. I would come to deeply miss the relationship of trust I had known with Mr. Hawley.

Mr. Nasser was a no-nonsense guy and ran a tight ship. There was not a lot of fun or frivolity when he was around. We resented him at first, but soon learned he was a good man we all came to respect.

So it was an unusually quiet and reflective group of boys in the branch rolling our papers when Bruce popped in the door. He had come for his papers too, and what a surprise! All decked out in a black tuxedo, he sported a huge grin as he danced across the concrete floor and whirled on his toes. Even Mr. Nasser chuckled.

Bruce got his stack of papers and moved to a spot at a table next to me. Then he made a big show of wiping his hands on his jacket.

"Be careful, Bruce," I said, "You'll get that printers ink all over your tux."

"That's right," he loudly announced to the room, "I paid a lot of money to rent this thing for the prom last night and I'm gonna get my money's worth outta this son of a bitch!" Then he dived down on the dirty concrete floor and wallowed around like a dog.

We all hollered and laughed as he made a spectacle of himself. Things had lightened up a lot as we got our papers rolled and stuffed into our satchels. Then we filed out one by one. Bruce looked pretty disheveled as he blasted away on his motorcycle to deliver his papers.

The prom. Wonder what that was like. I'd never been to a dance. But truthfully, I really didn't want to go to a dance. I felt a kind of contempt for those boys who knew how to dance—thought they were silly and careless, thinking about fun all the time. They weren't serious and conscientious like me. I seemed like a different breed from them, and while I despised them in some ways, I felt a desperate longing to be a part of their fun-loving lifestyle.

The night before, while others went to the prom, I'd been to another White Citizens Council meeting. Instead of having fun like most of the other boys, I was focused on what was happening to our country. It seemed like every time I went to a Citizens Council meeting, I learned about some new threat that shook me up.

All morning, I thought about what the speaker had said the night before. Later that morning I went to church with my family. My mind wandered back to the night before and the fearful prospects that the speaker had lain in my lap. I hardly heard a word the preacher said, but that wasn't unusual for me. I usually daydreamed through his sermons.

In the afternoon, I met my friend, Walter Henderson. We sat on his front porch for a while, just talking. "You should have gone with me last night to the Council Meeting. That speaker really scared me. You should have heard him."

"Scared you how? What did he say?"

"Ace Carter introduced him. His name was Dr. Albritton. He talked about fluoridation—and then he introduced a speaker from out of town. That man spoke about another communist plot involving fluoridation. It was really creepy."

*   *   *

A year had passed since I had first heard Ace Carter, and he had broadened his pitch. At first he was consumed by the threat of forced integration of the races by the federal government that would lead to the "mongrelization" of the white race. He hammered on state's rights and other constitutional issues to defend our state laws which required separate but equal schools.

Maybe Carter feared his constitutional arguments wouldn't be persuasive that caused him to change his technique. Or maybe his call to action had not sufficiently mobilized the massive resistance to integration of the races he sought. In any event, he diverted the gathering floodwaters of forced integration that he'd been obsessed about into the tidal wave of Communism as it threatened to swamp America. If he could show that the efforts of civil rights workers in the South were an integral part of the communist plot—now *that* would be the key to firing up the super-patriotic Southern people!

And that was not so farfetched. It was common knowledge that J. Edgar Hoover and the FBI were concerned about whether Rev. Dr. Martin Luther King Jr. and other civil rights workers had ties to the communist party.

Carter claimed that racial unrest in the South had not been initiated by "our Southern Negroes." They were merely pawns in a game played by other more powerful interests. Everyone knew the Soviet Union intended to convert the entire world to Communism by whatever means possible, even by force. It was a frightening prospect, as I worried about the ever-intensifying Cold War that presented two world views, the United States and the western world, on the one hand, and the Soviet Union and their satellite states on the other. Korea had been a hot spot in that Cold War. The early fifties had been a time of suspicion in our country. Senator Joseph McCarthy led a witch-hunt for Communists in Hollywood among the film-making industry and in our government. He made a big name for himself by "outing" those people in our country with communist connections. His technique and the period became known as "McCarthyism." In 1954, in his Congressional investigation of Communists within our Army, he went too far, and his star began to decline.

As Joseph McCarthy eased off the world stage, Ace Carter, at least in our part of the world, took up his mantle. He was big, burly, heavy-jowled, and dark, just like McCarthy. It was amazing how much they looked alike. They could have been brothers.

Carter asserted that the Soviet Union and its International Communists were being assisted by various organizations and groups who were either directly supporting the communist effort or who were "fellow travelers." He railed against the federal government. He was suspicious of ethnic groups and immigrants. When he organized the north Alabama White Citizens Council, all members were required to profess Christianity, thereby barring Jews from membership.

Then he began to throw his net ever wider and found even more enemies who were directly involved in the communist conspiracy. And now, there was this new dimension he had found in Dr. Albritton, a local dentist, who had been for some time a vocal opponent of adding fluoride into our water system, In fact, it was then a current issue before the Birmingham City Commission.

It did seem plausible. If fluoridation were approved throughout the land, then an "enhanced" fluoridation might be substituted and our water system employees would inadvertently kill or demobilize us without ever knowing of the plot. I went home from that evening's White Citizen's Council "lesson" grim with fear, and I worried about the fluoridation conspiracy for months, wondering when the plan would be triggered.

*   *   *

Walter grinned. He gave me a funny, quizzical look, as if to say he didn't believe me about this new conspiracy.

"Creepy? How could a speech be creepy? You mean 'boring.' That's what it was."

"Boring? Are you crazy? Nobody went to sleep. This guy had us listening to every word. It was so scary, I could hardly go to sleep last night."

"Well, what'd he say?"

"He said fluoridation didn't have anything to do with the health of children's teeth. No! He said it was a communist conspiracy! He said if it was approved, then it would be a legal way to add chemicals to our drinking water, throughout the entire country. We would think it was for our health, but no! He said if it was approved, it would be possible for the communists to add chemicals to the fluoridation in all the water systems, all over the country. They would poison us, or tranquilize us—the entire country—at one time and we would be powerless. Then the Communists would have defeated us—our whole country—without firing a shot and we would be their slaves."

Walter's mouth had fallen open. He was surprised, I think, at my speech.

"Well, it sounds like a lot of crap to me."

"You shoulda been there. It wasn't just me he scared. When he got done with his speech, there wasn't a lot of clapping and carrying on like Carter always causes. Everybody was pretty quiet and looked real worried and grim when they filed out."

"Yeah, well, I wasn't there so I don't see why you got so lathered up over it. I got enough to worry about so I'm not gonna worry about that."

*   *   *

Some years later, when I had been practicing law about ten years, my firm occupied space in the City National Bank Building, formerly known as the Empire Building. We needed more space, and rented a suite of offices on the eleventh floor, where I moved my practice. Ironically, I found I was sharing a thin, sheetrock wall with Dr. W. Klyde Albritton. He was then an elderly gentleman, lean and spry, and he spoke kindly to me when we met in the hallway or on the elevator. His anti-fluoridation posters were clearly visible through the glass front of his offices. I viewed them every day as I went to and from the elevators. He never spoke to me of the fluoridation issue, and I never asked him about it.

Isn't it strange how the wheel turns? Dr. Albritton had introduced the speaker who had scared me for months with his talk of communist plans to take over our country by dumping poisonous chemicals into our drinking water (and who I had forgotten years earlier). He was now back, and he was again invading my thoughts. Every day, all day long, through the thin sheetrock wall we shared, I could hear the vibrating shrill z-zzz-zzzz, z-zzz-zzzz of his drill, and the occasional frightened, muffled squeal from someone in his chair, as he was hard at work, again distracting me from my own.

32 • Tobacco Road

Scrubbing the sticky brown stains from my face and neck, I stared into the smeared mirror in the filthy, unvented, malodorous service station washroom. I scrubbed diligently with trembling hands soaped from a greasy, gritty bar. It was only 8:30 on a Saturday morning, and already my day was ruined.

Only a few minutes before, I had been making my rounds, collecting from my newspaper customers. I had mounted the porch of a house on Twentieth Avenue and knocked on the screen door. The morning was already hot and muggy, and the door stood open for ventilation. I saw her through the dusty screen door coming from the back of the house. She was barefoot and dressed only in a slip. She moved languidly, uncertainly toward the door, almost losing her footing a couple of times. With each step, her breasts and hips and thighs swelled against the fabric. My heart skipped a beat. I held my breath.

She pushed the door open, leaning from the waist as she did so, and creating a vista down the front of her slip. Two naked breasts swung right before my startled eyes in the morning sunshine. After a moment, I came to myself and blocked the screen door with my shoe. She straightened up, then slouched heavily against the door post, setting off in a teenage boy's eyes something like a cosmic collision, breasts ebbing and flowing, nipples surging against the silk. I was powerless to look away, like watching a coiled snake.

"Whatta you want?" she asked, her voice flat and garbled.

Embarrassed, I looked into her face for the first time. She was about the age of my own mother. Hair dark, in disarray. Face damp and pale. Eyes looking through me, fixed on something only she could see. Lips compressed, as if she were carrying something in her mouth. Crusted, dark brown tracks down both sides of her chin, like hideous birthmarks. In an instant, the excitement I felt turned to revulsion. I had seen those tracks before, had seen the amber juice dribble from mouths of old men and women in the country as they rocked on the porch and spat into open tin cans they carried for that purpose. I had seen old women pack the space between their bottom lips and teeth with snuff where they would taste it with the tip of their tongue for hours. Was it possible this woman here in the city would dip snuff? But nothing else would explain the ugly tracks and the juice dribbling from her mouth.

I averted my gaze from the mess around her mouth to her eyes, and said, "Collect for the *Post-Herald*, please." Her dark eyes reflected like a mirror. She seemed to look through me, as if she were looking at something a thousand yards away. Or at nothing.

In one slow deliberate motion, she shifted her weight off the door post and lifted her arm toward me. I watched her breasts as she slowly rested her open hand flat on my chest. Then she slowly, deliberately, closed her hand, the fabric of my shirt caught inside her fist. *What's she up to?!* I glanced to her hideous face for direction but her eyes were blank and lifeless disks. Then she began pulling me through the doorway into the living room. "Come on in," she said flatly, looking through me, tobacco juice dribbling down her chin.

"Yes, ma'am," I said, and was pulled through the doorway, not completely cooperating with her, but reluctant to openly resist. After all, as a Southern boy, I had been taught to respect my elders, and particularly women. The screen door banged shut behind me. The room was unlighted, humid and airless. My customers often asked me to step inside while collecting their change, for a quick conversation, but this was radically out of the norm. As she pulled me into the room, I looked wistfully back through the screen, where hundreds of dust motes were floating freely in the air. I was trapped. I hoped she would let go of my shirt and bring me my money. But no such luck. She continued to pull me through the living room. Confused and uncertain, I politely resisted at first, saying, "No, ma'am. I've gotta go." But her insistence was frightening. Now I began to resist in earnest, braking against the force of her tugs. Then, with her other hand, she seized my belt buckle and dragged me toward the back rooms. "Come on. Let's go back here," she said irritably.

Her intensity, her grip on my belt buckle and the strength of her tugs shocked me into high alert. Suddenly, it hit me—it became clear to me she was tugging me toward the bedroom. My heart leaped with fear and revulsion. Miss Talley had just toyed with me. This woman was serious.

But it was the blankness, the vacancy of her eyes that scared me. She was not normal. Something otherworldly was at work within her.

Now as she tried to drag me across her living room, I made up my mind I would go no farther and dug in my heels. When she could move me no farther, she wrapped one arm around me, pulled me to her and kissed me on my mouth before I could jerk my face away. A sickening, syrupy taste burned my lips and throat. She began to kiss my face and neck, searching for my mouth, as I craned my neck this way and that, struggling to avoid her hot, heavy breath and the cloying taste of her mouth.

In whipping my head to the side, my vision fell on the form of a large man lying on the sofa not five feet away, naked, hairy, motionless, either dead or asleep. In a flash, I remembered the papers I delivered every day told stories, multiple stories, of shootings and stabbings arising from situations—just like this! *Is he dead? Is he asleep? Will he awake? Does he have a gun? A knife? Will he kill me?* Terror-stricken, I snatched free and whirled toward the door.

She grabbed me again, one hand gripping my belt buckle and the front of my jeans, the other my upper arm and jerked me around. "Don't worry, honey. He's passed out. Come on back here with me," she insisted.

"No, ma'am. I really gotta go." I plowed backwards. She followed like we were dancing.

Then she threw her arm around my shoulder and kissed me again, her breath hot on my face.

I pushed her away but she wouldn't let go. Though I couldn't pry her loose, I forced my way back to the door hoping not to awaken the man.

She was now wrapped around me like wisteria, kissing my face and neck, searching for my mouth.

I struggled to the screen door, dragging her with me, and leveraged myself onto the porch. The antiseptic sunlight caught her full in the face. Stunned by the glare, she released her grip. Her eyelids fluttered as she struggled to focus. Then her eyes centered on mine for the first time, a fleeting, furious look of despair, then they slid into abstraction. "Why…?" she began, her voice slipping away as well.

I jumped off the porch and left her there squinting in the sunlight, slouched against the door jamb, one arm extended toward me, fingers drooping lifelessly. I raced for my motorcycle, kick-started the engine, and blasted away without looking back. I wanted to rush home and wash the shame and embarrassment from my face with cold water, brush my teeth, rinse the taste from my mouth, but I could not face my mother. So I rode to the nearest service station to wash away the sticky stain, to cool my hot, sweating face and neck, to slow the pounding pulse in my temples.

I studied the mirror, satisfied that the worst of the tobacco juice had been scrubbed off. Though the morning had ripened to thick humidity, the temperature now in the nineties, a wave of cool, fresh air swept over me as I stepped from the stifling washroom.

It seemed over the past year the embarrassment resulting from my first kiss had lessened, and now had gradually merged into a low grade lust for another kiss; but the kiss I'd just received was not at all what I'd daydreamed about. I never dreamed that my second kiss would be so repulsive, so thought provoking. I'd thought many times over what a fool I'd made of myself in front of Miss Talley and her roommate. Embarrassment was one thing, but this woman really scared me. She seemed as crazy as the street lamp guy, just as addled with some weird urge as he had been. I had not yet resolved the puzzle of the female breast, but I was now engrossed with a larger, more daunting and altogether incomprehensible mystery.

I kick-started the engine on my new Triumph Tiger Cub. I had bought it only a few days before and planned to take it out on the highway when I finished my collections. I wanted to let it run, see what it could do. After the experience I had just suffered, I wanted to abandon my collections and dash for the highway now. But I knew I couldn't do that.

I returned to my route, resolute but wary. I parked my Triumph at a customer's walkway and shuffled slowly on rubbery legs up the stairs, mounted the porch and found myself staring at the front door. I hesitated, gathered my courage and rang the bell. While waiting, I opened my route book to the customer's account.

The door opened.

My voice, untested since my ordeal, surprised me as I croaked, "Collect for the *Post-Herald*, please."

My customer nodded, said, "Just a minute," and closed the door.

She did not invite me inside. And that was just fine by me.

33 • A Wrong Address

I bumped my Triumph Tiger Cub over the curb and came to a stop on the sidewalk, far across town from my home neighborhood. I looked around in disbelief at the seedy thoroughfare. Mr. Carter was an important man. I expected to find an office building. He wouldn't have an office here, on this busy road, amid used car lots on the western outskirts of Birmingham.

Maybe there was a mistake. I checked my handwritten note on which I'd copied the address directly from the latest issue of *The Southerner*.[11] I sat astride my Triumph and looked up and down the block. It was clear I had parked at the only building that could possibly be 2005 Bessemer Road. There didn't appear to be an address on the building, but this had to be it. It was an old two-story brick building with a marquee in front. A neighborhood movie theater, it appeared to have been closed for some years, and was now abandoned. I thought of my own theater in Norwood which I had attended on some Saturday afternoons, until it too closed a few years earlier. There, my brother, Eddie, and I would see a double feature, usually two shoot-'em-up Westerns, on those Saturday afternoons we were lucky enough to get to go. I supposed some neighborhood theaters may have survived, but this one and mine had not.

I'd come a long way. I might as well check it out. I parked my Triumph beside the building, and went to the front door. I was surprised the door was unlocked. I cautiously entered and found the place dark except for a bare bulb at the top of the stairwell, which threw a dim light down to the first floor. The theater had a lobby and an upstairs office area. I hesitated. Hmmm. Should I go up those steps? I was going to see a man I'd heard speak on several occasions but whom I'd never met in person and who wouldn't know me. But was he here? Could this be his office? The appearance of the building and the darkness inside had me buffaloed. From the outside it looked abandoned. I stood there in the half-dark vacillating over what to do. It had not occurred to me to call for an appointment. I almost left the building, but then, I'd come all the way across town, at least ten miles; I should make certain Mr. Carter was not here.

I had no idea the man would see me without an appointment. And even if he were here and agreed to talk with me, what was it, exactly, that I wanted of him?

I began my cautious ascent up the stairs wondering if I were making a big mistake exploring an abandoned building so far from home. I was about half-way up when a big man suddenly burst onto the landing at the top, directly beneath the light. He faced me, standing tall, arms akimbo, ready for trouble.

"Whatta you want?"

I froze in place on the stairs, my head tilted back, my heart pounding. I recognized Mr. Carter, but I panicked.

"Uh, I'd like to see Mr. Carter please," I croaked.

"Yeah, what about?"

Rattled, I managed to say, "Just wanted to, uh, talk about the Communist conspiracy…," and let it hang there, mainly because my throat closed.

"Yeah, come on up," he ordered, without enthusiasm, as he whirled and disappeared from view.

It sounded more like a challenge than an invitation. I paused to gather my courage and gripped the handrail to steady myself. I said to the empty landing above, "Thanks. I'll be right there." Then I lifted my heavy, cast-iron shoes one at a time up those stairs.

*   *   *

I'd heard Ace Carter speak at some of those meetings of the White Citizens Council I attended with my father. I'd been carried away on several occasions by his oratory. He knew how to rev up a crowd with speeches about the evils of integration of the races as he lambasted what he mockingly called the "International Communist Conspiracy" and our own federal government, who he said were responsible for the social unrest. Even without his speeches, I knew integration of the races was wrong because that's what I had heard all my life.

But lately, two things had converged to cause me to question my own convictions.

First was Mrs. Miller and those Saturday morning talks that we had over the past eight months since she had moved onto my paper route. Her ideas were the opposite of what Mr. Carter said, and I found myself in school struggling to find the balance between the two.

And the second had to do with music.

For the last year or so, I had been listening to Elvis Presley and other musicians who were belting out a new brand of music called rock 'n' roll. All the adults seemed to hate it, including my parents. But Mr. Carter had gone off the deep end, calling it "negroid" music, which he said was aimed at breaking down the racial barriers. I could follow his logic when he spoke of the International Communist Conspiracy and their drive to create a race war in America, and particularly the South, which would lead to the collapse of our country.

But I could make no sense of how rock 'n' roll was part of the conspiracy. This is a quote from a long article in *The Southerner*, Vol.1, No. 6, August 1956, written by Carter concerning a protest at Birmingham's city auditorium by members of the Alabama Citizens Council outside a rock 'n' roll show which sponsored interracial entertainers:

> The purpose [of the protest] was to call to the attention of white parents everywhere, that rock 'n' roll, negroid, animalistic music is being used to drive the white youth to the level of the negro; to bring the realization before the public that if young white girls and boys are induced to think as negroes, act as negroes, enjoy with negroes their negroid expressions of baseness and immorality, then they will be easily integrated with the negro. Ace Carter FIRST hit rock 'n' roll, in his speeches, outlining it as only ONE facet of the communist integration warfare.

I thought he made a lot of sense when he spoke of the real dangers of communism, but I wondered what could be wrong with a bunch of teenagers listening to a concert? The more Mr. Carter railed about all the component parts of the conspiracy of the international communist movement, particularly rock 'n' roll, the more I wondered about the entire conspiracy. I had begun to doubt his multiple conspiracy theories. I couldn't help the questions that kept popping into my mind that made me feel disloyal, that challenged my faith in him. I began to wonder if maybe there was a stone missing in the arch that held it all up, not the keystone perhaps, but the arch seemed to be quivering.

I was now seventeen years old and was soon to enter my last year of high school. Even though I knew I was at an age that I had been told was characterized by rebellion and confusion, questions about my faith and my culture were painful nonetheless. I was more and more at odds with my parents. I just didn't seem to fit in anymore. There was no one I felt comfortable to talk with about any of the things that were troubling me, except for Mrs. Miller. And I had dropped my bucket into that well too many times. She was always helpful, but I always left her house with more questions than answers.

*   *   *

As I trudged up the stairs to Mr. Carter's office, I hesitated. I was unable to articulate even to myself why I had traveled across town to see him. Maybe I wanted to know him better. Maybe I wanted assurance from him. Maybe I hoped he could patch up my faith in his cause. I had no idea what I would say to him.

I was pretty shaky as I entered his office. It was dark and dingy and dirty. A lamp cast its light on his cluttered desk, but the room itself lay in deep shadows. Old newspapers were stacked around. Ashtrays were overflowing. His desk was heaped with books and files and papers.

He stood at his desk as I entered, then dropped into his chair as if exhausted. He waved me into a chair across from him, and lit a cigarette. He ignored me as he pulled a deep draw, then looking up at the ceiling, slowly let it out. The smoke rose up, then billowed across the ceiling.

He eyed me suspiciously. "Okay, what can I do for you?" He was big and beefy, with black hair, black eyes and black stubble on his face. He looked the same as I remembered him from his speeches, except that his white shirt was open at the collar, his tie askew, and he looked tired and disheveled.

For some reason, I had expected him to greet me warmly. His hostility had thrown me off. I stammered around for a moment about attending the White Citizens Council meetings, that I'd heard him speak, and that I wanted to meet him. He watched me in a disinterested way without comment. In desperation, I continued, telling him I had read *The Southerner*, the magazine he edited, and that I got his address from there.

He brightened.

"*The Southerner*, hunh? I'm glad you like it."

He rubbed his dark chin for a moment as if in thought. Then he asked me where I was in school. After some preliminary conversation about me, he turned back to the publication.

"How'd you like to write an article for my magazine? I'd get it in the next issue. Whatta you think about that?"

I'd never thought of writing an article before until Mr. Miller challenged me to be a newspaper reporter. It's true I had rolled that around in my mind, but figured it was years away. The idea of writing something other people would read was overwhelming to me. I was surprised he wanted me to write an article, and admit I was intrigued with the idea.

"Uh—I don't know. Don't know if I can. What kind of article?"

"Well, you're a teenager, in high school. That rock 'n' roll music is taking over with young people. You know that. Elvis Presley is a disgrace to the white race, singing and shaking his hips like a Nigra. That's going to be the downfall of the white race. It's gonna lead to race-mixing ..."

My blood ran cold as Carter continued, ranting and clenching his fists. " ... and you know where that leads—to inter-marriage, and ultimately to the mongrelization of the pure Anglo-Saxon race. We gotta stop it!"

Then he breathed deeply, looking over my head at something far away. After a moment he settled back in his chair and stubbed out his cigarette, spilling ashes from the overflowing ashtray onto his desk.

"How 'bout write that article for me, from your point of view, from the point of view of a white kid, you know, what's wrong with that Negroid music, the dangers of it. Kids don't listen to adults, you know, but an article from another kid—now that's different."

He lit another cigarette, blew the smoke up, and studied the ceiling, very satisfied, as the smoke rolled across the ceiling into the shadowed corners of the room.

"Yeah, that might be good. Looking for material for the next issue anyway." Then he drilled me with his black eyes. "Will you do it? Write an article about that Negroid music?"

I studied the dusty floor and mumbled that I'd think about it, but knew in that instant I'd never write such an article. I'd feel like a traitor among my classmates. I'd be the butt of a thousand jokes at school, would probably get beat up. All the kids liked rock'n'roll, including me. The only difference was they openly enjoyed the music. I felt guilty as I enjoyed it. But the fact was, I loved Elvis Presley and nothing my parents had said, nothing Mr. Carter was saying, made any difference. I was an Elvis Presley fan through and through.

I made some excuse that I had to get moving, and left as quickly as I could. I mounted my Triumph and slumped for a moment in thought, disillusioned. The rock I'd built my ideas on was crumbling into sand. I kick-started my engine and absently bumped over the curb and into the street, and began my return toward home.

I couldn't get over it, was stuck thinking about it for days. Asa Carter was such an important man, the executive director of the White Citizens Council and the editor of *The Southerner*. Yet his office was a disgrace, situated in an abandoned building. He had no secretary, no clerks, no employees.

I've thought a lot over the years about my motive in locating Ace Carter and visiting his office. I think the real reason was a need for solidarity. I'd gone looking for Ace Carter, the man who was in many ways the architect of my important ideas, wanted to find him—the real man—to confirm that I fit into a pattern and was part of a community, to escape my isolation and belong to something bigger than myself. I wanted Ace Carter to patch the crack Mrs. Miller had found in my resolve, and been chinking away on Saturday mornings.

Yes, I found the man I was looking for, the big, burly orator Ace Carter, whose speeches had in the past two years wound me up like a toy soldier. I found him in his natural habitat. There were no crowds of people, no stage lights—just a slovenly man behind a cluttered desk in a dark, dusty, smoke-filled room. Yes, I found the man I was looking for—found him at 2005 Bessemer Road.

But it turned out after all to have been a wrong address.

34 • Brave New Goals

In early 1956, the *Birmingham News* and the *Post-Herald* announced to the various paper branches across the city that they would hold a contest. Those paperboys who got the most new subscriptions would win a free, all expenses paid trip to Florida that summer. That was an exciting prospect for me. I had listened to my classmates talk about their vacations to Panama City, but I'd never been there. In fact, I'd never been to Florida except for two times my family had driven down to visit my father's uncles in Lake City. From there, we had taken day trips to the beach, once to Daytona and another time to Clearwater. I was certain a day trip was wholly inferior to a real vacation on the beach. Plus, those trips were long ago, when I was a child.

In fact, as I thought about it, I'd never had a vacation, period, since I began delivering papers almost four years ago. I delivered the *Post-Herald* in the morning and the *News* in the afternoon six days a week, delivered the Sunday morning paper and spent all day Saturday collecting my accounts—over three hundred in all. My job was seven days a week. There was simply no time for a vacation.

Mr. Nasser told me I had a chance to win because my routes were so large and because any new subscription would count, whether the *News* or the *Post-Herald*.

Yes, a vacation sounded good to me. I decided there was no reason I could not win the trip to Florida. I could probably generate a lot of new customers if I put my mind to it. And I knew if I won the trip, my brother Eddie would handle my routes for me for a week. I had handled his routes for him a few times on special occasions.

Exhilarated with the challenge, filled with hope, I began a drive for new customers on each Saturday when I collected my accounts. I called at every house and apartment where I left no paper. I kept records of the people in the houses and apartments who said no, and why, and those who were not home so I could call again.

On my *Post-Herald* route, I also began calling on those businesses in the commercial district along Twelfth Avenue that didn't already subscribe for a paper, such as Wood's Drug Store, Norton's Flowers, Benton's Draperies, Chick's Creamery, and Dr. Goins, the chiropractor.

*   *   *

My buddy, John McDonald, and I strolled along the boardwalk, and then onto a huge wooden pier on pilings that went out into Jacksonville Bay, gawking at the sights like country boys come to town, looking for a familiar face. All the hard work paid off and John and I were the winners from Norwood. We had arrived in Florida on a white bus that looked like a school bus with—

The Birmingham News–Post-Herald

—painted on the sides. There were over thirty newspaper boys from across the city who went along with several branch managers as chaperones.

We'd been told there would be food vendors and picnic tables near the end of the pier and that's where our group would meet for supper. But what a surprise John and I had once we got close to the destination.

We heard shouting and saw violent movement near the end of the pier. We knew whatever was going on down there involved our crew. We sprinted down the pier to catch up to our buddies and ran right into a great swirling melee of shouting and cursing and flailing. Suddenly, a large boy atop a picnic table charged across and leaped at John and me. John, a short, red-haired, pugnacious boy, reacted instantly, stepped forward with right arm cocked, and unleashed his fist into the face of the jumper. The blow hammered the unfortunate jumper in mid-air, flipping him like a pancake and he slammed at our feet on his back with a thud, his face covered with blood.

The fighting surged around us. Mr. Rocket, the branch manager from East Lake and one of our chaperones, threw his hands in the air and shouted for attention as he tried to separate fighters. I moved around, alert and self-protective, trying to find my way out of the mob.

The police arrived on the run, as the local toughs who had attacked us slipped away leaving only our group to sort things out. Mr. Rocket and the other adults explained to the police that we were newspaper carriers from Birmingham who had won a trip to Jacksonville. After a half hour of negotiation, the policemen left without arresting anyone. Then our chaperones conducted a quick inventory, and found only bruised lips and black eyes, but no serious injuries. Thank God, no knives or guns were part of the brief battle.

That was the summer of 1956 when weapons weren't common in teen-age fights.

*   *   *

Not more than three months after we'd returned from Florida, the newspapers announced a city-wide contest for the Newspaper Carrier of the Year. The winner would be a single carrier in the Birmingham area who obtained the most new subscriptions. And the prize? A car! Not a new car—a 1950 Ford—but a car nonetheless.

I was seventeen, and I wanted that car more than anything. The trip to Florida had been okay, but nothing to brag about. It was over and done with, and mostly forgotten. I had used up my one big opportunity to win a contest on that Florida vacation. My paper routes were now full. All the prospects on my routes I had already worked. How could I win the Ford? Well, there was just no way I could win the car, no way at all. No one could imagine how depressed I was as I considered the futility of my situation.

Meanwhile, Jimmy Osborn continued to flash around in his new yellow and black convertible. What I wouldn't give to have a car like that. Or any car. My motorcycles had certainly given me some status, but they were for boys. A car was the real measure of when a boy becomes a man. A car was my ticket to maturity, to adulthood. With a car, a new lifestyle would open up to me. A car would be my introduction to girls.

I had earlier discussed with my father getting a car and he had always said no. Even though I was putting my own money in a savings account and had enough to buy a car, he always said my earnings were for college. So I was certain the only way I could own a car in the near future was to win the car in this contest. The reality, however, was clear. I had no real source of new subscriptions.

Saturday morning came around, and time for collections. I'd been thinking about Mrs. Miller all morning as I went from house to house, hoping she would have a few minutes to visit with me. She always knew how to make me feel better, to pump me up. She would always find the right words to make me want to do my best. I sure hoped Mr. Miller didn't answer the door. It was his wife I wanted to see.

"Oh, hi, Sonny. It's nice to see you. Sit down there and I'll get your money." Good fortune was with me.

And when Mrs. Miller came back a few minutes later she brought my money and a glass of water.

"Here, I know you're thirsty after working all morning. Is everything okay with you?"

"Uh, yes ma'am. I guess so."

"Well, what's wrong? Looks like something's on your mind."

"Well, there is one thing I'm kinda worried about. The Newspaper's having this big contest to see which paperboy can get the most new customers. Well, I'd really like to win it because," and here I got animated and stood up, "the prize is a car! A 1950 Ford!"

Her eyes widened. "Wow. That's great. Are you going to enter?"

"Well," then I let out my breath and dropped my arms, and my chin drooped on my chest, "I don't see how I can. You know, I canvassed everybody on my routes about six months ago when I won that trip to Florida. There's just nobody else to get." I paused, then lamented, "Guess I'll just have to pass it up. There're just not enough new customers out there to make any difference. To win, I'd have to get dozens of new customers."

She sat quietly for a few minutes, while I slouched and studied the wooden flooring of the porch. "Now, Sonny, where does your paper route go? From where to where?"

"Well, my afternoon route is over on the Boulevard. But this route—my morning route—is a lot bigger. It goes from the railroad ...," pointing east, "to Twenty-third Street, the next block over ...," pointing west, then I turned and pointed south. "And it goes south toward downtown, down to Eleventh Avenue and then north to Twenty-first Avenue. That's a lot of territory, but I've called on everybody in there. Most people take the *News* and they don't need two papers. There may be a few new customers since I last made the rounds, but just a few. Not enough to win the car." And I plopped into the chair, dejected. I could tell from the serious, faraway look in her eyes that she was thinking over my latest problem.

Why do I always take my troubles to Mrs. Miller? It isn't fair to her. She never says no. She has two little boys to look after and, now, she's pregnant. How does she manage everything and still have time for me? She must think I'm an idiot. But she always seems honestly interested in me and my problems.

"Sonny, does some other paperboy have the blocks between Eleventh Avenue and downtown?"

"I don't think so. But that's only the railroads and a bunch of warehouses and colored houses along the railroads."

"Well, do you think another paperboy covers those houses?"

"I don't think so. It's a pretty small area and then you get to downtown. I'm sure somebody has downtown, but I doubt anybody covers those old houses along the railroad."

"Well, maybe that's your answer. If there's no one else covering the margins, cover it yourself. Expand your route. Fill the vacuum."

I thought about it for a moment. "But Mrs. Miller, they're colored. I don't want to deliver papers to colored people. You know how I feel about that," and I turned my palms up and shrugged imploringly. I sure didn't want to set her off. She'd give me another lecture about Negroes if I was not careful. And I wasn't in the mood.

"Listen, Sonny. You're just being silly. They are people just like white people. They read newspapers, too. I'll bet nobody is delivering papers to them. That could be your answer."

"Yeah, but—but what if they won't pay me? What if—?"

"So what? That's a risk you take with any customer, isn't it? Haven't you had white customers who moved off without paying? Sure you have. So why not give it a chance? You might get twenty, thirty new customers."

Then she looked at me very seriously, leaned toward me.

"But more important than getting new customers or winning that car—much more important—is getting to know some colored people. You really don't know any, do you?"

"No ma'am."

"Everything you know about colored people is what you've been told?"

"Yes ma'am." I was really uncomfortable, ready to go. This time Mrs. Miller was not making me feel better.

"You really need to make up your own mind, you know. Don't take what other people tell you as the gospel. Find out for yourself!"

I scrambled to my feet. I wanted out of this conversation. It had gone so wrong. What I'd wanted was some understanding, maybe a little advice. But she had stretched me out on the horns of a dilemma. She had shown me how I might have a chance to win that car if I was willing to take the chance. But a white boy delivering papers in a colored neighborhood—that could be a calamity of who knows what proportions. My head was just beginning to spin.

And then she said, just as I was stepping off the porch, "Keep this in mind, Sonny, if you do this. I know the car is important to you. But I'm more interested in your growth—your growth as a person. That will be its own reward. The car then, if you win it, will be a surprise. It'll be a great bonus you didn't expect."

I thanked Mrs. Miller for her time and went to my next customer, pondering the things she had said. I was in a quandary, a real pickle, a dilemma about principles and values. On the one hand, I wanted to win that car. But my routes were tapped out. The only way I could possibly win was by following Mrs. Miller's advice. I knew she was right—I must go to the colored neighborhoods along the margins of Norwood if I wanted to win. That frightened me and repelled me. Not only was I physically afraid to go into their neighborhoods, but it would violate my principles to serve colored people. But then I remembered the Professor. Surely he would have been an exception. I'd be glad to deliver his paper.

Would there not be others?

The resolution came to me slowly as I mulled over what Mrs. Miller had said. She was right of course, but could I do it? That was the question.

After I had delivered my afternoon papers, I wheeled my Triumph through North Birmingham toward the highway and then opened it up. I needed fresh air. I needed to think. Best I could tell, girls didn't like me. They didn't even notice me. It was like I was invisible. I knew if I had a car it would make all the difference. I still wouldn't know how to talk to girls or dance with them. But they would know that I was alive, at least, if I had that Ford. And if I wanted a chance with girls before I was an old man out of college, I had only this one shot.

My engine screaming, I streaked down the highway at seventy, the wind ballooning my jacket and pants and threatening to rip them away. I squinted so narrowly into the wind I was surprised to feel my tears squeezing out and speeding across my temples.

I was no daredevil, but I loved the sense of freedom out on the highway, away from home and school and church and the paper branch, away from all the constraints that squeezed me shut at every turn. My life was regulated in every way, from morning to night. I wanted to stretch my arms wide and breathe deep and dash for the horizon.

A car represented freedom—my coming of age—my independence. And that was important because—well, it always came back to girls.

I cut back my speed to a gentle cruise. For the first time in days, I felt great. In fact, I was elated. Suddenly my mind was clear. I would do it. I would take the plunge. I would rush in where even angels feared to tread. It would be a big gamble, but I would go into the colored neighborhoods and ask them to be my customers. I would go into the alleyways and along the railroads and solicit the people along the margins of my routes, even though it might be dangerous for a white boy and would probably shake me in my boots. Maybe the colored people wouldn't turn me away. Maybe there would be some like the Professor. Maybe I could get dozens of new starts. Maybe I did have a chance at that car. I was excited. I lowered my head, twisted my handlebar grip inboard and blasted through the dusky evening, wind whipping my face. My heart pounded but my mind was clear. I would begin tomorrow. I slowed, found a place to turn around, and headed home.

As I cruised toward home, I was jittery with dread over whether I should serve colored people and with exhilaration over the possibilities before me. A car. Privacy. Music. Taking a girl for a drive. The possibilities crowded out the dread. As I thought about most of the girls I knew, I thought how silly they were, what silly things they talked about, what silly things they did.

What I really wanted was a girl who was serious and sympathetic, who had strawberry blond hair, and blue eyes and a peach-fuzz softness in her face. For over a year, I had wanted a girl like Mrs. Miller. I was pretty sure I'd be looking for a long, long time for someone like her. And then it happened. I had found such a girl . . . though her hair was black . . . and her eyes were hazel and deep with mystery and meaning. She lived on Norwood Boulevard.

But, now having found her, what would she find in me? That was the question. I was just a paper boy with a motorcycle. I was convinced I'd need more than that. Much more.

What I needed to get the girl, I knew, was to win that car.

I was *going* to win that car.

35 • Racked By a Setback

Back in the 1950s, back before department stores abandoned our city and moved to the suburbs, downtown Birmingham was a dynamic venue for shopping. At Christmastime, even if one had no money, what a joy it was to share the sidewalks with families of window shoppers, hands in pockets, breaths fogging the air, all feasting on the holiday scenes in the windows. Oh, the store windows. They were all lit up with festive lights, scenes of holiday cheer and mannequins moving to the sound of music. Even on Sundays when the downtown stores were closed, families stood on the sidewalks and watched the holiday shows in the windows.

And I was there, too, wandering around downtown, thinking about Christmas and gifts for family, remembering when my own family had strolled in front of those very same windows, and feeling a tinge of regret that I had outgrown most family occasions. But in this particular Christmas season, I was mostly concerned with what else could I do to increase my subscribers. I was desperate to win that car. I had followed Mrs. Miller's advice, albeit with a lot of trepidation, and gone into the colored enclaves on the margin of my route and knocked on doors. I was not surprised. It had not gone well. For every three or four houses I tried, maybe one would subscribe. I'd had much better luck with whites, but I had already canvassed all the white people on my routes.

Though I had been apprehensive about entering those colored neighborhoods along the railroad tracks and in alleys and at the end of dirt roads, no one threatened me or was outwardly rude to me. Many refused to answer my knock on their door, and the eyes of those who did were hooded with suspicion because the only white people who knocked on their doors were bill collectors. But I was surprised that when they learned I was a paper boy, most were pleasant and treated me in a friendly way.

After a month or so of canvassing in those colored neighborhoods that were bordering my route, I was making progress, but it was clear I'd never get enough new subscriptions to become "Newspaper Carrier of the Year" and win the car. It just wasn't in the cards. And my frustrations were ruining the holiday season for me.

As I wandered along the street alternately enjoying the window scenes and fretting over finding new customers for my paper route, I noticed something I'd seen a thousand times—a newspaper rack. There, chained to a lamp post, was a newspaper rack, a simple wire contraption designed to hold fifteen or so newspapers with an attached coin deposit. The rack was open to the elements and operated solely on trust. Anyone could simply lift a paper and deposit nothing. But it was clear from the number of newspaper racks in downtown Birmingham that somebody thought he could make a profit in spite of all the risk.

Then it hit me—Norwood Hospital was on my route. Every day I left a morning paper at the Emergency Room but until now had never thought about other possibilities. Wow! A paper rack in the waiting lobby of the hospital would be perfect. Surely, people just sitting in the waiting room with nothing to do would buy newspapers. And it was inside, out of the weather, where my newspapers would be safe.

I dropped everything and raced to the hospital. I tried to contain my enthusiasm, almost certain there would be paper racks at the hospital already. Surely, the adult who operated the paper racks around town would have already thought of the hospital. I darted into the hospital lobby and looked all around. I could hardly believe it. There were no paper racks in the lobby or anywhere else in sight!

The next day, I approached Mr. Nasser about how I could obtain newspaper racks and what they would cost. He told me the rack was free if I would order at least fifteen papers. I asked him if there were any restrictions on where I could put them.

"No," he said, "as long as you keep them within your route."

It was an incredible opportunity, but there would be risk, too. If I placed papers in a rack and they failed to sell, or disappeared, or were damaged by the weather, the loss was mine. And I had no control over such possibilities. It would be a big gamble, but I had to try it. I reasoned that even if there were some pilferage, so long as it was not as much as fifty percent, I wouldn't lose money. I thought it would be a safe bet that more than half the people would drop a nickel in the slot. If I put a paper rack at the hospital and one in front of the drug store, I could order about thirty more papers. That would make a real difference. I might qualify as "Carrier of the Year."

Within a week, the paper racks were delivered to me. I set one in the hospital lobby and the other I chained to a telephone pole on the corner, adjacent to Black's Drug Store and across the street from the hospital. Initially, I ordered twenty-five newspapers for my racks, fifteen for the hospital lobby and ten for the drugstore corner. I loaded the racks that first morning with a prayer. All day long in school, I wondered if my papers were selling, if I was being paid, if people were stealing them.

Next morning, I could hardly wait to get to my racks.

I rolled all my newspapers except twenty-five, which I kept neat and flat for the racks. I stuffed them in my canvas bag, dropped it on my gas tank, threw my leg over my Triumph and roared off. Norwood Hospital was only one block away. I parked in front, dropped my satchel on the sidewalk, and ran inside the waiting room with fifteen papers. I held my breath as I jammed the newspapers into the empty metal rack, then unlocked the coin deposit to retrieve my money. The change poured out into my palm—two nickels and two pennies! *Twelve cents!? But I put fifteen papers in the rack yesterday. At a nickel each, I should have seventy-five cents. This is a disaster*, I thought. *I've gambled and lost.*

Dejected, I returned to my bag. At the drug store, I got the other ten flat papers and put them in the rack. then opened the coin deposit to find, with some relief, thirty-two cents. It wasn't fifty cents as it should have been, but at least I'd made a small profit.

After two weeks, I was more than breaking even at the corner rack. I had some losses from pilferage, but most were from the rain. How discouraging on those mornings to remove sodden newspapers, my capital investment, and dump them in the nearest trash can.

But if the corner rack was discouraging, my hospital rack was a big bust. For the fifteen papers left in the rack in the waiting lobby, I should have collected seventy-five cents. But my average take was no more than fifteen cents, and some days less. There were never any papers left unsold.

I just couldn't believe the average person sitting in a hospital lobby would steal a newspaper. But it went on this way for several weeks. I had decided to discontinue the paper racks and unsubscribe for the twenty-five papers. And that would be that. I would have no hope of winning the car.

But before I pulled the plug, I asked my father if he would help me. I explained the situation to him. Then I said, "I can't sit in the lobby all morning and watch those newspapers. I've gotta go to school. Daddy, could you on your off day sit in the lobby and watch my papers?"

My father was furious to learn that people were stealing my papers, and quickly agreed to watch the rack at the hospital on his next off day. I think he looked forward to it. And when the big day came, he went to the hospital early and counted every paper. Then he sat and waited, as any other hospital visitor would do.

He told me that evening, with fire in his eyes, that nothing happened for about an hour. "Then," he said, "a nigger orderly came in the lobby. He looked all around, real careful-like. Then he grabbed all the papers—every one of them—and quickly left.

"I followed him down the hall and watched him go from room to room. He was selling your papers to patients! After he'd sold several, I cornered him and we had some words."

I imagined the words they had. My father had a temper like lightning that flashed without warning. In my mind I could see his big hands, strong from a lifetime of wrestling the steering wheels of trucks and buses, at the orderly's throat. He was fuming.

"I took the papers away from him an' I told him he better never take another one! Then I put the papers back in the rack and went to the office and made a complaint—demanded he be fired! But I don't think they will. They gave me no commitment."

He reflected for a moment. "You know, it don't make any sense. If he'll steal papers from a paper rack, he'll steal anything else from the hospital. How could they have someone like that working there?"

I was apprehensive. "If they don't fire him, do you think he'll keep on taking my papers?"

"Well, even if they don't fire him, I don't believe he'll take your papers again." He raised his right hand before his face and flexed his fingers. Then he made a fist. His big blue eyes darted from his fist to my face. "He knows I know."

Then he relaxed and looked thoughtful for a moment and added, "You know, you just can't trust a nigger with anything. That's the way they are."

I was furious. After all my worry, to find out it was just one person taking my papers and selling them. I had to agree with my father.

Mrs. Miller told me that colored people were no different from whites and to give them a chance. Even though I found it hard to believe her, I had tried it her way. Strangely enough, based on what she had said, I'd really begun to feel that maybe I'd been wrong all those years about colored people. And now, just as I was feeling more comfortable with colored people, here comes this bum and ruins it all by proving what I'd always heard, and once believed, and now believed again.

The next Saturday when I collected from Mrs. Miller, she asked me how I was doing with my new subscriptions. "Oh, it's going good," I lied, but then, somehow, I couldn't help myself. I told her what happened at the hospital. I concluded by telling her that it looked like to me that some colored people are not trustworthy. I wanted to say "all" but I didn't want a lecture.

She said I was lucky to have a father so committed to helping me, and she was confident he had solved the problem. She said some people have no character, whether they are white or colored, and that character is color blind. Some have it and some don't.

I had been in business long enough to know a lot of white people had no character. She was right about that. But just as I had begun to believe her about colored people, I had suffered a mighty setback. I found it awfully hard not to repeat to her what my father had said. But I smiled instead and said thank you and moved to my next customer.

I was convinced Mrs. Miller would always give people the benefit of the doubt. I was convinced, too, that Yankees must be naive, by nature, and wondered how many years Mrs. Miller would have to live in the South to understand the Southern point of view.

36 • While They Were Sleeping

Vanderbilt Road, Birmingham, Alabama. If you didn't know better, such an address might carry an aura of wealth, of country club houses in a high-class community. To the contrary, Vanderbilt Road is a narrow, mean, two-lane stretch of asphalt, slashing from south to north, abruptly terminating Norwood Boulevard, and creating the eastern boundary of our neighborhood. Vanderbilt Road's right of way is crowded by junk trees and undergrowth, then plunges quickly into heavy industry, pipe shops, metal crushing plants, fabricating plants, scrap yards, including pockets of company-type housing occupied by colored workers and their families. Norwood Boulevard, on the other hand, winds sinuously and gracefully through our neighborhood, its two lanes separated by a generous parkland where electric street cars once traveled.

My paper route ran along Norwood Boulevard until its intersection with Vanderbilt Road, marking the terminus of both the boulevard and my route.

And there I was in the dark on a frigid Sunday morning in January of 1957, at 5 A.M. on Vanderbilt Road. I had delivered my newspapers along one side of the well-lighted Norwood Boulevard, and ordinarily would have traveled Vanderbilt Road the short distance across the width of the park before turning up the other side of the Boulevard to deliver papers on the other side of the street.

But today I had business on Vanderbilt Road. I turned my Triumph to the north, raced by Mr. Monte's tiny grocery store and plunged from my neighborhood down that dark road toward the industries. It was cold and I trembled in the frigid January pre-dawn. The moment I could no longer see the road, save for the narrow beam of headlight probing the darkness, I became instantly alert, forgetting my freezing hands and feet. The single beacon seemed to create a tunnel through which I traveled, accentuating the thick underbrush, the canopy of bare trees, and the low-hanging clouds. There were no occupied houses or other structures along the road for a quarter mile or more, and no street lights.

Norwood was an island socked in on the north, east and south by heavy industry. On the west, our neighborhood joined Druid Hills, another residential neighborhood. I was intimately knowledgeable of my entire neighborhood, but I had explored none of the industrial areas that surrounded us.

I cautiously pushed on for a quarter mile and slowed to search for the narrow dirt alleyway running perpendicular to Vanderbilt Road. Down the unpaved alley were about twenty shacks. That alley was not on my paper route, nor was Vanderbilt Road, but I figured no one else was covering this God-forsaken area and I might just give it a try. This was Mrs. Miller's strategy for increasing my route, and I had to admit, it was working for me. I came up with one new account in that alley, Sam and Mattie Broadnax. I had been delivering their afternoon paper for several weeks, but the Sunday paper was delivered well before daybreak, and their alleyway was hard to find in the dark, and the houses were located at the end of a long, empty, narrow dirt lane.

I located the mouth of the alley, mostly because there was a break in the tree line. I surely couldn't see the alley itself. Turning, I shut off my engine and coasted down the long empty lane for two reasons. First, I knew on Sunday morning all the people in the little company houses would be asleep. Those shacks were built right against the alleyway and I didn't want to disturb their occupants with the clamor from my motorcycle engine. And second, those folks had dogs. Coasting down the alley might stir up the dogs, but wouldn't anger them the way the racket of my engine might. At least, that's the way I had it figured.

In my neighborhood, dogs barked at colored people who came through.

Now it was my turn, as I intruded into the colored enclaves. This was all new to me. And very unsettling. I had never had any problem with dogs until I began working the colored neighborhoods. I knew many of those residents distrusted me. I guess they had their reasons. I suppose that was reason enough for their dogs to distrust me as well, but it sure hurt my feelings when their dogs barked at me as if I were some kind of alien.

Just as I expected, a couple of dogs darted into my path, snarling and barking, but they didn't try to bite me. I coasted to a stop at the Broadnax house, its front stoop bordering the lane. I knocked down the kickstand, swung my leg over, all the while crooning low and sweet to the dogs. I swung my heavy satchel of papers to the ground and, taking a single issue of the Sunday newspaper, quietly mounted the single, low step to the front stoop.

I wondered then if a single customer was worth the risk I was taking by being the only white down a dark alley with mean dogs, and among colored people who distrusted me at least, and hated me at the worst. Besides, would any self-respecting white do this?

I stopped in my tracks, there on the stoop, and wondered whether I should simply drop the newspaper there and leave. I was worried about doing what I had been asked to do.

I sucked in a great breath, gritted my teeth and turned the doorknob to the front door. Just like she had said, it was unlocked. Gripping the doorknob, I pushed the door open a couple of inches and waited. The dogs had quit barking, but I could hear them snuffling around in the alley. Otherwise, I could hear nothing, save the buzzing in my ears from my own vigilance.

I pushed the door open a foot or so and waited. Nothing. No sound. At last, I sucked up what little courage I could muster, and slowly lifted my foot and tentatively stepped over the threshold into the room, just one step, and waited. Then I shifted my weight onto the floor inside, holding tightly the doorknob, ready to explode out the door if need be.

There, in the next room, only a few steps away, Mr. Broadnax snored. I froze in place, didn't move a muscle, couldn't think clearly for a moment. The pitch-black room tilted. *What in the world could I possibly have been-thinking, coming into their home while they're asleep? Was I crazy?*

An acrid stench from a coal fire only recently smoldered out suffused the room and left a taste of coal dust and grit from the air I sucked into my mouth and lungs. I tucked the newspaper under my arm and muffled my nose and mouth with one gloved hand, still gripping the door knob.

I slowly closed the door and released the doorknob. I had been in this room once before, when I called on them to ask if I could deliver their paper. The room was small, only large enough for a few chairs before the coal grate in the fireplace between the two windows. The room was now so dark on this moonless night I could scarcely make out the windows, heavily draped against the cold. Then I cautiously padded a few baby steps and stood before the fireplace though it was virtually invisible. My leg bumped a chair onto which I quietly laid the newspaper. Then I removed the other glove. The only thing I could see was my breath ghosting into the air. It seemed as cold inside as out. I waited for my eyes to adjust, hoping soon I would be able to see, and wondering why I had put myself in this vulnerable place in their home while they slept.

*   *   *

It was on Mrs. Miller's earlier suggestion that I solicited new accounts from colored people along the margins of my routes. That brought me to meet Sam and Mattie Broadnax. Though I had met them only three weeks earlier, a lot had happened since then. Standing in front of a mantel I strained to see but could not, my mind jumped back to the events that brought me here, how I'd first come into this area near the McWane Pipe Plant and other heavy industry.

I had completed my collections that Saturday, and was thinking about Mrs. Miller's challenge. I cruised down Norwood Boulevard to its intersection with Vanderbilt Road and turned north. That was alien territory to me. I knew there were only a few if any residences along that road, and that it quickly became industrial in character. It was clear to me that this territory was not a part of my route. It was not even a part of my neighborhood. That area would belong to East Birmingham or some other paper branch. But that was all positive in a way. Whatever residences were there would probably not be served by some other newspaper carrier. To my knowledge, all the newspaper carriers were white, and I just didn't believe they'd go out of their way to deliver papers to colored folks.

I found, just as I expected, that the road was almost deserted, only a few abandoned houses before the heavy industry began. But then I spotted an alleyway leading off Vanderbilt Road. And that's how I came to find this enclave of company housing and to meet Mr. and Mrs. Broadnax.

When I'd first knocked on this door, a middle-aged colored lady answered the door.

She looked me over with suspicious eyes.

"Oh, hi," I said, "I'm a paper boy—I deliver the *Birmingham News*, and wondered does someone bring papers here on this street."

"No. Never seen anybody bring papers down here."

"Well, I'd like to talk with you about that if you have a minute. I deliver the afternoon . . . ."

"Son, come in here where it's warm. You gonna freeze standing out there."

She opened the door wider and motioned me in. I hesitated, didn't want to go into her home. I'd never been in a colored home before. *How can I say no?* I edged inside the door, and she gestured toward a couple of straight chairs before a glowing coal fire in the fireplace. I waited for her to take a seat, and then I seated myself.

"Thank you. It sure is nice and warm in here. I hope I'm not bothering you. I'm just trying to get some new customers for my paper route."

"No, son, no bother at all. Glad to see you."

As we talked, she looked toward the front door as it opened, and I followed her gaze. A huge man in a dirty blue work uniform filled the doorway. I leaped to my feet as I'd been trained all my life to do when an adult comes into the room. He was looking me up and down, watchful and suspicious, his face a dark scowl.

"This is my husband, Sam."

Automatically, my hand shot out, and my stomach contracted. Whites never shake hands with coloreds. I certainly never had. Though I don't remember anyone laying down that principle to me, I had never seen any handshake between the races, though a number of times I'd noted how a white man and a colored man would meet each other for the first time, each man with his arms kept tightly by his side.

But it was too late for me. I had been raised to always be courteous. I couldn't take back my hand now. In that instant I may have wavered, but I didn't withdraw my hand, even though my body seized up.

"Sam, this is Sonny. He wants to bring us the newspaper."

His face relaxed, and puzzlement replaced the scowl. He might have thought I was different from the rest of the whites, but he would have been wrong. Mostly, I was desperate to make a sale to whomever I could. I was determined to increase my route no matter how awkward canvassing among these colored people would be.

Then he relaxed all over. It was almost as if his muscles went loose, like a cat when the crisis is over. He took one long step and gave me his hand. I tried to do what my father had always told me, "When you meet a man, grip his hand, look him in the eye, make him think you're somebody." But gripping Mr. Broadnax's hand was like gripping a catcher's mitt. His hand was hard and flaky and pliable, like my leather bicycle seat, weathered from years in the sun and rain. I tensed, thought he might crush my fingers, but his handshake was docile, as if he were afraid he would injure me, like he was holding a hamster.

And in the space of a breath, I was overcome with the sense that here was a formidable man, a man who works with his hands, who is steady and dependable, a man who does what he says he'll do. This was no boozing layabout, the stereotypical Negro character presented to me so many times in so many ways.

"Glad to meet you." Then he signaled for me to sit. "Si' down, son, si' down."

I sat back down.

"Now, what's this about a newspaper? Why you wanna bring a paper way down here fo' us?"

"Uh, well, I'm just trying to get some new customers. Just trying to make a little more money."

"How much you charge to bring it to us?"

"It's a nickel for each paper, fifteen cents for Sunday. So that's forty-five cents a week."

"You mean the same price I pay at the sto'?" Mrs. Broadnax asked, surprised.

"Yes, ma'am." I flinched, almost involuntarily, for saying yes ma'am to a colored woman. But this lady was as nice to me as any white woman on my route. I had been raised to be polite, first and foremost. So as I sat there I resigned myself to use the same terms of respect I would use for whites. After all, I was asking them for their business.

"Sam," she asked, "How can we say no? He's charging the same price as we pay at the sto' and he'll bring it to us. And he's such a nice young man." She gave me a smile.

"Thank you," I offered, and opened my route book. "Let me get your names and address, please."

I struggled to find my pencil among my coat, sweater and other coverings.

"Take your coat off, son. It's warm in here," Mrs. Broadnax said.

"Yes, ma'am." I took it off, located my pencil and got their names and address.

We transacted our business, but I had just taken my coat off and felt awkward to jump up and put it on again. I looked around the small room and saw pictures on the wall.

"Are those your children?"

Mrs. Broadnax beamed. "Yes, we have five children, all grown up now. They live all around the county. We so blessed. They all good kids, married with they own families." She smiled at Mr. Broadnax and continued.

"We so lucky. We helped all five to go to college. All we ever wanted was for them to have an easier life than we had. We ain't got much but we got that." She smiled again to her husband. He didn't say anything, as he studied the pictures on the wall.

So strange, it seemed to me, that this colored lady had spoken the same words I'd heard from my parents, so many times. In fact, those were the exact words I'd heard my parents say.

I thanked them again and excused myself.

*   *   *

And, now, here I stood inside the Broadnax home as they slept.

Carefully, I extended my hand and found the mantel. I slowly swept my hand across the top until I felt coins. Quietly, I swept the three coins

into the palm of my hand and made a fist. Then I carefully opened the
door and edged outside. I eased the door shut and shuffled off the stoop
into the alleyway. The dogs were snuffling around me, menacing and unpredictable. I spoke softly to them, as I switched on my headlight and
opened my palm under the beam. There, in the light, shone a quarter and
two dimes. Just as Mrs. Broadnax promised.

I slipped the coins into my pocket, shoved my freezing hands inside
my gloves, lifted the heavy satchel of papers and swung it onto the gas
tank of my Triumph and with my foot snapped the kickstand into place.
Then I wrestled the Triumph in a half-circle there in the alley, and heaved
it up the slight incline toward Vanderbilt Road, the dogs swirling and
snarling at my feet. I pushed the motorcycle for about a block, until the
noise of the engine wouldn't wake the neighbors. Then I threw my right
leg over and kicked it to life. The dogs jumped away, barking, as I roared
off to complete my route.

When I had finished my deliveries, I pulled my Triumph over to the
curb to think for a minute, to reflect on my visit inside the Broadnax
home.

I thought about Sam Broadnax, his stolid build, his weathered face,
his powerful hands as big as shovels. It was clear to me that he was a hard
worker, industrious and dependable. And Mrs. Broadnax? She was kind
and warm and friendly, as nice as any grandmother in Birmingham. She
knew it was inconvenient for me to make a special trip to their home `to
collect. She suggested I collect on Sunday morning when I delivered the
paper. My money would be on the mantel. The door would be unlocked.

Then I thought about what I'd heard all my life about colored people,
what Ace Carter preached at the White Citizen Council meetings. *Is it
all a lie?* I wasn't sure about that yet, but one thing I did know for a certainty—it was a lie when it came to Sam and Mattie Broadnax. I thought
about Mrs. Miller. She had been right again. Is it possible she could be
right about everything?

And standing there, straddling my Triumph, my hands and feet and
face aching from the cold, I watched the dark sky above the tree line to
the east begin to pinken. I felt something warm flow into me. I couldn't
dislike these people, Sam and Mattie Broadnax, no matter what Ace

Carter said, no matter what anyone said. These were good people with good values. Their hopes and dreams were identical to those of my own parents. And they trusted me to come into their home while they slept.

I sat down, tucking my hands under my arms and felt warm even as I could see from the first dawning the rolling and swelling of low, dark clouds. I kick-started my engine and slowly pulled away from the curb. I couldn't have cared less had the bottom dropped out.

37 • Facing the Music

It was my senior year, and graduation was just around the corner. I had somehow avoided thinking about it, but now it came down on me—I would soon have to give up the one thing that had given meaning to my life.

Mrs. Miller had bugged me the entire school year to take my studies more seriously—that my paper routes were not that important in the big scheme of things. She just didn't understand how important my paper routes were to me. They were my single claim to success.

But in truth, I had begun taking a little more interest in school. My twelfth grade English teacher, Ms. Holliman, had pulled me aside one day last fall and asked me why I was making such poor grades. She said I could do a great deal better than I was doing. "You're bright," she said. "There's no excuse for you not making an A in my class."

I didn't make an A in her class, but I did make a B, an unusually high grade for me. Her lecture caused me to try my hand at school work with more confidence. So far as I could recall, she was the only teacher who had ever told me I was bright.

She assigned the class to read a play. I visited the library and casually browsed through the section entitled "Dramatic Arts," convinced this was another chore I'd hate. Reading a play sounded so boring. While I had always enjoyed reading, I avoided most of the books assigned to me by my teachers. I assumed they all would be boring. Meanwhile, I happily read those paperback westerns and mysteries my father read, most of which he inherited from passengers who left them on his bus.

I finally settled on a play called *Mr. Roberts* written by Thomas Heggan, mainly, I think, because of the Naval scene on the cover. It was the first play I'd ever read, and I was greatly surprised to find I liked it. I learned that the play was based on a novel, which I then also read with great interest. Mr. Roberts was a much more complex character than the heroes in the westerns and private eye books I had been stuck on for several years. I've since seen the movie several times, and Mr. Roberts, in the person of Henry Fonda, became and continues to this day to be my ideal for what a man should be: strong, courageous, compassionate, fair, and, yet somehow humble.

A month or so later, I browsed through the library and pulled from the shelf Thomas Wolfe's *You Can't Go Home Again*, and thumbed through it. I think I may have reached for it because of its sheer size. There must have been seven or eight hundred pages. I had never handled a book as thick as that and wondered if it was in me to read such a book, but once I began I could hardly put it down. I had never before read a book with such complex sentence structure, such fine description and moving introspection.

The title of the book was as compelling to me as its intriguing size. *You Can't Go Home Again*, for me, a senior in high school with graduation only a few months away, raised some interesting questions. First, I had never left home, but for the past year or so, I had experienced impatience with my parents. I increasingly felt isolated and alienated from them. Leaving home was just around the corner. I could hardly wait, yet I was apprehensive. My plan was to give up my paper routes at the end of May, then work a summer job at Hayes Aircraft arranged by our next door neighbor. Finally, in September, I would head to Nashville, at my parents' request, to enroll in David Lipscomb College, a small Christian college.

So here was this big book with a title that suggested to me I'd not be able to come home again once I left. I learned that George Webber, the protagonist in the novel, had himself written a best-selling novel that offended the people in his small North Carolina hometown, and he was not welcome to return home. I had no illusions about writing a book, but I wondered nonetheless whether a son could truly return to his home if, like George Webber, his values changed, particularly if he no longer saw the world in quite the same way as his father and mother. How quickly I would come to learn the accuracy of Thomas Wolfe's proverb.

While I took a little more interest in my school work, I also worked harder than ever on my paper routes, still thinking about that car some paper boy would win. I had long since tried to put the contest out of my mind and just do the best job I could, but it was impossible to completely forget that '50 Ford. I found myself day-dreaming in my classes about the car and the independence from my family I'd win. I could listen to the kind of music I wanted.

And I had met this girl who lived on the Boulevard. I had always been fascinated with and attracted to girls, though after my first kiss by Miss Talley and then my second by the Tobacco Woman, I was mortally afraid of them. Maybe even more afraid than delivering my papers in the early, pre-dawn darkness and the terrors of plunging down dark alleys. But the Boulevard girl was different, and my *third* kiss was warm and tender, as I dreamed it might be. She was now at center stage in every daydream. Somehow, Mrs. Miller's teachings had coincided with my yearnings over the Boulevard girl. It seems the passions I had felt about preserving the Southern way of life had somehow partly drained away, replaced by passions of a different kind. We were just good friends, but I had high hopes. If I had a car, maybe I would have a chance.

I continued canvassing in the colored areas, as Mrs. Miller had suggested, picking up a new customer here and there. But my real opportunity was the paper racks. My father had resolved the pilferage problem at the hospital. I felt more secure and ordered several more racks, and chained them to lampposts in other commercial areas on my route. Then I stocked them with the *Post-Herald* every morning and in the afternoon would restock them with the *News*. I had increased my routes by over fifty papers per day. I was then delivering each day approximately three hundred *Post-Herald* newspapers and about one hundred copies of the *Birmingham News*.

My days were full with an increasing interest in school. I read more books. I handled my morning and afternoon paper routes, and stocked my paper racks. I was so busy, the contest fell into a file somewhere in the back of my mind.

One day in early April 1957, shortly after I turned eighteen, my new branch manager, Mr. Abbott, told me the head of the newspaper circulation department at the *News* wanted to see me. He told me to go by the *News* building right after school a few days later, on April 13. He said he understood I would be late picking up my afternoon papers that day, that he would wait for me.

My heart skipped a beat. This must be about Dr. Goins, I thought. What else would it be? No way I could have won "Newspaper Carrier of the Year." I mentioned it to my parents who, surprisingly, seemed to know about my appointment with the circulation manager. But their faces were inscrutable. They told me to come straight home that day after school and they would drive me to the *News* building.

That didn't make much sense to me. Phillips High School was located only about four blocks from the Birmingham News Building, and I could've walked there more quickly than going home first. But I didn't argue. I was pretty jumpy all that day as it became clear to me that the meeting with the circulation manager was about Dr. Goins's neon sign I had broken a month or so earlier and never reported.

That was a day I'd never forget. It was a Thursday, I know because the papers were so heavy. I had rolled and tied my papers that morning as I always did. It was still dark as I passed by Dr. Goins's office, a Victorian style house set back from the street and located in the commercial area of Twelfth Avenue. In front of his office, a high pole sign perpendicular to the street announced in huge red neon lettering on each side—

Dr. James S. Goins
Chiropractor

— The neon lettering was so large it lit up that side of the street. Believe me, if I had thrown that newspaper ten thousand times as I passed by on my motorcycle I couldn't have done it again. I swung that heavy rolled paper over my shoulder, launching it stiff-armed like a basketball hook shot. It looped high, end over end, in an arc headed for Dr. Goins's front porch, and then, as it passed by the neon sign—it cleanly swept all the letters off! As if they had never been there. My heart stopped.

I brought my cycle to a stop, then cautiously turned a circle there in the street. The paper had landed on the porch, its flight uninterrupted. But now, one side of the pole sign was dark. I held my breath as I surveyed the pole sign, dark on one side, and glass scattered on the ground beneath. *Oh, no! What will this cost? Hundreds of dollars!*

It would take me months to pay for this damage.

I drove off to complete my route not knowing what to do or how to handle it. I knew the right thing to do, of course, was to go back to Dr. Goins's office after school and own up. After school that day, I temporized, deciding to put it off until Saturday when I collected. *I'll do it then,* I promised myself. All day Friday I agonized over it.

That Saturday, as I collected for the paper at Dr. Goins's office, I did not own up, but instead held my breath and said nothing. He said nothing, and I was thankful. *Did he know? Did he suspect?* I still remember the event as if it were yesterday. I can see clearly in my mind that heavy rolled paper skimming the side of the sign, dumping all the neon lettering into a pile of glass slivers on the grass.

After a couple of weeks, it was too late to own up to what I had done. It may not have been a lie in a technical sense, but there's no question in my mind I had an obligation to set the record straight and I failed.

They're going to fire me!

I was so keyed up I couldn't keep my mind on my classes. I imagined being dressed down in front of my parents by the big boss, whose name I didn't even know.

That afternoon when I came home from school, my mother insisted I wear a sport coat, though I really didn't need a jacket at all in April. "You need to look nice," she pleaded. For a fleeting second, I considered the remote possibility that I'd won the contest, but it disappeared like a snowflake on a warm car hood when it dawned on me that Mother knew, as lawyers in the courtroom know, the worst criminal might get the benefit of the doubt if neat and well-dressed.

We showed up at the outside loading dock of the *News* building on Fourth Avenue where the delivery trucks are loaded with newspapers. We were to wait for the circulation manager there. That's where I would face the music. We stood in silence, the three of us. I felt like a soldier waiting for the general. On the far side of the loading dock, a white school bus was parked—

The Birmingham News–Birmingham Post-Herald

—painted on the side. I thought of my trip to Florida in that very bus the previous summer. Then he showed up. I say "he" because if I learned his name, I've long since forgotten it. A little later, when he held out a set of car keys to me, I must have collapsed into some catatonic state. I have no memory of anything that was said, nor do I recall actually taking the keys to the two-tone blue 1950 Ford that was parked there at the loading dock. I don't even remember the *Birmingham News* photographer taking a picture of me sitting in my new car, but I do have a copy of the photograph as evidence, and these words on the reverse side in my mother's handwriting:

> Car was presented to Sonny by the *B'ham News*
> on April 13, 1957, as winner of contest.

Wow! A 1950 Ford Custom Deluxe Sedan, with a V-8 engine and manual shift, three-speed gearbox, white-wall tires and fender skirts.

And she was all mine.

I pushed the clutch pedal to the floor, turned the key and pressed the starter button. The engine rumbled. I smiled, waved to my parents, pushed the clutch to the floor and slipped into first gear. Easing the clutch pedal up, a very difficult job for a new driver, I gently depressed the accelerator—didn't want to mess up in front of them and the manager by jerking out of the parking lot like a fifteen year old learner—and smoothly edged out into the street. As I pulled into the traffic, I reached for the radio and turned the knob, searching for the station where Shelly the Playboy bantered between the rhythm & blues songs he played. He was the colored disc jockey everybody listened to after school—except me, of course. I delivered papers. Little did I know he had moved on to another city by then.

What a feeling! Cruising along in my own car, engine rumbling, windows down, music thumping. I turned the corner, shifted into second and headed toward Norwood. Everything will be different now. I can almost taste the change. I shifted into third, now speeding on my way.

Exhilarated, my eyes were locked straight ahead as I raced down Twenty-sixth Street like a horse to his barn. I would turn right on Fifteenth Avenue, go under the railroad and then to Norwood Boulevard. I'd cruise around the Boulevard and swing into her driveway and knock on her door. She was so pretty. I could see her now. Black hair, short bob cut. Smooth olive complexion. Direct, hazel eyes, sometimes as serious as Mrs. Miller's and sometimes sparkly and playful.

I'd pick her up, and we'd cruise down the Boulevard, where, formerly, we had often walked, hand in hand, to the drug store. My destination now that I had a car was to Ed Salem's Drive-In, the local teenage hangout. I'd never been cool before, but I'd be cool now. I'd pull into a parking slot and rev my engine. The waitress would come over and take our order. I would unroll a pack of cigarettes from my turned up short sleeve, shake one out, and put it between my lips, unlit, and just let it hang there, like James Dean. Then, I'd turn to her and say something cool and she'd laugh and touch my arm. It was exciting to imagine those things, but I knew it was all futile. I'd never before tried a cigarette nor said anything cool.

And then, just as I turned onto the Boulevard, I remembered how protective her parents were. Would her mother let her go for a ride with me, especially on a school day? I backed off the accelerator and slowed. I had to think this through, get the right words together about how safe I'd be, where we'd go and when we'd be back. And just then, just as I got it all together in my mind, just as I was about to turn into her driveway, it hit me—Mr. Abbot is waiting for me at the paper branch.

I have my afternoon papers to deliver—a hundred of them.

38 • Leaving Home

My Ford was gassed and my bags were packed. College. Nash-ville. Freedom. A new world, a new way of living, lay north on U. S. Highway 31.

My heart thumped with eagerness—my stomach churned with fore-boding.

I hugged my mother, tears in her eyes, and Dale, now a fifth grader. I bantered with Eddie, teasing him about whether he could handle all those papers he now delivered—his and mine. I was wary with my father, with whom I had a love/hate relation, even as I shook his hand, about to fly the nest. He gave me a final piece of advice as I climbed into my car. "Always be humble, boy. Always be humble." I had heard that before, and I still didn't get it. It seemed inconsistent with his other advice: to stand tall, to look the man in the eye, to defend myself when necessary. It would take me years to figure that out.

Little did I know that September morning in 1957, when I pulled away from home, that I'd be towing an anchor behind me. I lugged it up the hill to Seventeenth Avenue, where the street was level for a couple of blocks. My mind darted back a year or so to when I ran along this same street beside my little sister, Dale, then a nine-year-old, as I taught her how to ride her bicycle. She was a good learner, and it didn't take long.

Then this anchor, an anchor of memories, dragged me to a halt at the traffic light at Seventeenth Avenue and Twenty-sixth Street, just around the corner from my home, the very intersection where my adolescent life had burst into bloom. I looked south, up the highway a half-block to where the car had knocked me down with my load of papers. Across the street was the paper branch, where a dozen motley motorbikes were usually parked in front. For a moment, I missed the camaraderie of the boys inside the branch joking as we rolled our papers. And across the street from the branch stood the big chinaberry tree on the vacant lot from where I had spied on the boys so long ago. It had now been more than a year since Mr. Hawley had retired or been fired, and I still missed him and his gruff friendship.

There on the corner, Johnny Graffeo had not yet opened his grocery store for the day. And in the road, there in front of Johnny's store—that's where the truck hit my brother and dragged him down the street. How Eddie survived that collision I'd never know.

The light changed. Turning north toward Nashville, I slowly dragged along Twenty-sixth Street. Hills rolled above both sides of the highway where blocks of neat cottages nestled, cottages where I had left my papers every morning for more than three years, building up a reservoir of good memories of good people.

During the five years I delivered newspapers in Norwood, I had a series of routes that covered much of the neighborhood. I learned that Norwood was an old, established neighborhood occupied by all kinds of people—the well-to-do, the middle class white collar, the blue collar, the poor, the old and the young and ages in between, the friendly and the rude, the sophisticated urbanites, the country folks like us, and the ethnics, the Italians, the Greeks and others. Norwood was a residential community, but there were all kinds of commercial activities in our neighborhood: a hospital, doctors' clinics, restaurants, drug stores, corner groceries, churches, a funeral home, beer joints, flower shops, hardware stores and the like, as well as Norwood School. Norwood was a self-contained neighborhood of great diversity, a diversity which I had appreciated more than ever during the past year, as the Boulevard girl was Italian and Catholic. She and I had become close friends—my girlfriend, I dared to think.

That diversity and self-sufficiency made Norwood, to my mind, the perfect cocoon for a young boy. It was the perfect neighborhood. It sustained me. It gave me a way to learn discipline and hard work. It allowed me on my paper routes to become self-sufficient in limited ways and to feel a sense of independence. It gave me room within which to grow. It introduced me to a variety of people of all ages and persuasions. We are who we turn out to be because of our parents and all our experiences and the varied influences that come to bear during our youth.

Three blocks of memories, and then I passed the Tobacco Woman's house. *Ugh!* That broke my reverie, and then my paper route was behind me. I was headed north through North Birmingham and then out Highway 31 toward Nashville. Happily kicked back in the driver's seat, I let the hammer fall. I was gone, alone on the highway with my roadmap—a new school, new friends, a new city, unfamiliar and unexplored.

A new life. Freedom.

39 • Stretching My Wings

I failed my first big test as a college student. I failed it before I ever opened my first text book or attended a class.

I blame my failure on the fact that my life had been constricted for so long it was natural that I falter a time or two as I tested my wings of freedom.

When I registered for classes at Lipscomb College I was assigned a roommate. His name was Billy. He couldn't hear, and as a result his speech was almost unintelligible. I felt awkward that first day for my inability to communicate with him. It was freedom I wanted, freedom from responsibility and constraints. I didn't want to bother with him. I wanted the freedom of a roommate who could take care of himself, the freedom not to be burdened by Billy.

I fretted for a day or so over my discomfort and frustration, failing to take into account Billy's courageous efforts to be normal.

My new freedom was too much for me to handle. I'm the one who before had empathized with the underdogs, yet I went to the administration and got a new roommate. Yes, I made my decision. And it's a decision I've lived with all the rest of my life. I'm still haunted by it.

I'm not proud of several of my decisions that first school year away from home. For the previous five years, all my time was dedicated to attending school and tending my newspaper routes. I had saved most of the money I had earned and had three thousand dollars in the bank when I entered college in the fall of 1957. That would be equivalent to approximately thirty thousand in current dollars.

I had enough money to attend college for the entire school year and pay all my tuition and room and board. For the first time, I had no part-time job.

What I did have was freedom—for the first time in my life. And I was ill-equipped to deal with it. I was like a bird let out of a cage. I became distracted upon my discovery of Nashville and the larger life available to a man with a car and a spirit of adventure. Among the things I discovered was Vanderbilt University. I often hung out at the coffee shops around Vanderbilt, reading and dreaming of the day I could transfer to that campus.

Another thing I discovered in Nashville was Gene Nobles, a disc jockey at WLAC, a Nashville radio station. He became my favorite. He and the other WLAC disc jockeys, Hoss Man and J. R., were white I learned later, but for a long time I thought they were colored. They played rock 'n' roll and rhythm & blues. It was from them that I learned about B.B. King and Bobby "Blue" Bland and dozens of others. Learning about this new style of music I found so compelling pushed me into a broader and more respectful view of colored people and their talents. Something about the blues spoke to me in much the same way Hank Williams did. The blues tapped into that part of me that searched for something I couldn't identify, maybe something I'd lost—or never had in the first place.

Gene Nobles, in particular, fascinated me not only because of his music but because of his off-color humor. It was cold that winter in Nashville, so cold I worried about my car freezing up. Many evenings, I would go out late at night, crank my engine and drive around for a while to keep it warm and listen to the radio. I can hear Gene now, his voice raspy, raucous, smoky:

> It's cold out, people—freezing out there. Bring in your dogs
> and cats, and don't forget—heh, heh, heh—your brass mon-
> keys—heh, heh, heh.

Gene pushed his commercials in funny, suggestive ways.

> Every man in the world—every young blade—know you
> gotta have a jah' of White Rose Petroleum Jelly in the
> pocket of yo' cah'—man, it's the best. You never know when
> you may need—heh, heh, heh—to fix a squeaky do' hinge.

As the school year passed by, I often thought of the girl on the Boulevard. I missed her and, because she was away at Convent School, I had not been able to correspond with her. But now I felt an awful conflict. I was in college. She was still in high school. It didn't seem right to me; yet, I could hardly wait to see her and to pick up our relationship, which I hoped she had not forgotten during a school year of absence.

I don't know when it occurred to me that I was homesick. Freedom is good. But gradually during the school year, I became aware that the flip side of freedom is untethered—isolated—lonely. At the end of the school year I had run out of the money earned during five years of delivering newspapers, but I was also ready to return home, home to my family, home to Norwood and the Boulevard girl.

I managed to make Bs and Cs that first year, enough, I hoped, to get into Vanderbilt or some other college after working for a year and saving up my money again. I knew without a doubt I wanted to go back to college. I had discovered Hemingway and Steinbeck and Dostoevsky. I had discovered the beauty and power of words, words to transform the moment, to set a mood, to trigger a laugh, to cause my heart to stutter, to send a shill down my spine, to catch my breath. The force of words to cast me into the heat of a desert sun or the chill of its starlit night. The mystery of words to create a moment, reaching the well-springs of my deepest emotions. And I had discovered that I thoroughly enjoyed talking with other students about books.

So it was time to return home. Obviously, I could go home, but could I really go home? The question was, of course, could I go back and pick up as if I'd never left?

I thought a thousand times about Thomas Wolfe and his maxim that "you can't go home again," and I wondered if it were true. During the time

I was gone, I had become aware of this painful paradox—that we long for the day we can leave the place we call home—to stretch our wings and fly the nest. And then, once we've flown, no matter how far we've gone or how old we become, or how our vision of the world has changed, there remains in us like a lodestar a longing, a yearning, a hope, to go back to that place we first so badly wanted to leave. I knew in my heart that Wolfe was right—that things would never be the same.

40 • The Truth Shall Set You Free

How many times during the last year I'd been away at college had I imagined myself revving my hot Ford and rolling into Ed Salem's Drive-In?[12] All the girls would look my way. I would swing open my door and put a foot on the ground real cool like, slow and casual. I would salute the girls by sliding my open hand toward them, palm down, out and away, smoothing the waters, just like James Dean. I would saunter toward the restaurant, between cars lined up for curb service. Teenagers would be huddled in little groups. Maybe one of the pretty girls would recognize me and ask where I'd been. I'd say "college," and she would say "ahhhh," nodding slowly.

But I didn't rev my engine when I pulled into Ed Salem's parking lot. And I didn't park right down front for curb service. I cautiously nudged my Ford into a spot back in the corner of the parking lot. I ventured cautiously toward the restaurant, weaving my way through the cars parked in the service area. Kids were sitting on car hoods and gathered in groups, girls and boys, all atwitter and flitting from one group to another, laughing and talking. On the margin, out in the driving lanes, were the "hoods" in t-shirts, their cigarettes rolled into their sleeves, making obscene gestures and cutting up.

No one looked my way. I slipped off my heavy, black Buddy Holly-type glasses I hated and stuck them in my pocket. Then, with both hands, I smoothed my ducktail haircut. I had been away a year, and I felt as if I'd never been to Ed Salem's at all.

Actually, Ed Salem's had always been pretty much off limits to me. Not even as a senior in high school was I allowed to go by there except for a quick burger. My parents thought it was not a place for teenagers, even though they didn't sell beer or wine. It was just a hamburger and milkshake place where all the kids hung out.

Except, of course, for me.

I suppose the thing my parents were concerned about was the loud music from outside speakers that made the restaurant seem wilder than it was. The juke box was full of rock 'n' roll music—Elvis Presley, Buddy Holly, Chuck Berry, Fats Domino, and dozens more singers belting out lyrics to make kids act crazy.

A few years earlier, a white audience would have listened to popular music, like Frank Sinatra or Ella Fitzgerald, or sung along to hillbilly music with Hank Williams or Ferlin Husky. Colored people listened to rhythm and blues. But then, a strange thing happened. White singers like Pat Boone began to record sanitized versions of R&B hits. They were called "crossover" artists. By 1958, white audiences were listening to colored artists like Fats Domino sing what became known as rock 'n' roll, and white artists like Elvis Presley became music idols, adored by white and colored folk alike. Music, it seemed, was setting its own cultural attitudes in the deep South among teenagers, regardless of Ace Carter and his existential fears.

As I twisted my way through the parking lot at Ed Salem's, past cars full of kids with trays hanging at open windows and past the carhops in short skirts who served the parked patrons, I was caught by the pounding piano beat of Danny and the Juniors belting out their big hit, "At the Hop." Even if I weren't jiving to it. Even if everyone there was utterly oblivious to me.

I opened the door and the pounding outside merged with the pounding inside. The smell of hamburgers, fries and grilled onions enveloped me as I stepped inside. Uncertainly, I squinted around the room hoping to see someone I knew, someone I could join. I didn't have many friends before I left town and now that I'd been gone for a year probably had none at all. I remembered my glasses, slipped them on and quickly re-looked. But I didn't see anyone who might know me.

And no one noticed me. Embarrassed, I sat down at an empty booth, trying to look cool and detached, but feeling lonely and isolated. There was a line of kids feeding the jukebox. I ordered a burger and coke and sat there, on the edge of my seat absently bobbing my knee to the rhythm of "That'll Be The Day," a great Buddy Holly hit from a couple of years back. Why on earth I had imagined that coming here alone would be fun was lost to me now.

I had returned from my first year in college only a few weeks earlier. I now had a job at Hayes Aircraft working the graveyard shift, from 11:00 P.M. to 7:00 A.M. the next morning. In fact, I had to be there—I looked at my watch—in only three hours.

As I sat alone in the booth feeling sorry for myself, I reviewed my current love life. It was just as I had feared about going home—nothing was ever the same. When I had set out from Nashville I could hardly wait to get back home so I could call on the Boulevard girl. I wanted to renew our friendship and explore the possibility of seeing each other more. But insurmountable obstacles lay in my path. First, she was still in high school and I was now a college dropout working the graveyard shift like any other blue collar worker. That didn't seem right to me, and I worried that it wouldn't seem right to her parents. And then, second, for the big clincher, she had recently confessed to me her confusion about the future, and whether to give her life to the Church—to become a nun. I was thunderstruck. *Is this her way of keeping me at arm's length . . . Is she seriously considering throwing away her chance to have her own children, her own family?* How could I honorably press her for a deeper relationship when she was so young and so unsure? To go down that road would be wrong, I knew, but I was helpless to my own yearnings. I was faced with the classic paradox: to give up that which I loved best because, most of all, I wanted so desperately to hold on; and to hold on would not be in her best interest.

I knew in my heart that I must quietly fade away. Distraught and disheartened, I worried endlessly over how I could possibly withdraw, even as I continued to call, though it was clear to me that was the only course I could follow.

Thankfully, the waitress appeared at my table and interrupted my rumination over how it had all gone so wrong, and, then, to my horror, as she took my order I saw him across the room, over by the jukebox.

Oh, my God, I thought. *I could use a friend right now—almost anyone would be okay—someone to help me take my mind off the Boulevard girl—but just not him!* Danny Kilpatrick was a neighborhood acquaintance a couple of years younger than I. I knew him primarily from the newspaper branch office where we went every day to get our papers, before I went away to college.

When it happened, only a year earlier, I had just graduated from high school. I had taken a job at Hayes Aircraft for the summer and turned my newspaper route over to my brother, Eddie, both my morning and afternoon routes, all except for the paper racks which our new branch manager, Mr. Abbot, insisted were not transferrable. I learned later he had his own paper racks downtown, and he added to his account the rack locations I had worked so hard to assemble. I was furious, but there was nothing I could do. He was an adult, and Eddie and I were not. We had to let it go.

Danny was Eddie's age. He delivered his papers from a bicycle, the same way Eddie and I had delivered ours the first year we had our routes. I had delivered mine that last year on my beautiful, black Triumph Tiger Cub! He desperately wanted to buy my motorcycle. Since I owned a car and no longer needed it, we worked out a deal, and I sold it to him. But I didn't tell him it wasn't running well, and had not run well the last few months. I hadn't been able to fix it. Of course, it was over a year old when I bought it, and the dealer had sold it to me "as is" and wouldn't take responsibility for the problem. Danny didn't ask me, and I didn't offer to him that anything was wrong with the motorcycle or whether it ran well—but the fact is, I should have warned him.

Danny waved to me and approached my table as I stood up, feeling sick to my stomach. I'd known for a year a confrontation would probably happen, and now I was caught, having to face up to my lie of ommission.

*　　*　　*

The first time I told a lie, or the first one I remember, was a big one, deliberate and bald-faced. I was in the first grade. The boys in my class were in the bathroom, and we were urinating in a common trough, shoulder to shoulder. The boy behind me, waiting his turn, was pestering me. Then he pushed me or hit me. I turned around and peed right down the front of his pants. He was furious! He ran out into the hallway crying, his jeans soaked, and told Ms. Barnett what I had done. When I came out of the bathroom, she was waiting for me. She bent down to me, her hand on my shoulder, and looked into my eyes.

"Did you urinate on Jerry?"

I looked into her eyes, terrified, and said "No, ma'am."

Just like that, and my heart seized up.

Then she grabbed Jerry by the arm, dragged him down the hallway, shouting at him and spanking him. I was stunned as I heard her say, "Jerry, why do you always cause trouble? Chervis always tells the truth."

I told myself then I would never, ever tell another lie.

I've pretty well lived up to it.

But then, life does get complicated, doesn't it?

My second big lie?

Well, I *wish* it had been a lie.

I guess I was about fifteen. I had really begun to look at the girls and wished for the talent and ability to talk to them. So, when this girl called me at home one evening and wouldn't tell me her name, I hardly knew what to say on the phone. She asked me if I liked a particular girl, as if that particular girl were an acquaintance of hers, and whether I thought she was pretty. I said no, because that's what I thought, but I would never have said that to the girl's face. Except that I did, because I heard her catch her breath, and her voice became tremulous as she said she had to go, and I knew she was the girl. Then I realized that sometimes a little white lie is better than the brutal truth.

The truth is my conscience still bothered me to no end about Dr. Goins's neon sign. That was not simply a little white lie by any measure; but even with *that* disaster on my mind, there was yet one more lie, the real whopper, the one that tore me up—it concerned the deal I made with Danny for my Triumph Tiger Cub. It all began with a lofty view of

myself as a top-shelf mechanic, which was based on my working knowledge of several Harleys I had owned . . . which was well before my prized
Indian Arrow had conquered and defeated me.

*   *   *

Over the years *before* I acquired my Indian Arrow, I had bought a series of Harleys. My first was the 125, which I rode for a while and then
eventually gave to Eddie. Then I got a used Harley 165 and later a *new*
165.

During those early years, I did a lot of motorcycle maintenance. All
kinds of work—adjusting and cleaning my carburetor, changing spark
plugs, and other minor repairs. A couple of times, I broke down the 165
engine block and changed the piston rings and replaced the head gasket.
I came to see myself as a master mechanic. Meanwhile, my father was
telling me there was no future in that. I could be a pharmacist, he said.
But somehow grease under my fingernails was a lot more grown-up and
romantic to me. It was so manly.

One day, a guy turned up at the branch with a beautiful old Indian
Arrow. He was showing off, blasting up and down the street. It was a lot
bigger than a Harley 165. It had a one-cylinder engine like mine, but it
was a 218CC OHV engine, and the frame carried a much larger profile.

While it had four gears, one was missing. It went from one to three,
then to four. He said it was nothing, that it could be easily fixed. He said
he would sell it.

I bought it and proudly rode it several days. Then I decided to fix it
myself. I took the transmission apart in our basement, carefully noting
the use and location of every part. But there were so many parts. I cleaned
it up and put it back together. To my dismay, I now had only one gear,
third. When I tried to go, the engine conked out unless I was pointed
downhill.

So back to the basement I went, took it apart again, and put all the
parts in a pasteboard box so they wouldn't be lost. I sat and studied but
couldn't figure it out. My career as a master mechanic just faded away
after that.

There was no Indian mechanic at the Harley shop. The Indian and its parts sat there in my basement a few weeks while I pondered.

I heard about a motorcycle shop in Tarrant, a town adjacent to Birmingham. I rode over there one Saturday and looked around, thinking that maybe they had a mechanic who was familiar with Indian transmissions. When I walked into the shop, a black Triumph Tiger Cub seized my attention. It was almost new and was for sale. It was a 1956 model, made by Triumph Motorcycles in Britain, the first year the Tiger Cub was produced. The Triumph was smaller than the Indian, at 199CC, but it generated fourteen horsepower and had a four-speed transmission. It was gorgeous. Suddenly, the Indian lost all its power over me. I didn't need a mechanic. I was in love with the Triumph. I wanted it so badly I could taste it.

"How much?" I asked. He told me the price. "Will you take a trade?"

"Whatcha got?" he inquired.

"I have an Indian Arrow, but it's not running so well. You'll have to come get it."

After some haggling, we made the trade. I returned home, got my money and told my brother about the trade. He carried me to Tarrant on his Harley. I completed the trade and rode the Triumph home. The dealer brought a truck to my house for the Indian. He was furious as he carried the pasteboard box to his truck. I can still hear his curses.

*   *   *

I reached out and shook Danny's hand, hoping my confession wouldn't be as bad as I feared.

"Danny, it's good to see you," I lied, yet again. If he noticed my discomfort, he didn't show it.

"Hey, man, how you doin'? I bet it's been a year since I seen you at my shop. Where you been?"

"Oh, I was out of town at college in Nashville all this past year. You still delivering papers?"

"Nah, gave that up. Too much trouble."

Oh, no, it must have been the Triumph! He had to give up the paper route because he couldn't keep it running. Elvis Presley was throbbing in the background, but I was too distracted by Danny to notice which song. We were shouting to make ourselves heard over the beat.

"You going back to college in Nashville next fall?"

"No, ran out of money. I'm dropping out for a while. I've got a job now at Hayes Aircraft. I'll work there, save my money, maybe get back in college later."

The music had slowed down. Now Pat Boone was crooning, "Ain't That A Shame," which had hit the number one spot on the Hit Parade a year or so before.

"Nashville, hunh? That's cool. Hey, man, you ever run into Pat Boone? He's from Nashville, right?"

"Yeah, he is, but I don't believe he actually lives there."

"Whatta you think of his recording," and he pointed to the jukebox, "compared to the one Fats did? You know, a white version of Fat's song."

"Well, to tell the truth, I like Fats Domino's recording a lot better. It's got soul. The one I really like, though, is Fats's newest one, 'Sick and Tired.' You heard that one?" And in my head, I kind of sang to myself, *I'm sick and tie-uhed . . . of foolin' 'round wit'choo.*

Then Danny changed the subject.

"So, what's Eddie doing? I haven't seen him for months."

"He's okay, still delivering papers."

The conversation continued. Small talk. Who's seen whom, school stuff . . . all the while, I was waiting for the shoe to drop. I knew it was coming. He was going to nail me about the motorcycle.

Now, here we were together. I was so tense I could hardly follow what he was saying, for fear the next question would be, 'Why did you cheat me? You didn't tell me it wouldn't run good.'

Danny talked and talked about friends we knew from school and the neighborhood and what all he'd been doing this summer.

Finally, I couldn't stand it anymore.

"Danny, how's my old Triumph doing? I'd sure like to see it. Would you let me take it for a ride?"

"Ha," he laughed, throwing back his head and slapping me on the shoulder.

"You'll never believe this. It's just too crazy! Not one week after I bought it from you, not a week! Our garage burned down and burnt it up! You shoulda seen it!" And then he laughed some more.

Danny didn't notice the color drain from my face. He was too busy matching the driving rhythm of "Sweet Little Sixteen," Chuck Berry's latest hit which was zooming up in the charts.

I managed to point to the open booth across the table from me and croaked over the music, "Hey, Danny. Sit down. I'll buy you a shake."

He glided into the booth, snapping the fingers on both hands to the driving guitar rhythm. As I listened to Danny talking about various things I couldn't follow, I promised myself, yet again, that I would never, ever tell another lie.

*   *   *

I have always been a worry wart about things in general, my various life issues and concerns over complicated legal matters. It was much later after a lifetime of worrying about those things I had no control over that I learned for myself what a lot of other people already knew – that only about ten percent of our worries are worth the trouble. I think Calvin Coolidge said it best: If you see ten troubles coming down the road, you can be sure that nine will run into the ditch before they reach you.

41 • My Dream Job

J was as jittery as a boy on his first date as I introduced myself to Mr. Thornley. I couldn't imagine why his office had called and made this appointment. It seemed odd that I was summoned to meet the head of the Birmingham Public Library, particularly since my part-time job had not been important enough for him to interview me in person when I was hired six months earlier. Something was clearly amiss, and I had no idea what could have led to this meeting. But Mr. Thornley's smile was disarming as he directed me to a chair across from his desk. Maybe this was routine. Maybe I had just been seeing ghosts that weren't there.

He was friendly as he asked me first about my classes at Birmingham-Southern College where I was now in my second year of college, after having missed a year earning the money to resume my studies. He then asked about my job at a neighborhood Branch of the library.

My tension had just begun to subside when suddenly his smile disappeared, he leaned forward into his desk, parked both arms on the flat surface and gazed at me. I flinched, caught my breath, and waited for the shoe to drop.

"You need to know that a complaint has been filed against you," he said flatly, without emotion, "and I've got to get to the bottom of it."

I stiffened in my chair and felt the blood drain from my face.

He paused, watching my reaction as he let the news sink in.

A complaint! Who had I offended?

For the past six months, I had worked at the small library, where I stood behind the counter smiling, checking books in and out and assisting patrons with book selections. Those interactions had all been pleasant to my knowledge. I couldn't think of anyone I might have offended.

Cautiously, I asked him what the complaint was about, but he didn't answer my question. His eyes bore into me. I felt defenseless. I couldn't explain away an offense I didn't know about, nor could I suggest any justification or excuse. I couldn't even offer up an apology. All I could do was wait. At last, in a voice that was not accusatory, he smiled and said, "I understand you've spent some time talking with the custodian."

"Oh, yes, sir," I answered innocently, "Annie's a nice old lady."

"What have you talked with her about?"

I shrugged. "Just ordinary things, you know, her family, the weather, stuff like that, nothing important."

Where was this going? I understood the "code" of the South that allowed only minor conversation between the races, enough to transact business, but never on a social basis. Did someone think I had crossed over the line? Was that it?

*   *   *

It had been almost three years since I last delivered newspapers to Mrs. Miller, but I still thought about her and her straight-forward advice about getting to know colored people. She insisted the only way I could learn for myself that we were much more alike in our values and dreams than we were different was to actually get to know some colored people.

But my paper delivery days were over. I went to college for a year, dropped out and worked for a year. There was no opportunity presented in either setting to further my education about the races. The only colored people I saw at college were the lunchroom ladies. And later at Hayes Aircraft, there were no colored workers among my crew.

Mrs. Miller had shown me how to rise above my narrow views. But Birmingham was so thoroughly segregated in the late fifties that few opportunities had presented themselves to me for meeting and getting to know someone of color. It was now almost six years since *Brown v. Board of Education* and there had as yet been no integration of schools in Birmingham. Rev. Fred Shuttlesworth did attempt to register his children at

Phillips in September 1957, the semester after my graduation, and he was brutally beaten by the KKK at the school right in front of his children. Nothing had changed since then in Birmingham, except that resistance by whites was more desperate than ever.

I was struggling in my own awkward way to take the first steps out of my racist history, but I didn't know how except to follow Mrs. Miller's lead. So, the question banged around in my head, *Had I been too familiar with Annie? Had I crossed that line?* I couldn't imagine that I had, and yet Mr. Thornley was asking me about it.

In the instant all of this was turning in my head, I remembered an event that occurred about a year earlier, when I was returning home from my job at Hayes Aircraft. A young colored man at the edge of the street was "thumbing" a ride. I pulled over and waved him in. Why had I done that, you might ask. I was experimenting. I simply wanted to talk to a colored person my age—just to see what it was like. As he approached my Ford, there was that look of caution in his face. His eyes were averted from mine. He opened the door, pulled the seat forward, and started to climb into the back seat.

"No, sit up here, in front."

"You sure?" He hesitated in the open door, crouched to enter, looking down into the seat.

"Yeah, up front. I'm not your chauffer."

Compliantly, he eased the seat back into position and slipped in, never looking at me. He was probably hoping the same thing I was: that the Klan doesn't see this transgression and teach us a lesson we'd never forget.

"Where you going?" I asked.

"West End," he answered, looking at something far up the road.

"I'm headed downtown. I'll drop you there."

"Thanks."

We rode in silence for a few minutes as I tried to think of a way to begin a conversation with a guy who seemed reluctant to speak. I wound up driving him all the way to West End, and during the time I asked a few questions but was not able to get any significant conversation going. Was he paralyzed by fear that we might be seen by the Klan? Did he hate me, as a white, so deeply he was unable to give more than the barest answers to my questions. Did he feel he had violated his sense of propriety by crossing the code of conduct laid out so perfectly for colored people in the South? Or was he simply aloof or shy? He answered all my questions courteously but with no enthusiasm and nothing to add. When we arrived in West End, I pulled up to the curb. As he opened the door, he turned to me, momentarily looked me directly in the eyes for the first time, and said, "Thanks."

Then he was gone.

*   *   *

"Have you talked with her about her paycheck? How much she makes?"

That question straightened me in my chair. "No, sir. Just ordinary things, like I said."

He waited, as if he expected more.

"Mary—Miss Jones, my manager—and I are there all day talking with each other and with all the customers who come in. Annie has no one to talk to. It's just the three of us. All day long, she cleans and dusts and keeps things straight. I just try to be friendly."

His eyes narrowed. "What is your opinion of labor organizations?"

"Well, I'm in favor of labor unions. My father's a union man. I sometimes wonder where I'd be today if it weren't for his union, what it's done for my family."

"Are you some outside agitator trying to stir things up in Birmingham?"

"No, sir!" My response was quick and brisk. "I've lived in Birmingham my whole life. What do you mean, 'stir things up?' I don't understand."

This was the strangest conversation I'd ever had in my life. I had no idea where it was going.

"I've been told you may be trying to organize a union among our custodial workers."

"What!"

I was flabbergasted, speechless. I gripped the arms of my chair, pulled in my breath and blurted, "That's absurd! I'm a student. I don't know anything about organizing unions."

He must have seen the shock on my face. He leaned back in his chair, made a pyramid with his fingers and thought it over, while I sat at attention in disbelief.

"So there's really nothing to the union rumor?" He asked quietly.

"No, sir!" I firmly replied.

He smiled again.

"You live in the Deep South, son. You know about how things are done down here. Now I'm not offended by your efforts to be friendly with a colored woman. I think it's high time we changed our policies about segregation. But, you know, there are a lot of people around here who get offended if they see a white person making polite conversation with a colored. They think it's wrong to socialize between the races. Maybe that's what we have here. Maybe someone has taken offense and jumped to the conclusion that you were organizing."

As I listened to Mr. Thornley's possible explanation for the complaint, I knew there was only one person who could have made the complaint and that was my supervisor, Miss Jones. And the instant that became apparent to me, another possibility leaped to the front. It became difficult to keep Mr. Thornley in focus as he droned on about the South and our arcane social patterns. Was that the real reason she had made the complaint? Or was there another reason, a possibility I knew I could never discuss with Mr. Thornley?

*   *   *

Following my first year in college, I dropped out and worked at Hayes Aircraft for fifteen months. Living at home, I'd saved enough money to go back to college for another year. After a four day trial run at Auburn University, where my registration was never completed, I threw in the towel and drove back to Birmingham. In one quick afternoon, I found myself registered for classes at Birmingham-Southern College.

Though I had never taken any courses in business, I was astute enough to know my money would run out long before my remaining three school years were complete. It was obvious I would need a part-time job to get me through. I found the perfect employment at the Birmingham Public Library, a job where I could make a little money and simultaneously spend my working hours speaking with patrons about books. What a deal! Where else would someone pay me for talking about books in a house surrounded by thousands of volumes?

I was placed at a neighborhood branch in a small but beautiful old rock building in a public park. There, I worked with Miss Jones, a middle-aged, unmarried woman, and the custodian, Annie, an elderly black woman.

In addition to speaking with our visitors who came in sporadically all day, I was charged with returning books to their places in the shelves and other miscellaneous chores while Miss Jones worked at her desk. But there were times when we were free to chat. She, like myself, was a book-lover, and we spoke at length about what we were reading and the authors we valued.

While she dressed about as frumpily as a middle-aged librarian was expected to in those days, when she would turn and reach for a book on an upper shelf, I had noted the obvious curvatures that the heavy, dark fabric failed to conceal. But it was just a note. I had the romantic illusion back then that one ought to be in love before good things happened.

After a few months, Miss Jones asked me to call her "Mary," and I was glad to do so. As we talked more about books, she became almost vivacious in our conversations. What a great job it was to spend a good part of the day in animated conversation about books. But then one day, it changed. She asked me if I had read some specific book—I don't recall which—and I told her I had not. She recommended it to me and sug-gested I read it. Then she added, "I'd like your opinion about the sex scene. It just didn't seem realistic to me." She stared directly into my eyes and waited. The floor tilted, and I looked away in confusion. Then she plunged on. "In my limited experience," she said, "people don't talk that much while having sex." There was a moment of embarrassed silence, at least on my part. I gazed out the window to the park beyond in stunned inertia, my feet glued to a shifting deck.

"What has been your experience?"

She waited.

I shot a glance at her in near panic. Her eyes were locked on mine. I looked back to the park. My throat closed. I couldn't answer her question. I couldn't say a word. I was mortified that a woman the age of my mother would ask me such a question, and I was too humiliated to admit to her that at twenty years of age, the sum of all my experience on that front was absolutely—zero. I wanted to bolt from the building, dash through the park and disappear into the distant trees. I muttered something incoherent, and then stood mute, hoping she didn't have any more questions. Thankfully, she quietly returned to her desk.

The following week she asked me to go with her to the symphony on Saturday evening. I politely declined, explaining I had a date with my girlfriend.

During the next couple of weeks, there were no more embarrassing moments, but the chill in the air was perceptible. Or was it all my imagination? Had I jumped to a conclusion?

*　　　*　　　*

"Well, I guess that must be what happened," I heard Mr. Thornley say. "Someone must have jumped to a conclusion." He leaned forward again, a course of action now clear to him. "I'll speak to the person who complained and work it out. I'm sure there'll be no problem. Everything will be just fine."

He reflected a moment, his fingertips meeting again in prayer, "Forget about this little conference, son." He smiled and then confided to me, "I have to supervise more than a hundred women," as if it were a secret just between us menfolk. "I get these kinds of problems a lot—these misunderstandings. Just go back to work next week like nothing happened. I'll take care of it."

Then he rose, smiled broadly and shook my hand. I wandered away in a daze.

The next few weeks were miserable. Even though I was working among thousands of books, in a setting I loved, and with customers I had grown to like, it was as if there were some poisonous gas floating in the air. She avoided me, never made eye contact. Any communication she made was terse. My conversation with Annie was now only a quick, "Good morning."

There was nothing I loved like a library, and working at a small community library was a dream come true. But now it had all changed. Instead of a place of joy and learning, it had become a house of stress and unhappiness. Anyone could see it was time for me to go. How unfair, I thought. In order to hold tight to my love of this sanctuary, to not have it tainted by the hostility that now permeated the small, rock building—it fell to me to give it up.

And so I found another part-time job, this one as a night auditor on weekends at the Thomas Jefferson Hotel, in downtown Birmingham. I have no memory of my resignation from the library. I assume the exchange with Miss Jones was quick and perfunctory. But the aftermath has lingered long.

I've wondered ten thousand times how my life might have changed had I accepted Miss Jones's invitation to the symphony. What, after all, was the harm in that? Why had I been so moralistic—so cowardly?

And should I have told Mr. Thornley about those conversations with Miss Jones? No! I would never have besmirched the name of a woman in defending myself to Mr. Thornley, particularly since I had the nagging notion that my interpretation of her motives was based on nothing more than my hyper-active, sexually charged imagination. You would think, then, that if I had misgivings about Miss Jones's objectives, that uncertainty would dilute or temper my creative imagination. But, no; for years afterward, in spite of my doubts, my fantasies were big and bold and in vivid color.

42 • My Unmooring

When I showed up for work at the Thomas Jefferson Hotel on my first night, the afternoon crew going off duty learned I was a college student. One of them suggested I might be interested to know that a writer had lived at the hotel several years earlier as he wrote a book. That caught my attention. The writer, she said, was William Bradford Huie,[13] and the book she said he wrote was *The Americanization of Emily*. I had heard of Huie but had not read him. I checked out the book from the library, and I learned that Huie was a prolific Alabama writer, who had published, at that time, at least a half-dozen books. *The Americanization of Emily*, published in 1959, was a dark, cynical, and comic anti-war novel about a naval officer in World War II. That book was later made into a movie.

I never learned whether Huie actually wrote that book while living at the hotel, but that legend became real to me. For a time, it gave meaning to my midnight tedium. I hoped that this tenuous connection to literary greatness might somehow rub off on me.

But that mystique quickly gave way to boredom.

As the weekend night auditor at the hotel, I not only balanced the day's receipts, but was expected to stand tall and erect behind the counter and check hotel guests in and out, greet those who came through the lobby and generally be the face of the hotel during the graveyard shift, eleven P.M. until seven A.M., on Friday and Saturday nights.

The night shift was old hat to me. I had worked the night shift for fifteen months straight at Hayes Aircraft. But there, the work kept me busy and active for eight hours. The hotel became deadly quiet after 2:00 A.M.

The long weekend nights at the hotel were unusually quiet. We had a low occupancy on the weekends. I wondered why that was. Mr. Mansfield supplied me the answer. He was a tall, handsome salesman who often stayed at the hotel. He had wavy dark red hair and I admired his impeccable suits and ties. He would bring his bottle of Scotch down to the counter well after midnight and talk with me. The kitchen was locked up, but I always had access to a quart of half and half for coffee and a supply of saltine crackers. Everything else was locked away for the night. I would lay out the heavy milk and crackers on the counter. Unbelievably, he would pour a half glass of creamy milk into a shot of whiskey. That was his standard drink, he said, because of his ulcer. Though I hated the texture and taste of half and half, I would pour myself a glass (no whiskey added) and join him as we sipped our drinks and ate crackers, he to feed his ulcer and I to stave off hunger.

"Birmingham," he said with great authority, "is a boring city. No night life. No self-respecting salesman would be caught dead in Birmingham on the weekend." But there he was, smiling as he said it. He whiled away many hours leaning on the counter, nursing his toddy, and talking with me. I can still remember his face after all these years.

Mostly, though, the hotel lobby after midnight was boring. I would have the accounts balanced shortly after midnight, unless there was a party in the ballroom or Mr. Mansfield was there. After that, there wasn't much to do but lean on the counter. There were no stools to perch on. Bennie, the bellman, did offer some diversion, though I quickly tired of his all night routine. He weighed at least three hundred pounds, and spent most of the night leaning back against a support column, flexing his shoulders and moving from foot to foot in a hilarious attempt to scratch his back. Bennie was not much of a conversationalist, though he was willing from time to time to enlighten me on his many sexual exploits. I declined to inquire of him the big question his stories begged me to ask: How, exactly, could a man of his girth . . . . But, then, I really didn't want to know.

When all activity had stopped for the night, I would pull out a book and try to read, but it was exhausting to stand there at the counter struggling to stay awake when the clock struck three, then four. I needed to look fresh about six when activity began again.

One evening, Birmingham churches sponsored an "All Night Singing" at Boutwell Auditorium, an event that brought gospel quartets and singing groups from across the South. Hundreds, maybe thousands, attended those affairs which lasted until well after midnight. A well-known gospel quartet were our guests. About midnight, the four of them blew through the revolving doors and didn't pause to notice me. They were dressed in tight, western-style clothing and their high, swept-back, black pompadours shone with oil. They didn't look particularly holy, I thought. They may have even looked slick, but I assumed they were fine, Christian men to follow gospel singing as a career. They strode through the lobby, jumped on the elevator and were gone. I thought no more about them.

It was almost one A.M. and very quiet when I heard the revolving door and looked that way as it ejected, one at a time, three hot-looking blondes and a redhead, all in short skirts and high heels. They quickly lined up, side by side, and paused as they looked the place over as coldly as four gunslingers in a western saloon. Then they marched up to the counter, four women on a mission. They looked me up and down distastefully, as if I were a scrawny, harmless, shifty-eyed barman. The redhead, hands on hips, thrust out her breasts, popped her gum, and slapped the counter with one palm. "Those gospel boys! Room number!"

"Uh, I'm sorry, but, uh, I can't give you the room number." I flushed the deep crimson color of the carpets.

"Oh, yeah?" She gave me the evil eye. "You just call 'em! You'll see."

As I vacillated, her hard face gave way to a giggle. They all laughed, I'm sure at me and my consternation, as I was caught in the helpless dilemma of gazing at their bodies and long legs while debating in my confused state how best to handle her demand.

I held my breath, wondering if I would get in trouble for disturbing important, celebrity guests; but could that be worse than the trouble I might be in for refusing to call if these ladies were expected and welcome? And more importantly, how long could I stand the pressure of these lively women regarding me as insignificant as a bar room piano player.

I picked up the house phone, knowing full well I was making a big mistake. Those gospel singers were religious men. They sang gospel songs for church people. They'll be offended if I call. I pulled the cord as far as it would go, seeking privacy in a little alcove, and dialed the number of one of their rooms. I craned my neck to check on the women. They were snapping their gum, grinning and shifting their hips in provocative ways.

"Hello," a wary voice answered.

I jerked my head around and, in a secretive voice, answered, "Is this the room for the gospel singers? This is the night clerk downstairs. Some ladies say they're here to see y'all." I paused. "Want me to send 'em away?"

"Oh, hell no," he laughed. "Send 'em up."

Shocked, I told the women the room numbers and they strutted to the elevator, entered one by one, and turned to face me. One of them smiled and blew me a kiss as the brass door slid shut. I checked the clock and wondered how long they might visit our celebrity guests. The book I had opened on the counter was particularly boring as I fantasized over what might be occurring on those upper floors.

When I clocked out at seven the next morning, they were still up there. So much for religion, I thought. I had become increasingly disillusioned over several years about my church and its fundamentalism. It had become difficult to square all I'd been learning and reading with the teachings of my church. And now, those gospel singers had come along with an ax and taken a mighty chop at the few moorings I had left.

43 • A Regrettable Exchange

𝕵t was almost midnight. I was hard at work behind the counter balancing the day's receipts from the hotel café when the razzing began.

"Hey, Chervis, is that you back there?"

Startled, I looked up from my ledgers as a young man and woman, all decked out in evening clothes, lurched from the Ballroom across the lobby toward me. His arm surrounded the tipsy girl, but he looked as if he could have used some help himself. His bow tie was askew, his clothing rumpled.

The band had distracted me for the past hour, but I had not bothered to learn who had sponsored the party. To my chagrin, I learned it was a fraternity from 'Southern.

"You workin' back there?" he asked incredulously, as if he had not yet discovered where money comes from. "On a Friday night? You gotta be kidding!" And he laughed, as he squeezed her around the middle and leered into her face. She giggled as if he'd made the cutest joke.

I had gone through fraternity rush the year before at the insistence of my girlfriend, a sorority girl who was concerned that her social life would be incomplete were I not in a fraternity. She was a fine student, directed toward and focused on a successful and productive life. I was more concerned about whatever book I was then currently reading than I was about my own future. Until she mentioned it a half-dozen times more, I hadn't thought much about fraternities and sororities. Most of my friends were independents who hung around the Cellar. She continued pressing me, and, so, I went through rush and had become acquainted with guys in all the fraternities on campus. That's how I happened to know this particular guy, who was having a good old time ragging me at work in front of his date.

"Yep," I smiled. "It's called work. Somebody's gotta do it."

I turned back to my task at hand and ignored them.

During the next hour, the party-goers flowed out two by two and in flocks. I endured a seemingly endless course of ribbing from those guys for the benefit of their dates.

And that evening was not the only fraternity party held at the hotel. There were several such parties over the two years I worked at the hotel, and they always served up the same kind of guys with the same cute comments at my expense. And they all ended the same way. After they had all left, I was planted at my post, alone, and humiliated.

That is the problem with fraternity boys, I decided, even though at that point I, too, was a fraternity boy. *They may not all be rich, but they are comfortable. They can afford to go to big parties. I have to work to eat.*

In order to go to a party or to a movie with a date, it fell to me to earn the money. Birmingham-Southern was a private, liberal arts school. Tuition was expensive. I couldn't afford tuition and fun, too. So, I didn't have much fun.

My first year at 'Southern, which was my second year in college, I lived at home where my mother fed me well. But my third year, I wanted out. The restrictions on when I came in, the constant harping about church, and my need to be closer to campus, to not be a day student, caused me to give up food for freedom. In this, my third year of college, I rented an apartment several blocks from campus with my buddy, Charlie Clark.

My school day began with coffee from the "Honor Pot" in the cafeteria. Sometimes I would drop in a penny or two. Then I would fortify cup after cup of coffee with milk and sugar. Thank God for the Honor Pot. That was my breakfast.

My fraternity brothers repeatedly harped on me to join them at their table in the cafeteria for breakfast. I sat with them only once. They talked incessantly about hunting and fishing and water skiing. I had nothing to add to their discussions and wanted nothing to do with those outdoor sports I knew nothing about. I had grown up on the sidewalks. I'd never seen a pair of water skis. But the main reason I didn't join them again—I simply couldn't bear to see them crush their cigarettes in their half-eaten eggs and grits when all I could do was squeeze my empty cup in painful silence.

I had joined a fraternity the previous year. I was now an active member. The fraternity rush season had concluded, and it was time to consider those prospects for membership who had participated in rush.

A freshman from the Northside of Birmingham had latched onto me at a party and expressed to me how important it was to him that he be accepted by our group. He had graduated from Phillips High School, as had I. He was not particularly impressive, but I liked him. He was honest and straight-forward.

At the fraternity meeting, my first to consider membership, the name of each rushee was submitted. The term "blackball" was not new to me. I understood in a general way that it was the method by which the fraternity selected its new members.

And then the name of my friend came up. I made a short plea for his acceptance and assumed everything would flow smoothly. But someone suggested he was not very attractive and that he had pimples. When the votes were counted, several blackballs had been dropped.

I was embarrassed, and after a short, impassioned plea, asked for re-consideration. After some discussion over whether a re-vote would be proper, they consented at my insistence. This time he had almost ten blackballs. Did they vote against him because they didn't like him—or because, like me, he was from the wrong side of town? Or could it have been because I had challenged the system?

In any event, I was upset. This was not the way I intended to select my friends, and I certainly didn't want others to select my friends for me.

What a paradox, I thought. Those who need the comfort and security of a fraternity or sorority can't get in—while others like myself, who didn't need it or couldn't have cared less, were courted by all the groups. It wasn't fair.

Then, to make matters worse, following the meeting one of the brothers said something to me, with obvious pride, as if aware that my feelings had been hurt by the process and that we should all be proud of our selectivity. "You know," he said, "our fraternity has never pledged a Mexican or Jew."

Though I knew no Mexicans and had only the barest acquaintance with several Jews at school, the statement was like a slap across my face. While I recall exactly the words of his statement, I cannot remember how I responded, if at all.

I was well aware that we were a homogenous group. We were all from Alabama except a few others from surrounding states in the Deep South. And most it seemed were from prosperous families. So far as I was aware, not a single brother had a part-time job. I felt I was the only misfit.

I had not seen Mrs. Miller since the summer of 1957, four years earlier, but I had not forgotten her. The advice she had given me about judging people from minority groups had taken a long time to sink in, but her efforts to save me from myself had apparently, unconsciously borne fruit. She had opened the door for me to be touched in a special way by *The Grapes of Wrath*, John Steinbeck's novel of the Great Depression and the plight of the "Okies" as they migrated to California in search of survival.

I had grown up something of an outcast, always on the outside looking in and wishing I were on the inside. Now, as an adult, I discovered that being on the inside was not at all what I had considered it would be. It came with some burdens I had not imagined. The inside was not for me.

I was never one for drama nor confrontation, particularly in this situation. I liked all my brothers and had the highest regard for them. It was the system I didn't like. I quietly withdrew, pledging to myself to never again join an exclusive organization.

How strange, I thought afterwards, when it dawned on me what had happened. At the beginning of the previous school year, I had moved from my home to an apartment near campus, away from my mother's good cooking, with the full knowledge that my resources, even with my part-time job, would leave me little money for food. I had willingly traded food for freedom—the freedom to broaden my circle of friends, to extract myself from my parents' control, and to transform myself from the timorous character I was to the bold young man I wanted to become. Food for freedom—that had been my stark choice, a choice I fully understood when I made it.

Could it be that by joining a fraternity, I had unwittingly traded the freedom I desperately yearned for—and had so hungered to achieve—in exchange for an unspoken servitude of the social kind? Was my fraternal affiliation so imperceptibly confining and restrictive that I had failed to notice my core beliefs slipping away, carried to the curb by culture and convention. Was I becoming a slave to a tradition I no longer believed? Those questions—and the answers to those questions—swept over me like a tidal wave when the blackballs fell, and I realized, yet again, that life is never simple.

44 • The Dangling Conversation

Before my disastrous conversation with Tom toward the end of my junior year, 1960-1961—Tom was a classmate and close friend of mine at Birmingham-Southern College—I had grown pretty satisfied with myself. I was convinced I had overcome my prejudices about colored people, but, then, following the awkard and unhappy conclusion to that same conversation with Tom, I found myself, once again, sick at heart: I was clearly not the social progressive I thought I had become. Why is it so hard to change, to truly change?

But, then, I get ahead of myself . . . perhaps I should slow down and go back to the beginning of my sophomore year—well before the moment I would betray my friend Tom—to explain how my life had been changing and my studies improving so dramatically since I had entered Birmingham-Southern.

*   *   *

In the early 1959 fall semester (my first year at 'Southern and my sophomore year), I was ineluctably drawn to a smoky campus coffee shop called "The Cellar," where many of the English, philosophy, and other liberal arts students met to talk about the deep, existential questions of life that only college sophomores plumb. Even though my grades up until that time had been average, I was nonetheless attracted to those students who were bookworms like me. One girl in particular, who regularly visited the Cellar, was known for her top grades. She was a member of the "President's Scholars," a select group who met each month with Dr. Henry King Stanford, our school's then-president, to talk about a specific book he had selected for the occasion. She had approached me one afternoon in the Cellar with a question, delivered in a somewhat frantic manner.

"Hey, Chervis, you read a lot. Have you read Golding's *Lord of the Flies*?"

"Yeah, sure. Read it last year, why?"

"It's this month's selection for the President's Scholars. I finished reading it last night. We meet," she looked at her watch, "in about an hour, and I'm confused."

I was jealous that she was in the President's Scholars and I was not. But, then, I knew she was really smart—I'd heard all about her grades. I could never qualify for an honor like that. *Why does she need me? Of course! She doesn't know I'm only an average student.*

"I just wanna kick it around with you a moment—make sure I'm on the right track. Did you like the book?"

"No. It was interesting, but I didn't like the ideas behind it."

"Well, what do you think it was about? I'm sure it was a religious allegory. Don't you think so, too?"

Religious allegory? Is she joking? Where'd she get that?

"No, I didn't see that at all, Betty. All I saw was an attempt to show that if you strip away our civilization, we become animals. Maybe it's some kind of argument for naturalism or something. Maybe Darwinism. But there's no religion there I could see."

She looked incredulous. "Are you sure?"

I nodded. "Yeah, I'm sure," I said, and even as I said it, I had that old feeling of uncertainty I'd lived with for so long and wondered if I might have been wrong.[14] (I had once been so certain of things, back when I was a teenager, before Mrs. Miller had proved me so wrong in so many ways.)

She wandered away in a daze, leaving me to consider how she, an all-A student, a President's scholar, had missed the mark so badly, while I was the C student. That singular event served to wake me up to the possibilities I had never before considered—that maybe I could be an A student—maybe I had undersold myself all those years. And, indeed, the three years I was at Birmingham-Southern College would prove much later in my world to have been a life-changing time for me. It was there that I found myself, and I discovered that I did indeed have the ability to make competitive grades and that reading and education do matter in ways much more rewarding that mere money and power.

But that was only one of the positive indications that my life was in fact changing. I lived in an apartment near school during the 1960-1961 school year. Most of my time was spent on campus. I was hardly aware of the "sit-ins" by colored students occurring in Birmingham and around the South at that time (there was so little coverage of it in the newspapers), but I continued to read the newspaper when I could, and I admired the letters to the editor I saw signed by "A. Berkowitz," who spoke out about Bull Connor's policies.

I visited my home regularly, but rarely had to listen to my dad's frustrations with his job. By that point, his bosses had made it clear to him that he could no longer re-arrange seating patterns as he wanted to do.

It was now May 1961, and I had heard about the Greyhound Bus carrying Freedom Riders that was burned by the KKK in Anniston, some sixty miles east of Birmingham. I was relieved to learn my dad was not the driver. Because of my changing viewpoint about race, I was no longer obsessed about the threats to the "Southern way of life," as I had been as a teenager. Although the racial pot was boiling in Birmingham, it was all happening outside the scope of my view. Mrs. Miller's talks with me had begun to bear fruit, as I read more and more books that offered me broader views.

Five years had passed since I first met the Millers. Mrs. Miller had done her best to make me see the light, back when I delivered her newspaper. There's no question, I did see the light, even then, but it had flickered during those two years I delivered her papers, like the guttering of the flame of a candle just before it catches on. The flame had finally leveled out those past few years in college, as if I'd placed a glass chimney over it, and it was now burning brightly. And that was because of books I had read, such as Lorraine Hansberry's play *A Raisin in the Sun*.

That play caught my attention. Written by a colored woman about the Younger family, a colored family in Chicago, it came alive for me. Near the end of the play, they signed a contract to buy a house in a white neighborhood. And then a representative from the neighborhood visited them in an unsettling scene that's been hard to forget. This was the first book I had read from the colored point of view and it had me reflecting about and regretting my past attitudes.

*   *   *

So, yes, at the time of my conversation with Tom at the end of my junior year, I had indeed grown content with myself. Now, a thriving college student majoring in English and Philosophy (after a lifetime of average grades), I was, at last, competing at a much higher level. I had become socially enlightened, or, rather, that's certainly the way I felt. I now viewed myself as a sophisticated college student, liberated from the old racism that the Millers had observed in me as I collected for their newspaper four years earlier. You might even say I had become proud of my progressive stance and viewpoint. I was now convinced I had rid myself of any social prejudice.

But, unfortunately, that was before my converation with Tom.

Tom, a Chinese-American, confided in me his personal dilemma. He told me of his frustration and loneliness—there were no girls his age in Birmingham of Chinese extraction that he knew of—and he deeply feared crossing racial divides because of the atmosphere of hate in Birmingham at that time. He asked me whether I thought it would be appropriate if he were to ask a white girl to go out with him.

To my everlasting shame, I equivocated. I have no idea, no memory of the exact words I used to answer my friend Tom. Embarrassed, I blundered around and said nothing helpful or constructive, I'm sure. Fifty years have passed, and even now my blood runs cold as I think about my insensitive response to his heartbreaking question.

Yes, I had become a sophisticated college student . . . but I clearly was not liberated fully from the old racism that the Millers had found in me. I thought I was prepared to go all the way toward racial equality and reconciliation . . . but obviously I wasn't. There was still that one aspect of racial prejudice I had not been able to shake, and that was the old bugaboo, miscegenation—or as Ace Carter called it the "mongrelization" of the races.

Tom was too kind to let my failure damage our friendship, but I have never forgotten the incident.

*   *   *

Perhaps it was my failure with Tom that opened my heart to hear the truth a month or so later, in a book that's come to be a favorite of mine. This story written by a young man from Birmingham, Joe David Brown,[15] turned me upside down. He grew up in East Lake, a blue-collar neighborhood much like Norwood. Somehow, he had risen above the racism with which he must have grown up in this City. Brown had served in World War II. His novel *Kings Go Forth* was a war story, published in 1957. I've carried Brown's protagonist, Lt. Sam Loggins from Los Angeles, with me all these many years like the memory of a friend.

Sam was a working man. He didn't have the education and background to be an officer. But he was tough and determined, and was awarded a battlefield promotion to Lieutenant as his unit slogged up the boot of Italy. Brown's simple, straight-forward writing reminded me of Mickey Spillane's books from my high school days, and in some ways Sam was as tough as Spillane's alter ego, Mike Hammer, although it turned out that Sam had a heart.

His platoon was now in Southern France, dug in against a stubborn German defense. One of the men in Sam's platoon, a fresh troop from stateside, was Britt Harris, an enlisted man from Mississippi. Britt was educated, handsome, cultured, and spoke fluent French. He was everything Sam was not. He had been shaped as a gentleman from the Mississippi upper-class, while Sam was the product of a rough, blue-collar background.

A few days furlough in Nice brought Sam good fortune—Monique, a beautiful young woman with whom he fell in love. A few months later, after several visits, he introduced Britt to Monique. Britt impressed her in all the many ways Sam could not, as they carried on conversations in French that Sam could not follow. But Britt knew it was Sam who loved her. Britt learned her father was deceased, that he was an ex-pat from the

States—and a Negro. Then, the aftermath. To Sam, an orphan himself, her heritage was irrelevant. But she had fallen in love with the wrong man.

Racism is an abstract concept until it is made personal. Monique and Sam made it very personal to me.

Kings Go Forth—this story of unrequited love, of betrayal and treachery, of love gone wrong because of race—and revenge—gave me a lot to think about. I thought about Ace Carter. He was wrong again. What does race matter in the face of love? And I thought of Mrs. Miller. She had been right at every turn. I read many books that verified the truth Mrs. Miller taught me, but it was *Kings Go Forth* that hit me in a personal way, right between my eyes.

Most of all, though, I thought about Tom and our dangling conversation. But it was too late for me to make that right.

45 • Arizona

He pointed to large, raised letters near the end of the dusty eight inch steel pipe. With one swipe, I brushed them clean. "Made in Belgium," I muttered, as if he needed my translation. Then he stalked away. I studied the dozens of identical pipe stacked in the yard. The electric grinder he had given me, now hanging from my hand, seemed wholly inadequate for the job I had been told to do.

As I dithered, trying to figure out the best way to begin, I noticed the colored guy—they called him Arizona—watching me. His neutral face showed no emotion, but I knew he must have been amused to watch a college boy flounder in ignorance and incompetence.

How do I begin? I wondered. *Is there a place to sit? If I sit on the pipe, will it roll? There must be a trick to this somehow.* Arizona watched quietly. After a few moments, I looked at him. "You done this before?"

Quietly, he eased over and said, "You gotta block this pipe so it don't roll, son, like this"—and he showed me how to do my job.

"Now you get that grinder going, those filings gonna fly ever'where. Try not to breathe that shit—and cover yo' eyes best you can."

Then he was gone. I began the tedious work of grinding off the offending letters that I assumed would somehow make the pipe more saleable. I hated the job, of course, a summer job at a pipe distributorship, but it would earn me enough money to pay my tuition in the fall for my senior year.

When I reported to work that first morning in the summer of 1961, the foreman had me clock in and then he turned me over to the two yard men, tall and lanky guys responsible for loading and unloading the pipe from flat-bed trailers and physically handling the pipe to be stored in the yard. They were Billy and Lamar, two young men in their early twenties from the hill country of North Alabama and redneck to the core, both of them.

The foreman made a quick introduction of the two white men, ignoring the small, wiry colored man more than twice their age who stood close by, dressed in the same green work uniform. After we had shaken hands and they demonstrated their inability to get my name straight, one of them said, "Thi 'shere's Arizona," waving a hand in the colored guy's direction.

I stepped over and extended my hand to Arizona. "Glad to meet you," I said.

He raised his eyes and hesitated. The rednecks raised theirs too. Arizona dropped his eyes and reluctantly extended a grizzled, limp hand, as if the first time he had ever touched a white man. My efforts at courtesy were rewarded by two hostile stares from two clearly agitated white men and the shuffling of one deeply conflicted and embarrassed colored man.

In time, I came to think of Billy and Lamar as the white boys. They were ignorant and proud of it, and arrogant with authority. Billy was in charge of the yard and Lamar was his flunky. Arizona had worked there for years. His job was to do the white boys' bidding which involved mostly common labor. He never volunteered, never suggested a solution, afraid perhaps that his eagerness would somehow be translated as implied criticism of Billy or his know-how. But in time, I came to see that he could handle any problem the white boys called on him to do. *What a waste of talent,* I thought. He'd been working at the pipe plant for years and knew how to do it all. I watched as the white boys screwed it up time after time, and then in desperation called on him to step in and fix it. He did what he was told and he did it well. It took me only a few days to discover that Arizona should have been the boss of the yard, telling the white boys how to do it.

But that's not the way it was in Birmingham, not in 1961, when the

Jim Crow laws then in effect segregated the races in every aspect of life, and the customs of the time reinforced the assumption of white supremacy. That summer job was my first observation of those laws and customs being applied against someone I knew and respected.

It turned out to be a life-changing summer.

*   *   *

There's an art to unloading pipe from a flat-bed trailer. And there are dangers as well.

When the first tractor-trailer lumbered into the yard on my first day on the job, Lamar yelled for me to leave my grinding chore and come help. I ran into the yard. Billy was there on a forklift mobile crane, waiting for us to get in position. Arizona checked the wedge blocks that chocked the lower level of pipe in place before removing the side stakes and loosening with a winch bar the web straps that wrapped the pipe. Then Lamar scrambled onto the pyramid load and secured the cable around the middle of the upper pipe, what they called "hooking" the pipe. Then he got out of the way and Billy, by a single cable, lifted the pipe from the load. One end of the pipe shot skyward as he lifted while the other sagged in place. It fell to Arizona to provide the counter-weight to stabilize the pipe as Billy lifted it from the trailer. Then Billy slowly swung the boom and lowered the pipe to me, rotated the forklift and proceeded slowly onto the yard with me trailing behind and struggling to hold up my end of the pipe. When there, we laid the pipe on the ground, and continued the process until the stack of pipe had been relocated.

The problem, of course, was that Lamar couldn't find the center when hooking the pipe and Arizona and I had to use pure muscle power to wrestle the pipe from place to place.

As more loads came in, occasionally I would be told to hook the pipe. I learned early to call on Arizona. Though I was totally inept, I too was his boss and he was at my beck and call, although I never gave him an order. I simply asked him for his help. Unbelievably, he would invariably hook the pipe in the exact middle, and when it was lifted by the crane, I could follow the pipe stabilizing my end almost with my thumb and forefinger. That's how easy he made the job.

One day, in the middle of the summer when too many trucks had come in, Lamar had taken a shortcut. He failed to check one load to ensure the chock blocks were properly secured before untethering the straps from the load. The load shifted. Lamar bolted to the side. Billy backed the forklift away. We all knew it could dislodge any moment and come crashing down. Lamar shook his head, refusing to go near it. If there was ever a dangerous job to do, they sent Arizona to do it.

Billy looked at Arizona and gave a signal. Arizona hesitated, a cloud passing over his face, and then, as he moved to correct the problem, he waved me off. "Them pipes coming yo' way."

I don't know what happened or why. All I know was the pipe shifted and instantly the entire load exploded onto the tarmac, spinning, bouncing and surging like a Tsunami, with lightning speed and a thunderous racket. I ran like hell.

Afterward, we stood around looking at the scattered pipe and speculating how nobody was hurt. Actually, I wasn't surprised the boys weren't hurt. They got out of the way before it fell. And Arizona had waved me off. He must have ducked underneath the trailer when the load gave way. Where else could he have gone? We all expressed wonder we weren't hurt, but only Arizona had truly been at risk.

I had no doubt the white boys liked Arizona, in their own cruel way. How could anybody not like him? They teased him unmercifully in a good natured but unfair way because he couldn't tease back.

Apparently, Arizona had a severe case of hemorrhoids, because at least once a day one of them would sneak up behind him and "goose" him in the seat of his pants. He would invariably scream "son of a bitch" and flail the air with his fists. But the assailant always backed out of the danger zone. Then Arizona would compose himself and grin. One day, it backfired. Arizona and I were painting a wall. Lamar quietly came up behind us and gave Arizona a goose. He screamed and whirled with his brush before Lamar could back out of reach, and slapped him with a gray stripe across the face. We all got a laugh at that one, even Arizona.

Another incident was particularly cruel. It was a rainy, foggy morning and we had gotten damp in the yard. We found some work to do in the metal building. The boys suggested that the gas stove be lit to warm up the place. Arizona was afraid of the heater, but of course it fell to him to light it. He squatted before the heater with great caution, a lit match in his hand, stretching his arm as far as it would go into the heater while leaning backwards and turning his face away. Lamar had quietly moved behind the metal wall adjacent to the heater. He carried a steel rod, and, just as the flame caught, Billy gave the signal and Lamar slammed the wall. Bang! It sounded like the building had blown up. Arizona sprang backward and fell all over himself scrambling out of the building. The boys whooped and hollered. They thought it was a great trick. After a little while, Arizona came back to the warm heater with a sheepish grin to more teasing.

I couldn't decide whether I hated the boys for being bullies, or whether I felt sorry for them for their crude insensitivity and ignorance, or both.

But it wasn't just the boys and their cruel behavior that bothered me. It was the Jim Crow laws that required, even in an industry like the pipe shop, separate restrooms for white and colored. But there was nothing equal about the colored facilities. Segregation reminded colored people every day that whites viewed them as inferior, even where men sweated together in the workplace.

That's why the more I saw of Arizona the better I liked him. He never complained about the way he was treated, never groveled or wheedled, never showed fear or anger or any of the emotions he must have felt in his position of subservience. What amazed me was his ability to grin and bear it. His self-discipline was inspiring. It was almost as if he were able to transcend himself, like a monk.

I tried to find common ground with him—something to talk about. Having long followed rhythm & blues, I spoke to him of my favorites— B. B. King and Bobby "Blue" Bland, from my Nashville days, along with Jimmy Reed, Muddy Waters, Sonny Boy Williamson, and Willie Dixon. He knew the sounds of these artists. I learned he liked jazz as well, and we talked about my favorite disc jockey in Birmingham, Lewis "Luigi" White, who was known for his jazz hour. I wondered if he too were white, impersonating a colored voice like the WLAC guys from Nashville, though his voice, unlike theirs, was as smooth as velvet. But no, Arizona assured me, he was colored.

And we watched the women saunter down the dirt road adjacent to the plant as they walked to and from the store to their houses in the settlement, company houses that had been thrown down among the grit and grime of the industrial area. There was one woman in particular we watched. She was tall, dark and heavy-boned. Twice the size of Arizona, she sailed slowly, languorously, sensually, as graceful as a cruise ship and as regal as a queen. Arizona would smack his lips and express the thoughts he might have expected me to anticipate from him. I laughed and teased him about how he wouldn't survive five minutes with her, that she would crush him like an egg shell, but he cackled and took it in good cheer.

*   *   *

Colored people had always been a mystery to me. I had grown up in a segregated world. I had never really known any colored people, except for the few I had met on my paper route. While I had been taught as I grew up that segregation was required—it was the only way they said that whites and colored could live together peacefully in the same city—I had become aware that the "separate but equal" principle had been a lie. There was no equality at the "white only" chilled water cooler which sat next to a bare water tap marked "colored." Nor was there any equality on the city bus. The whites dropped their money in the fare box and sat down in the nearest empty seat. The colored paid at the front, then disembarked and went to the back door to again mount the steep steps to the normally crowded back of the bus. All that had been made clear to me by experience.

And I had read any number of books that had confirmed the truth of what Mrs. Miller had taught me. But until my summer at the pipe plant, I had never gotten to know any colored person except in a superficial way. My summer was coming to an end, and I felt that somehow I wanted to express to Arizona my thanks for his help and support and my admiration for him as a man.

The last day I worked at the plant, I told Arizona I wanted to have a drink with him after work. It was not possible that I could invite him to join me at a beer joint. Nor could he invite me. Jim Crow laws prohibited us from drinking together anywhere, anytime.

So after we clocked out, we sat in my car outside the gate of the plant and tuned in to WJLD. I had bought a pint of cheap whiskey and we sat there like two old friends, passing the common bottle between us, listening to the Blues, until the bottle was empty.

At first, we laughed and teased and joked, but after a while, the whiskey loosened his tongue. I asked him about his personal life. He was fifty years old. He had been married for many years, he said, and he and his wife had raised four children. He told me about each child. They were all grown and living up north. And then, he spread his grizzled hands in his lap, and stared into his empty palms. "With these hands," he said, "and not much else, I put my kids through school, four of 'em."

The whiskey was gone by then, but we were lit with its warm afterglow, encircled by the yearnings and hunger of the Blues.

I had a mild buzz. My summer job was done. I'd saved enough money to pay tuition for my senior year in college. I would return to school next week where I would read more books. My whole life so far had been thrust in an upward arc. The future looked good. I should have been content. But instead I was wound as tight as a tether around a load of pipe.

Arizona stared blindly to the west, toward the red-rimmed horizon as the sun sank fast beneath the gathering darkness. He looked like a tired, old man. Suddenly, I understood the brutal truth of his life. Arizona would continue to work as a laborer under Jim Crow until he physically couldn't do it anymore. And then, what? I realized his dreams were as empty as the bottle I clutched in my lap.

My stomach churned and burned, but it was not the whiskey. It was the injustice I had witnessed all summer.

I was desperate to say something, to try to make it right. But I was just a college boy, leaving a summer job and returning to school and an easy life. What could I tell a grown man that would make any difference?

My thoughts jumped around. Here we sat, in my car, near Tenth Avenue North, only a few blocks from my first paper route I delivered nine years ago. It seemed like a lifetime. I reflected on all I had learned in the past few years about the South and my city and our strange racial attitudes. It's true, I had learned a lot. I'd come a long way in some respects, but it had mostly been an academic journey—until now.

We sat quietly. There was no reason for Arizona to speak. The Blues had told his story his whole life.

As for me, I had something to say. Now, I had to get the words in order—and force them out of my mouth.

I gathered my courage the best I could, took a deep breath, placed my hand on his shoulder, and stuttered, "Thanks, Arizona. Thanks for all your help." I gasped another breath. "You're a good man—the best."

That was all I could manage to utter.

Three months at the pipe plant watching Jim Crow at work—that was the real lesson I had finally learned. And it had broken my heart.

46 • Sunday, September 15, 1963

For a news hog like myself, that period after college of almost a year was a time of total darkness. I lusted not only for the news but for the written word.

I graduated from college in May 1962, and was promptly inducted by the Armed Forces. I went through the induction process in Montgomery, the paperwork and the physical examinations, and was on the verge of serving in the Army for two years when I decided at the last moment that a six-month's reserve program might be less intrusive in my life.

I joined the U. S. Marine Corps Reserve and reported for duty on August 1, 1962. For three months, I did not see a TV screen or a newspaper or hear any news whatever—except one time. As the only college guy in my platoon at Parris Island, the drill instructors called me "the Professor," when they weren't using stronger names to describe my ineptness. I was charged with looking after the gear locker while the other recruits scrubbed down the squad bay. One day, there was a week-old newspaper in the gear locker. I was thrilled at my good fortune. Quietly, I closed the door and wolfed it down like a starving man. The only thing I remember about that newspaper—Marilyn Monroe had killed herself! Before I could digest that horrible news, the door opened. My drill instructor gazed at me in disbelief. Then he came in, closed the door and beat the hell out of me. Gaining news was discouraged in boot camp. They preferred to parcel it out to suit their needs—to rouse up fear and loathing of the enemy. At the time, it was the "gooks." I was amazed at how quickly it could change.

A few months later, I was in infantry training at Camp Lejeune, North Carolina. Again, no TV, no newspapers, no news of any kind. And again it was the gooks behind every tree.

Suddenly, one morning all our officers were gone, shipped out to sea, and replaced by non-coms. Gooks were irrelevant. It was now the Cubans, and we faced an unknown but existential peril. We were completely in the dark—had no idea what had happened. All we knew was what we were told by our trainers—"Learn well," they said, "because next week you'll be shipped out to war like everybody else at this base. This is the real thing."

Then after a few weeks, it was over. The Cuban Crisis is still a deep, dark hole in my personal history. I've promised myself one day to learn what happened and why.

I was released in the early spring of 1963, with six years of reserve duty ahead. But I was again a civilian.

I took a job as a teacher at the Alabama Boys Industrial School. ABIS was the state reformatory for white boys from ages twelve to eighteen, in Birmingham. There was a separate such school for colored boys near Montgomery. I lived on campus in a dormitory with the boys and took all my meals in the cafeteria. Again, I was in a cocoon, cut off from news except for an occasional newspaper.

During this time I served on active duty, I was given leave to return home for a week. My sister, Dale, was then a student at Phillips High School. She asked me to visit and have lunch with her. She introduced me to her speech teacher, Miss Green. She was a tall, thin, erect young woman in high heels, as tall as I. Her platinum blonde hair seized my attention until I looked into her almond shaped, amber-colored eyes that bespoke power and purpose. Tongue-tied, I felt myself wilt in Miss Green's sophisticated presence.

A few months later, when I returned to town, I called her on the phone. I was not surprised she had no memory of meeting me, but somehow I got my tongue working and convinced her to have coffee with me.

I learned her name was Martha and she taught, in addition to speech, a class in English. She was the dramatics director and debate coach. At that time, she had a company together for a production of *Our Town*, Thornton Wilder's play about the fictional town of Grover's Corner, New Hampshire. I made it my business to show up for play practice several late evenings to watch the proceedings and hope to take her to dinner afterwards. She was only twenty-one years of age, but she directed those big eighteen-year-old boys around with the same kind of authority I'd seen in the military.

Except for my forays away from ABIS at night, I was essentially cut off from the news.

I did receive some news from Martha, who told me about the marches in May 1963, which occurred several blocks west of Phillips. She saw little of the unrest, but her windows were knocked out of her classroom, and on one occasion her tires were slashed. There was little local news about the marches and the brutal tactics of Police Commissioner Bull Connor as the police and firemen suppressed even the children's marches with fire hoses and police dogs.

Based on the meager information I was able to gather, I sympathized with the cause—it was time to end the segregation. But I resented the outside "rabble rousers" who planned and led the marches, particularly Rev. Martin Luther King Jr. I read of the eight ministers and their letter to Dr. King asking him to give more time, to let it work out gradually. I sympathized with their point of view.

Later, I read Dr. King's brilliant response from the Birmingham jail, which he wrote on scraps of paper. I thought of Lorraine Hansberry's play *A Raisin in the Sun*, which I had read in college a couple of years earlier. I then thought of Langston Hughes's poem *A Dream Deferred*, on which her title was based:

> *What happens to a dream deferred?*
> *Does it dry up*
> *like a raisin in the sun?*

Suddenly, very suddenly, I understood how wrong I had been.

Martha and I married in the summer and moved into an apartment together. Then I was able to read newspapers again and see the television news on a regular basis. Bull Connor and the other commissioners had by then been removed from office by a change in the form of city government, and we were looking forward to the absence of Bull Connor and his cronies and to the harmony of the new Mayor-Council governance.

Perhaps it was only because I was newly married that the world became a friendlier place almost overnight. It did seem to me that violence in our city had waned, and that our future seemed more secure than ever before. But, no, our city had paused just long enough to catch its breath. Not even our new marriage could distract us from Birmingham's next violent spasm.

I was attending a weekend drill at Fort McClellan in Anniston, Alabama, on Sunday, September 15, 1963, when I heard the news about the bombing of yet another church in Birmingham, this time with horrendous consequences. The Sixteenth Street Baptist Church in downtown Birmingham had been the assembly and jumping-off point for the marchers facing Commissioner Bull Connor and the police dogs and fire hoses earlier in the year. It became the target of members of the Ku Klux Klan who planted a bomb, and four innocent young girls were killed by the blast as they were preparing for Sunday School.

Hardly had news of the church bombing stopped ringing in my ears when I heard that another youth had been killed. Johnny Robinson, a black sixteen-year-old boy, was shot in the back by a policeman for throwing rocks at a car in downtown Birmingham.

A third piece of awful news arrived on that same day, this one touching me in a personal way. Across town from the Sixteenth Street Baptist Church, and wholly unrelated to the Ku Klux Klan bombing, a young boy had been killed in the very neighborhood where I, a college student, had worked a summer job several years earlier surveying the residents about the need for a federal housing project. The senseless circumstances of his death took my breath, a shock wave that has followed me across fifty years.

Virgil Ware was thirteen years old. He and his brother, James, age fifteen, were traveling on Docena-Sandusky Road, headed home. James was pedaling. Virgil was balanced atop the handlebars. They were colored. Two white boys, sixteen-year-old Eagle Scouts, Michael Lee Farley and Larry Joe Sims, had attended a white supremacist, segregation rally the afternoon of the church bombing and were fired up, incited to mindless no-good. Farley had a .22 pistol and drove a motorcycle with Sims on the back. They were traveling on the same roadway as the Ware brothers, meeting them head-on. When Farley spotted the two colored boys ahead, approaching on their bicycle, he handed the pistol to Sims. Sims raised the barrel, took aim on the Ware boys and pulled the trigger, firing two shots. Virgil died in the ditch where he fell, in James's arms.

Two young men—only just old enough to get a license to drive, Eagle Scouts taught mottoes and lessons in helping others—whipped into a frenzy of blind stupidity and violence. Untouched, of course, as they always had been, were the men who had conducted the segregation rally— the white supremacists who pumped the boys full of poison, who put it all in motion.

One boy dead, a brother left to nightmares, two boys prosecuted for their terrible crime, and men walking away scot-free to stir up more of the same around the South.

I remember myself being riled up, white-hot with patriotic rage following those meeting of the White Citizens Council, when Ace Carter and other speakers would rant and rave about existential threats from blacks, Communists, foreigners, Jews, immigrants, our own federal government, and the myriad and manifold conspiracies they imagined. I, like Farley and Sims, had been sixteen years old riding my motorcycle and thinking dark thoughts, under the same evil spell. How many times have I thought of those Eagle Scouts and wondered if I had possessed more courage and self-confidence, could I have hurt someone?

I'm thankful for the Millers' counter-balance to Ace Carter's virulence. Would that there had been others like them who might have talked to other boys, like Farley and Sims. With their hands on my shoulder, with their words of reason, I had made it through those difficult teenage years when boys are apt to act before thinking.

And what of the two Eagle Scouts? For the record, only two years' probation. Off the record, who knows what shame they still bear, what dreams haunt their nights.

And Virgil Ware? He was gone, his memory seized in the swirl of horror at the church and lost in its overwhelming aftermath. Thankfully, *Time* magazine published an article titled "The Legacy of Virgil Ware," written by Tim Padgett and Frank Sikora, on September 22, 2003, marking the 40th anniversary of Virgil's death.

A lifetime after Virgil's death, I did some basic research, found the *Time* magazine article, and at last learned the identity of the man who conducted the segregation rally that Sunday before the two Eagle Scouts went for their ride. I knew it couldn't have been Ace Carter who set them off, as he had once set me ablaze with his oratory. He had become too important for local activities. He was by then busy writing speeches for Gov. George Wallace, and had largely disappeared from public view. When that article turned up the name of the man I was looking for, I was stunned. At first, I convinced myself it was a coincidence, maybe a father-son name relationship. But, no, there was no other conclusion. Rev. Ferrell E. Griswold,[16] Pastor of the Minor Heights Baptist Church, where the Farley family were members, was one of the men who spoke at the rally that Sunday, though he had learned of the church bombings earlier that same day and and counseled the crowd against any further violence.

Only eighteen months prior to Virgil's death, Ferrell and I had been in philosophy classes together at Birmingham-Southern College. We often had coffee together, sometimes he and I alone and, at other times, a group of us. He was at least ten years older. He was a pastor and had a church. That maturity allowed him a certain deference in our friendly discussions, most of which involved various questions raised in class. Occasionally, his fundamentalist approach would surface, though I don't recall our ever discussing racial politics. No doubt my rapidly evolving views seemed to him unanchored and sophomoric.

For a time, we had been friends.

How strange. For almost fifty years I wondered who may have set this chain of events in motion, and I now learn this participant in the tragedy was my classmate and friend. Suddenly, Virgil Ware's death takes on a new horror for me, for I now imagine had I been a better friend, instead of the cynical, callow college senior I was, I might have made the difference.

*   *   *

Yes, for almost a year, from August 1, 1962, until the summer of 1963, I lived in a news vacuum. I had missed the activity surrounding Birmingham's vote for a Mayor-Council form of government which ultimately forced Bull Connor from his office. And I had missed the protests and marches in the spring of 1963 sponsored by Rev. Martin Luther King Jr. and known as "Project C," a more confrontational approach to non-violent action to get the media's attention and to force Bull Connor's hand.

For the balance of 1963, I was fully engaged with the daily newspapers and television coverage as the catastrophic church bombing occurred and President Kennedy was assassinated in Dallas. There can be no doubt that in the history of Birmingham 1963 is a pivotal year; just as there can be no doubt that the Sixteenth Street church bombing became *the* galvanizing event in the Civil Rights Movement—and, for our nation, 1963 is truly a watershed year in the continuing American saga.

47 • Moving the Vatican

Following the horrors of September 15, the city simmered in unrest. I was blissfully unaware. I had my own problems.

While I lived on campus at ABIS as a single man and a teacher, I had no expenses—no rent, no board, no utilities, no commuting costs. Almost everything I made, which wasn't much, went into my bank account and stayed there.

But when Martha and I married and moved into an apartment, the reality of rent, utilities and other such expenses hit me in the face. Our furniture consisted of hand-me-downs and second-hand stuff. Martha and I together—two teachers—were not making enough money to break even after payment of our expenses.

But money, as they say, is not everything. We had each other, and that was sufficient. Until we learned we were going to have another, and that changed the equation.

With her pregnancy, we knew something had to give. It was up to me to find a better job.

Two things converged to again alter the course of my life. My cousin, Jackie Isom, had entered his first year of law school. And my friend, Charles Clark, my former roommate at Birmingham-Southern, had attended his first year of law school at the University of Virginia, but had dropped out for a year to work. All he talked about was going back to finish his studies.

Though I had never before considered, nor even thought about law school, the prospect lay before me, and in my desperation to latch onto some way to make a living, I gave it my full but cynical attention. It was literature I loved best. How could I read law? It seemed so overwhelmingly boring. Charlie gave me a book about President Harry Truman and his nationalization of the steel industry. Suddenly, the law came alive. Maybe it wouldn't be so bad after all.

I applied to Vanderbilt Law School. It was the one place I'd always wanted to attend, since the first year I was in college in Nashville. I have no idea how I came up with my application fee. It was a big number. And then we waited to hear from the application. Meanwhile, I began to interview for other jobs, just in case. Maybe something better would come along. After all, I had no confidence I could make it in the law.

While my personal life was in an uproar over our financial predicament, the aftermath from the church bombing continued. Perhaps it was the depth of my personal dilemma that eclipsed the continuing racial unrest, but it did seem that things on the racial front had quieted down. I was not prepared for how nasty the next round of hate would get.

John Kennedy was then our president. He had been elected in November 1960, our first Roman Catholic president. That factor alone generated a tremendous backlash. Many people in Alabama feared our republic was going to hell in a hand basket—that the election of a Catholic president marked the end times. It was another facet of the xenophobic view of Southern people, always suspicious of immigrants. Most of the immigrants coming to Birmingham were from Southern and Eastern Europe and most were Catholic. That antipathy toward Catholics arose in the early twentieth century and reached a crescendo in the 1920s. A recently published book, *Rising Road*,[17] explores that early history of Catholics in Birmingham and the murder of Father Coyle on the front porch of the rectory of St. Paul's Cathedral in downtown Birmingham.

All that distrust of Catholics was beyond me. I was thrilled by Kennedy's election. I had grown up in Norwood, a neighborhood that was ethnically diverse. I'd gone to school with Catholics. The Millers were Catholic. The Boulevard girl was Catholic.

Although President Kennedy had been in office for more than two years, the virulent letters to the editor persisted. The writers raged against the federal government and particularly our President. *Was it not time to get over it?*

*   *   *

It was late fall 1963. There was an atmosphere of anxiety, giving rise to all sorts of lunacy and conspiracy theories. The times were crazy, emotions overwrought.

My application at Vanderbilt was pending. Living off campus, I was taking only the noon meal while teaching at ABIS. Eating at home two meals a day was bad for my pocketbook, but it was good from a political point of view. I was able to avoid most of the paranoid politics I suffered at the dining table with the teachers. One of the elderly women teachers at lunch one day ruefully predicted to our group that John Kennedy would serve two terms, his brother Robert would follow with two terms, and then the baton would be passed to Ted. When that happened, the Pope would "move the Vatican to America," our republic would fall, and we would no longer be a free people. I was appalled. Until then, as the youngest of the teachers by far, I had kept my opinions to myself. Now, for the first time, I spoke up and said that was preposterous. I was met with disapproving glares and comments by the entire company at the table.

Am I going crazy, I wondered, *or has everybody else flipped out?* Thankfully, a few days later, I saw a letter to the editor of the *Birmingham News* published on November 14, 1963, indicating that the President is due respect. I glanced at the bottom and recognized the name: A. Berkowitz. That name I so respected. I hungrily read the letter, the letter that had given me hope that not everyone in Birmingham had gone mad.

Nine days later, President Kennedy lay dead in Dallas. It was a strange and horrifying time. Though I admired President Kennedy, most people I knew were contemptuous of him and his politics. But most of them were subdued in the face of this national tragedy.

The year 1963 came to a somber close. For me, a pall had been cast over my entire life. I couldn't get that conversation about the Vatican out of my mind. It tainted my relation with the other teachers and my view of my job. I was ready to move on to another job or to law school. But I was stuck and had nowhere to go.

Then came the good news . . . I had been accepted by Vandy. But it was not to be. After two trips to Nashville, Martha and I learned that no new teachers were needed. Unfortunately, that was the year the school systems of Nashville and Davidson County merged. I don't know now whether I was more disappointed about missing my opportunity at Vandy or losing my deposit.

Meanwhile, my brother, Eddie, was home from college.

"What do you plan to do with your English degree?" I asked.

"Don't know. I've thought maybe about law school."

"Oh, really? Me, too. Let's go."

It was about that simple. Two years earlier, Cumberland Law School had been acquired from Cumberland University in Tennessee by Birmingham's Howard College. With a law school, the college changed its name to Samford University. Eddie and I sought admission and were taken as a package deal with identical partial scholarships.

At that point, I should have been hopeful for the future. Instead, my fears and uncertainties had taken the wheel. We had no health insurance and the baby was on the way. How could Martha and I support ourselves and a baby for three years of law school? If, indeed, I could cut it for three years. I gritted my teeth. It was do or die.

*　　　*　　　*

The truth is were it not for my morning *Post-Herald* route, I would not have met the Millers.

The truth is were it not for the newspaper, countless men and women may not have been persuaded to act courageously and follow their wavering consciences in the face of ignorance and crass populism.

The truth is were it not for my reading the editorial page, I would not have known of Abe Berkowitz, and I wouldn't have come to respect him as a man, a hero offering a distinct voice in Birmingham, Alabama, writing of a truth that so few people were willing to accept.

His letter published on Thursday the fourteenth of November 1963, however, would come to represent, for me, the most powerful letter in a long series of letters he had been firing off to the *News* over the years. Taken together, the body of his editorials comprise an unparalleled public record of a heroic stance against racism, but it was this letter which filled me with hope for Birmingham's future.

November 14, 1963
Voice of the People
President Due Respect

The presidency of our country is a lonely office: its occupant a lonely man!

It is now public knowledge that, in retaliation of attack, the power and duty to destroy half or more of our world is at all times necessarily and actually within physical reach of the President.

Since the H-bomb, the awesome responsibility of the office has increased in a degree which permits little comparison with that existing before.

Political, economic and social tremors in the remotest corners of the globe cause instant necessity for consideration and, often, decision as well, by the President.

The world and all its ills follow him throughout the day and all the lonely hours of the night, wherever he may be and however engaged.

For these reasons in a world of turmoil and tension, I deeply deplore the local bitter, insensate, irrational and sometimes obscene personal attacks upon the young man who is our President. I would resent them no less, whoever might be the holder of the office . . . .

Criticism of our presidents and their actions is traditional in American history and a healthy right under our democratic system. Though criticism is seldom tempered with mercy, it would seem that some compassion, which takes into cognizance the burdens and duties of the office of President, ought to be an ingredient of it.

Particularly does it seem to me, from an examination of the letters on your editorial page, compared with those in other parts of the country, that the vulgarity and even obscenity of these personal attacks are endemic here.

I do not know the President. I doubt that few, if any, in our local community who vent their hostility and hate upon him know him either. I do know that he is product and representative of his age and era. This is his world and the world of all the fine young men of World War II, Korea, Vietnam, Berlin, the Cold War and all the other fronts we must man in the years to come to dike the floods which batter against democracy. He and they, his children and theirs, if there be other than cinders and ashes then to contemplate, will live to stand upon the threshold of the third millennium of the common era.

I do not know the ages of those whose letters fill your editorial page with such harsh and personal indictment of the President. This I do know—whatever their age, they cannot be young in heart. They must not know, as they should that this is an era of the young—an age of new and youthful ideas, an age of change with much error in it, no doubt, but one which cannot be gainsaid its trial and testing.

For my own part, since adulthood, I have felt and thought that each of our presidents was my President, whatever his political affiliation; that he was as good an American as I; that whether he sought the office for its power or accepted it only out of duty, I owed him the duty of respect, however I might differ with his policies.

Since 1789, just 35 presidents have guided the destinies of our beloved country. In terms of critical history, some have been better, some worse. In totality, no nation has been so fortunately blessed with such a long line of leaders, differing as they have in political affiliation and temperament, for each made some contribution to America's growth and greatness.

Thus, in varying degrees, our presidents have always reflected a full measure of our common intelligence and decency and, above all, our love of country; and we, as the citizens in whom there is the right and power of choice, have never permitted, with hardly an exception, the selection of any man who did not, with all his faults and virtues, represent other than the best common denominator of our own and America's special gifts!

Granting the right at all times in our free society to disagree with the President, or any of his policies, I think it wrong when we spit upon him, for then we spit upon ourselves.

A. Berkowitz
Bank for Savings Building

So, yes, the daily newspaper is essential to every community.

And, yes, indeed, it was bitter news to hear that the *Birmingham Post-Herald* would stop production in September 2005.

And, yes, I find it sadly ironic that just as I write this piece extolling the virtues of the daily newspaper that our own *Birmingham News* has announced a cutback to only three issues per week, including a Sunday edition for the weekend.

When I heard this tragic news, my first concern was the newspaper carriers. How could they make a living delivering three issues per week? Then I thought about the jobs that would be lost, including those of the talented writers and journalists. They would be on the street, struggling to find a place in a rapidly changing industry. And, finally, then I thought about the very real possibility that our city may not be able to support a local newspaper at all. A frightening prospect . . . for it is the local newspaper that historically has kept its citizenry apprised of events and provided an important voice of leadership in the affairs of the people.

Perhaps never again will the arc of someone's life be altered by newspapers as was my own case. But that's only a personal reflection. In a larger context, the exercise of a free press has been the bedrock of our social contract.

We must ask ourselves, Can we, as a society, afford to let our free press lapse by a "lack of interest?" It's clear the television networks are not filling the void, and, God knows, the bloggers and radio hosts appeal only to the lowest common denominator. Surely, somehow, we must as a society find a way to undergird this singular vehicle of leadership to our communities. After all is said and done, the very concept of our nation was founded on a free press.

48 • The Question, Part Two

Abe Berkowitz's Law Office
The Empire Building
Birmingham, Alabama, April 1965

𝕴 **want to know why you are here.**

Mr. Berkowitz sat, patiently waiting. After a few moments of strained silence, he prompted me, asking, "Who referred you to me? How did you come to me?"

"No one referred me," I stammered. "I know your name from reading your letters to the editor. I've been concerned about the racial situation here in Birmingham. Your letters have been inspiring. I admire your viewpoint, and your courage for publishing those letters. I need a job with a lawyer. You're the only lawyer I know. I'd like to work for you."

He leaned closer, placed his arms across the top of his desk and riveted me with his eyes.

Mr. Berkowitz asked me about my background, my education, my views, my values. I explained that my family had come to Birmingham when I was a small boy, my father was a bus driver, and that I grew up in Norwood, attended Phillips High School, delivered newspapers. I received a Bachelor's degree with a major in English from Birmingham-Southern College. I spoke of my father's union membership and that my opportunity to graduate from college and have a chance for middle-class success was directly tied to the union. I told him I was the first person in my family to go to college. I spoke of my concern for the "underdogs" of society, and that I had remembered my origins and where I had come from.

He probed deeper, and I told him that I had grown up with the racial prejudices endemic to our region. I told him about the Millers on my paper route and how they had planted in my mind the seeds of change and that books also helped to change my views.

Mr. Berkowitz inquired about the books that had been meaningful in shaping my worldview. I cannot now recall specifically the books we discussed, but I must have included *The Grapes of Wrath* by John Steinbeck and *From Here to Eternity* by James Jones, forceful stories about underdogs of society facing powerful threats with dignity and pride.

I explained to him that it had slowly dawned on me that perhaps the largest group of underdogs in all America are the blacks. I had read many books that contributed to the reconciliation of my views. Odd that I remember mentioning only one specific book—*Only in America*, a collection of essays by Harry Golden. Mr. Golden was a journalist. His writings had made a difference in my life and my views of the racial questions in the South. Mr. Berkowitz was familiar with Harry Golden, editor of the *Carolina Israelite* published in Charlotte, North Carolina, and told me he admired him as well .

Though much of the interview has faded in my memory, I do specifically recall that Mr. Berkowitz and I laughed about one of Golden's essays. It was in response to the clamor among the Southern legislatures to deal with the 1954 Supreme Court decision *Brown v. Board of Education*. The legislatures of Southern states were working overtime to arrange a plan to avoid integrated school systems. Mr. Golden, in his essay, "The Vertical Negro Plan," reasoned in jest that there had never been any problems in the South concerning whites and Negroes standing in the same lines at grocery stores, banks, government offices and such other places, and that whites and Negroes had always intermingled in the streets and in stores all while standing or walking. With tongue in cheek, Mr. Golden suggested, as there is no problem or danger with the vertical Negro, the school integration problem could easily be solved by removing all chairs from public schools and installing stand-up desks.

Mr. Golden's essays were alive with stories of individual human beings caught up in the hard knocks of life and the strength and malleability of the human spirit. As I spoke with Mr. Berkowitz, I remembered that only two years earlier, as I was transported by bus from Parris Island, South Carolina, to Camp Lejeune, North Carolina, we traveled through Charlotte. I had been thinking of Harry Golden. Then, as if by magic, we passed a large two-story home on a commercial street with a sign in the front—

The Carolina Israelite

—A wave of emotion passed through me and I wanted to get off the bus, go to Mr. Golden's door and ask for a job. I wanted to work for him just as now I wanted to work for Mr. Berkowitz.

We had been together for almost an hour when he began to close the interview, repeating that he had no position for me.

But then he brightened and said, "Look. Why don't you stay in school this summer?"

"I can't stay in school this summer. I don't have any money for tuition. I need a job."

"Don't worry about the tuition. I'll pay your tuition."

I looked at him in amazement.

"No, Mr. Berkowitz. I need a job so I can make enough money for tuition for the next school year."

"Don't worry," he said without hesitation, "I'll pay your tuition for the year."

I was dumbfounded. I stammered, "No—no, I can't do that. I don't want a loan. I want a job."

"It's not a loan."

Again I refused. I was embarrassed. I had never borrowed money in my life and no one aside from my father had ever offered me anything of tangible value. I was worried I was being ungracious. I thanked him again and said I couldn't accept that generosity.

Mr. Berkowitz then spun his chair away from me, thought for a moment, picked up the phone and made a call. After speaking for a few minutes with his friend about personal matters, he said, "Doug, I have a young first-year law student from Cumberland in my office. He needs a clerkship position this summer. I'm sending him over to see you." Then he added with emphasis, almost a command, "Give . . . him . . . a . . . job."

He then turned back to me and instructed me to go directly to Douglas Arant's office, giving me directions to Bradley, Arant, Rose & White, Birmingham's largest law firm, located in the building just across Twentieth Street. We then shook hands, and he wished me well.

As I left the office, I thanked the receptionist for her kindness and went directly to Mr. Arant's office. I approached the receptionist and asked for Mr. Douglas Arant. After a few minutes of waiting, I was shown to his office. I guessed Mr. Arant—tall, stooped, and gruff—was about seventy years old. He spoke with me for about fifteen minutes, learning I had a wife and child and actually "needed" a summer job. He took the opportunity to explain to me that he had attained thirty-seven years of age before assuming those obligations, and chided me for my foolish decisions. As I sat there in his office, I thought to myself, *What am I doing here? I can never get a job at this place.*

But much to my surprise, Mr. Arant told me based upon Mr. Berkowitz's recommendation the firm would offer me a job for the summer. He sent me to the office manager to make arrangements for employment.

I served as a law clerk for Bradley Arant during the summer of 1965. I was housed in the library, where I worked with several summer clerks and several law graduates from the most highly regarded law schools in the country—Harvard, Yale, Virginia. I was working with the best and the brightest. My summer at Bradley Arant was a richly rewarding experience.

I wrote a letter to Mr. Berkowitz and thanked him for his assistance. I did not hear from him again until the spring of 1967, my senior year, when I received a telephone call from one of Mr. Berkowitz's partners, who said Mr. Berkowitz had asked him to call me to arrange for an interview.

I was thunderstruck. I had not sent a résumé. I hadn't yet completed my last semester and had no idea anyone would talk to me before I had passed the bar exam.

I scheduled the visit, and showed up in the same waiting room as before, to the same pleasant receptionist and the same brass name—

Berkowitz, Lefkovits, Vann, Patrick & Smith

—I interviewed with Arnold Lefkovits, Vernon Patrick, and David Vann. I did not see Mr. Berkowitz. Several days later, I received a job offer.

I told my father of my offer, but had never told him what Mr. Berkowitz had done for me two years earlier. His emphatic advice: "Turn down the job. Jews will never treat you fairly. They stick together, you know. They look out for their own."

A day or so later, I visited with Dean Weeks, the dean of my law school, and told him of my offer for employment by the Berkowitz firm.

"Oh, I'm not surprised," he said, "I thought you would get an offer. Mr. Berkowitz has telephoned me every semester to check on your grades and to inquire about your progress."

*   *   *

Though I must have wondered ten thousand times about the sandstone statue on his desk—the one of the biblical prophet holding a broken sword above his head—I never asked Mr. B, as I had come to call him, what it signified. That question lay quiet on my tongue year after year.

One evening, as I read the first few chapters in the book of Isaiah, I found the answer. It was Isaiah who said, ". . . and they shall beat their swords into plowshares, and their spears into pruning hooks: nation shall not lift up sword against nation, neither shall they practice war any more."

Mr. B was a tough lawyer who aggressively represented his client. But the statue that stood silently before him as he sat at his desk day after day said it all: Mr. B, like myself, was a deeply conflicted man. He was paid to fight for his client, but, at rock bottom, he was a peacemaker.

And was it not Jesus who said in his Sermon on the Mount, "Blessed are the peacemakers; for they shall be called children of God?"

Mr. B is gone now, but what greater tribute can be given a man in a few words than that—that he was a child of God.

He died on December 1, 1985. I had the privilege to practice law with him for eighteen years before his body wore out at age seventy-eight. He was my mentor. I've missed him every day since then, an absence now of twenty-eight years.

49 • Reconciliation

By 1968 white flight to the suburbs was underway in Birmingham on a large scale, facilitated in part by the condemnation of large swaths of land through neighborhoods occupied by Birmingham's African American communities. Now, over forty years later, there is speculation that the routes of Interstates 65 and 20/59, and particularly as they interchange near downtown Birmingham, were deliberate attempts to disrupt and displace many of the black activists in the city. There is evidence to suggest that these interstate highways were built to maintain the separation of white and black neighborhoods, as they had been established by racial zoning patterns no longer legal.[18]

Speculation aside, blacks were indeed displaced, and as they moved into other neighborhoods, the white population flooded to the suburbs. Norwood became a favorite target of unscrupulous real estate agents, whose method was to encourage white folks to list their property for sale, a shrewd and disreputable practice commonly known as "block busting." The real estate agent would approach one or more homeowners on a block within the targeted neighborhood and make his pitch. "Get out now, quick, while you can. If your neighbor sells to a black, your values will plummet."

The result of this tactic was often a panic among white homeowners, who would rather sell at a sacrifice price than suffer the ignominy of being the only whites left on the block.

My parents finally succumbed in 1969, bitterly selling out to a black family at a low price, shortly after my daughter, Natalie, was born on Christmas day 1968. They escaped to Forestdale, an unincorporated community on the western outskirts of town, much farther from and less convenient to the Greyhound bus station where my father worked.

One year later, in 1970, my wife, Martha, and I bought a two-story brick house in Forest Park, an old neighborhood on Birmingham's Southside. My father begged us not to do it, urging us to move to the suburbs as he and my mother had done. They were concerned that Forest Park would soon be targeted by blacks just as Norwood had been, and we would lose our investment. He was unaware that Forest Park had already been labeled "blighted" a number of years earlier.

About twenty years later, blacks began moving into my parents' neighborhood. While they were agitated, they did not panic. In part because, upon my father's retirement from Greyhound in 1977 at the age of sixty-five, he had taken a job at Colonial Bank as a mail clerk—a job he kept until he was eighty.

The bank was located in the Empire Building, the building in which my firm was situated. He became well-acquainted with my mentors, Abe Berkowitz and Arnold Lefkovits, and came to see them as my partners and men worthy of trust and admiration.

During that time, my father also came into direct and meaningful contact with black employees of the bank, people he came to know, like, and admire. And, yet, he had a hard time reconciling his new feelings with his lifelong viewpoints. When we watched a ballgame together, for instance, he would take note of how many black players were on the respective teams, particularly if one of the teams was from Alabama. And I took note of how he used less and less often the "N" word.

One evening, much later, when my father was about eighty years old, he and I were watching a football game, when he told me blacks had bought the house next door and had moved in only a few days earlier. His voice fell with a familiar resignation, punctuated with a deep sigh. I held my breath, waiting for the tirade to ensue, and looked away, wondering what I could say to defuse the frustration. I remembered well his anger twenty-five years earlier as he felt put out of his home by the encroachment of blacks.

This time, however, he chose to say nothing. Surprised, after a few moments, I turned toward my father. He was staring faraway and seemed perfectly at peace. I slowly let out my breath and began to relax, though I was puzzled. Then, out of the blue, he said in his matter-of-fact voice, "Your mother baked a cake yesterday and we took it over and met them." Then, after a long pause, he continued, "They seemed okay to us. I think they'll be good neighbors."

He looked away and so did I, my eyes welling with tears.

I didn't say anything, afraid my voice would break.

What is it about fathers and sons that each conceals from the other his weakness? After I was grown, I never asked my father for any kind of assistance. Nor did I ever confess to him the fears and insecurities I had felt over the years. Neither did my father share with me, even in his last years, any of his own fears.

Only this: He was always a physical man, confident in his ability to "stand up" to other men, to take on any situation. He was a fighter. But in his last years, he would often show me his gnarled, arthritic hands and say, "Look at this, son." And he would draw his knotty fingers closed. "I can't even make a fist anymore."

My father died suddenly on the evening of September 11, 2000, one year before the horror and devastation in New York. He was eighty-seven. I served as executor of his estate. Among my duties was the organization of his bank account and financial investments. He had been loyal to his former employer, Colonial Bank, and had his bank account and certificates of deposit there. When I visited the bank, I presented my letters testamentary to Ms. Gilmore, a middle-aged African American lady. She told me she remembered my father. She devoted an hour gathering the information I needed. She was kind and helpful to me. When we were finished, I told her how much I appreciated her help. Her eyes misted over.

Haltingly, she said, "We've missed your father so much since he retired. We all loved him very much."

*   *   *

My father, the eldest son, raised in the despair of the agrarian northwest Alabama hill country, needed on the farm, an education neglected, a good, kind, and sensitive man never having known or even met a black person; my father, a man who married and in desperation moved his young family to Birmingham seeking a better life and who was then plunged into a Jim Crow culture of white supremacy and hate, eventually finding a job on the front lines of racial integration as a bus driver bound to enforce the laws of segregation in Alabama; my father, struggling with an impossibly frustrating job, having to make intolerable decisions in the wake of a growing movement of Civil Rights activism he was just beginning to understand.

He had swallowed the rhetoric of the time—that all the trouble was Communist-inspired—and then he became enraged by the rules of the Interstate Commerce Commission, which precluded the enforcement of local law regarding interstate travelers—yet, eventually, following his retirement from Greyhound at the age of sixty-five, he came into meaningful contact for the first time with African Americans he would work with and come to know at Colonial Bank, many of whom had by that time finally and rightfully earned responsible and rewarding positions in management.

We've heard it said that morality can't be improved by changing the law. That is clearly untrue. My father's attitude eventually changed, and he found reconciliation, only because the law had in fact changed. Fifty years ago, the Jim Crow laws completely precluded any relationship between members of the two races. When my father retired from Greyhound and took a job at the bank, the Jim Crow laws had been nullified fifteen years earlier, as a consequence of the hard-won Civil Rights Movement. Blacks were then in responsible positions at the bank, and over the fifteen years he worked at the bank, he came to know and respect—perhaps even to love—his black co-workers with whom he worked daily. Without my having noticed it, my father—one man—had slowly changed.

Birmingham too had slowly changed. It was the beginning of a new century. At the time of my father's death in 2000, it was a different time, a different day, a different Birmingham.

I would give anything to know the entire scope of the hardships and heartbreaks, the frustrations, and ultimately his reconciliation given the difficult choices he had to make in those terrible years and how he made them. Except for the frustration and rage he occasionally unleashed at the kitchen table, I can only guess about the nature of the internal struggles he must have faced and dealt with. Unfortunately for me, he, like most other men of his generation, was too strong and silent, too proud to speak of personal feelings to anyone, much less his own son.

Unfortunately, my father did not learn, until his later years, the lesson Mrs. Miller had tried to teach me in my adolescence—that it's wrong to view an entire people as a monolithic and stereotypical group—that each person should be entitled to dignity and respect. For it is only when we can come to know another and understand his viewpoints and his hopes and dreams that we begin to see the full commonality we share as human beings.

It's a lesson my father learned in his last years; and we are bound, each of us in turn, to learn the lesson in our own time.

50 • The Territory of the Heart

As a student at **Birmingham-Southern College** in the late fifties and early sixties, I thought I wanted more than anything else to be a writer. On several occasions, I sat at my desk for hours but nothing would come. Perhaps at the time I had read too many pocket book westerns and mysteries and private eye thrillers, and assumed that only action and plot were important to telling a story. I examined my life but there were no adventures, large or small, to tell about. I had lived an ordinary life with an ordinary family. My social life was barren. Even my fantasies were bland.

I reflected on the fact that I had for all my life been a wallflower, had only a few friends and had not acquired recognition in any field. There had been no defining moments in my life. There was simply nothing to write about. After a time, I concluded I really had nothing to say and tucked away my paper and pen. I gave up any thoughts of becoming a writer and began to think of more mundane ways to make a living.

But now, more than fifty years since I despaired before the blank page, it has all come into focus. I should have written these stories while in college, when my memory was clear, but none of it seemed then to have any significance. It was only much later that I read William Faulkner's acceptance speech for the Nobel Prize for Literature awarded him in 1950. There, he said the only thing worth writing about is the human heart in conflict with itself.

*   *   *

I've always been intrigued by how easily one may hold conflicting views of things which cannot be reconciled.

As a child, I grew up in the time of and was molded by the McCarthy era, and, like everyone I knew, I was a rabid anti-communist. But we were blue-collar, working class union people.

I grew up in Birmingham, in a world where the races were segregated. I attended school for whites only—never really knew any blacks. We never understood that by bringing together the poor whites and the blacks, we could all have worked together politically for the greater good. It was only much later that I learned the separation of the races and the fear implanted in whites over generations was much more diabolical than mere custom. It was a scheme by a handful of unscrupulous planters and capitalists to maintain their positions of power and wealth by separating the races by law, by custom, by fear and suspicion, thereby ensuring their continued economic exploitation of both poor whites and blacks.

How could one support the labor movement on the one hand and at the same time support the forces that separated the races? For together, the poor whites and the blacks could have created a formidable union movement.

How could one attend church regularly and call himself a Christian and yet support segregation of the races knowing full well that segregation meant treating one race as inherently unequal? How could one be a Christian and yet feel pride and perhaps exhilaration arising from a terrorist bombing of some pastor's home in the night?

But, it's true. We were able to hold those unexamined and conflicting views in our hearts because we were small. We had not the maturity nor the inclination nor the judgment nor the reason to sort it out.

We were not, as Walt Whitman wrote in his *Song of Myself*, enormous in our thinking so as to embrace all.

Do I contradict myself? Very will then I contradict
myself, (I am large. I contain multitudes.)

Would that I, too, were large enough in heart and mind to have contained multitudes. Then, I might at least have understood the contradictions that drove me.

I delivered newspapers from the age of thirteen until graduating from high school at eighteen. During that time, I grew in ways that school could not have reached. School, after all, was merely one aspect of our social microcosm. I was able, through my contact with a remarkable couple—Vernon and Helen Miller—as their paperboy, to be drawn outside the boundary of my normal social customs and educational background to view the world in a different way.

*   *   *

The year was 1955, and Birmingham was a boiling cauldron, a toxic racial brew that threatened every day to spill over and flood the streets in violence and hate. The Millers had moved their young family from the far north onto my paper route into the middle of that danger when he took a job in the editorial department of the *Progressive Farmer* magazine (later to become part of the Southern Progress Company).

But they were not afraid. In fact, as we became acquainted over the first year, they often shocked me with outspoken views on race and religion and other topics which seemed revolutionary to me. I had never before heard, first-hand, such talk, though I was aware from the newspapers that heretics with such crazy beliefs were "out there," but they lived up north, far from Birmingham. And now the Millers had come down from the cold north bringing radical thoughts and words right onto my paper route.

I felt concern that such nice people were so wrong in the way they looked at the world. And I felt a need to educate them. If the Millers were going to live down South, they needed to learn about the Southern point of view.

And so, on Saturdays, as I collected for their newspapers over a two-year period, we carried on a moving dialogue, but by no means always so serious. In fact, Mr. Miller was reluctant to join in when race or other heavy subjects came up. He preferred pleasant conversation to hot debate.

But Mrs. Miller was always ready to plumb the depths of my Southern attitudes, especially as concerned black people. Perhaps she feared that the xenophobia I spilled onto her kitchen table would mark the balance of my life. She tried to understand the nature and source of my attitudes about race, and to possibly find some antidote to such feelings.

And I can now say that the Millers, and especially Mrs. Miller, became for me in those and later years a quiet but insistent voice that caused me to question what I had been taught as a child, particularly about racial stereotypes. Maturity was a slow and painful process, but there's no question that my process of re-evaluation of a distorted world view began with Mrs. Miller's kind and patient words. The seeds she planted may then have lain dormant for a time, but they did germinate. I found that everything she had taught me was true and good, while much of what I had learned through my Southern experience and culture was poisonous to my soul.

Not that they taught and I immediately learned. Oh, no! I was far too immature to appreciate what Helen and Vernon Miller shared with me and too cussedly stubborn to actually acknowledge the impressions they made—this, even as I ruminated over the conflicts and doubts their teaching truly inspired. For the most part, their wisdom was in fact ignored, while I tried with all my might to rally cogent arguments to countervail their wisdom.

As I write this, I remember—the Bible speaks of pearls thrown before the swine.

I was full of bigotry and judgment and self-righteousness, having little or no logic to support my positions. The Millers always listened to me with interest and respect, surprised, I think, by the depth of my feeling about the South and the Southern way of life regarding separation of the races. As they were from the far north—Minnesota and Dakota—they not only failed to understand my views, but they brought ideas to me I'd never before heard. They stated their positions with kindness and respect. They were never dogmatic or impatient.

The Millers could not understand the attitudes in Birmingham about the blacks, and how all members of the black community were dismissed in a monolithic group as a people not worthy to associate with whites.

They could not understand the policy of segregation of the races in the face of the fact that some whites were ignorant, ignoble and evil while some blacks were well-educated, noble and charitable. The question, of course, is how could a person of normal goodwill view the black community as a monolithic, stereotypical group? They posed that question (or some variation of that question) to me multiple times over the two years I visited their home as their newspaper boy. Based on my uncertain memory, I may never have conceded they were right, but their lessons were germinating nonetheless, as I struggled to retain my culture in the same way I struggled to retain my faith in a fundamental view of Christianity I could no longer believe. The seeds they sowed did in fact sprout in spite of the rocky, impoverished soil on which the seeds had landed.

By 1963, I can attest that the plants had good and substantial roots. When I first heard Martin Luther King say, "I have a dream that my four little children will one day live in a nation where they will not be judged by the color of their skin but by the content of their character," Mrs. Miller's face flashed into my mind, and I remembered her kind and patient attitude as she taught me about the commonalities of all peoples, regardless of color or creed. While it was Ace Carter I had followed in those years, Mrs. Miller repeatedly warned me that he was a false prophet who called on the darkest side of my fears and uncertainties.

She was right, of course, about Ace Carter and everything else she taught me. I now better understand why we must be ever vigilant, why we must strive to enhance all those better aspects of what it means to be human while at the same time suppressing those negative tendencies we all experience as members of the human race. We must, as Abraham Lincoln suggested, call on "the better angels of our nature."

Somehow, after all these years, now over fifty years since I last saw Mrs. Miller, I felt the need to see her again, to say, Thank you for saving me from myself.

51 • The Better Angels

I **parked my car at the curb,** set the brake, switched off the engine and sat for a full minute staring at a house I had never before seen, wondering what I would now say to them. This would be awkward at best, and I was having second thoughts about whether I should be here at all.

My mind flashed back a half century to Norwood, to the neighborhood across town in which I had grown up, to Twenty-fourth Street North and the clapboard, two-story house where the Millers had lived and where I delivered their newspapers for two years and visited with them many Saturday mornings when they would invite me in for something to drink while Mr. Miller got the money to pay their weekly account. My hands now still locked on the steering wheel signaled my reluctance to carry through my commitment. I had a flash of nostalgia, for a moment a kind of longing for the vibrancy and joy resonating in that house on Twenty-fourth Street North more than fifty years before.

Shortly after entering the professional world in Birmingham, unexpectedly I saw the Millers on the street one day. I made small talk as I considered the words I wanted to say to them. I wanted to tell them how many times I had felt guilt and shame for initially rejecting their guidance, for those times when I posed instead my dogmatic positions that now embarrassed me as I thought about those days then not so many years before. But I couldn't bring myself to say the words that lay on my tongue.

Many years passed and I continued to think about the Millers from time to time. I wondered how they had fared during some fifty years. If they were still alive, I wondered if they would remember me, a paper boy, someone who only tangentially touched their lives.

On an impulse, I opened the telephone directory, knowing they would have to be more than eighty years of age, having no idea they might still live in Birmingham. My eyes scanned down the listings, and, sure enough there was the name—Vernon Miller.

I immediately dialed and Mr. Miller answered the phone, his voice so familiar it caught my breath. Awkwardly, I told him who I was.

He said, yes, he did remember me, and he and Mrs. Miller would be happy to see me. We set a time for my visit the next afternoon. We spoke for only a short time, and when I hung up the phone I wondered was he merely being polite? Did he really remember?

Now, I sat in front of their home. At last, I released my grip on the steering wheel, opened the car door, and slowly got out, wondering, really, *Why am I here? Why am I opening a door closed so many years before?* As I stood on their porch, about to ring the bell, I pondered again what I would say to them now, after all those years, and wondered if her eyes would be the shade of blue I'd remembered from so long ago.

*   *   *

"I don't remember any of it," Vern laughed, "but I do remember when you ran your motorcycle into the side of that car—now that was something!" And he threw back his head and laughed, a laugh I hadn't heard in fifty years, suddenly so familiar. A spasm seized my throat, and I joined him in laughter, though constricted. I was too jittery to feel the humor, anyway.

Helen sat very quietly, and when the laughing had ceased, in a quiet, unobtrusive way said, "I remember those discussions, I remember them well," her voice low and sincere. I held my breath and waited, afraid of what she was about to say.

"You were such a sincere young man, just a boy really. How old were you then? Maybe sixteen? And so certain of the truth. I had never met anyone who was so certain of the truth."

"Dogmatic, you mean," I corrected.

"Well, you could call it dogmatic, I suppose. There may have been some of that, but, no, you were passionate in what you said. You were polite and sincere. You seemed to pity my failure to understand."

She was pensive for a moment, looking at her hands in her lap. Then she looked to me and smiled. "We had a lot of friendly debates on those Saturday mornings. I remember them well, and pleasantly." She turned to Vern. "You do remember our talks, don't you, Vern?"

"Well, yeah, a little I suppose," he said and smiled. Then he laughed aloud. "All those serious discussions you had back then—they made me tired. Guess I just didn't take it all so seriously."

I was amazed. They were still just as I remembered—he so light-hearted and fun loving; she so serious and grounded. The exchange between Mr. and Mrs. Miller transported me back to those times when I was filled to the top with certitude about ideas that now caused me to flush in embarrassment.

I knew there was one thing I had to say. I might as well get it over with. I drew in a deep breath and steeled myself.

"I was the worst kind of racist when I met you. And I suppose I continued to be for some time after that. I don't think you completely changed me over the two years I visited in your home, but you cracked open the door. You made me doubt much of what I took for granted. You made me think it through, and if it weren't for you I would never have even thought to solicit in the black communities. I got to know black people for the first time. That opened the door for me. I began to see a bigger picture."

I paused a moment. I was so embarrassed I wanted to stop, but they were both smiling and seemed eager to hear more, so I clenched myself up and continued in what I feared was a tremulous voice. "When I got to college, I was open for new ideas because of you. I began to read and to talk with people who came from different backgrounds. It was a slow process, but I want you to know it began with you. It took a good part of my college career to break all the way through, and in truth, maybe I'm still evolving. But if the two of you hadn't spoken to me in the way you did, who knows when if ever my eyes would have opened."

My heart pounded, my eyes brimmed with tears, my breath came in snatches. I was thoroughly embarrassed. The Millers sat quietly, as if they were too stunned for words.

"And I'll forever be grateful to you for that," I choked out, regretting the telephone call I made the day before.

Then Helen said, "Here, let me get you some water." She pushed herself from the chair and made her way toward the kitchen.

Mr. Miller and I sat in silence for the few moments she was gone. Thoroughly embarrassed and upset over the emotion that I had brought into their home, I wished I had never looked up their number in the first place. I should never have opened that door so long ago closed.

But, by the time she returned and I had sipped some water and got a hold on myself, I began to feel better. Afer a few more moments, a sense of relief washed over me—I had finally done the thing that had hounded me for fifty years.

I had finally said "thank you."

Afterword

The awkwardness I had felt at their front door—and the embarrassment of my speech—were gone. We were soon telling each other about our families. Though fifty years had passed and the subject matter had changed, our visit was much like our earlier visits had been—friendly and sincere.

As we closed our reunion, and I had taken my leave at the door, the sense of closure I had sought escaped me. It was not the ending of something I felt. Not at all. I felt it was just the beginning. It was then I decided it was time to reflect on my history and what others had done for me and to write it down. I had spent forty years working for others. I would now use part of my time to work for myself—to write my own stories, those stories where my life had intersected with others who had taken the time and effort to lead me, to teach me, to elevate the arc of my life.

All those years I had been away, I had practiced law without looking back—keeping my hands to the plow as it were, following the mule as my forebears had done, but it was I who wore the blinders and not the mule. I had rarely thought of Norwood and the people I'd known there. I suppose the aging process, the growing sense of mortality, causes us to look back, to recall those past events, both precious and painful, and put it all into some kind of coherent trajectory of experience. Who are we, after all, but the sum of those experiences?

As I began the process of mining my own memories, of putting pencil to paper, I knew very well that Helen and Vernon Miller and Abe Berkowitz would be at the center of my stories, but I did not become aware until I was half done that my father would claim center stage as well. Now that he was gone, I discovered that he had been a powerful force in my life, a form of guidance I did not fully appreciate and most often resisted, but an energy that engraved my character as if he had turned me on a lathe.

As I began the process of writing, it quickly became clear that I would be unable to call up the key memories without some stimulus or help. More visits to Norwood were required, visits to the actual streets where I played as a child and where I delivered newspapers as a young man. I needed to be physically present with my past in a geographical way to trigger such memories.

And so I drove to Norwood several years ago, to Seventeenth Avenue where I had lived as a boy. I parked at the curb in front of the little house in which I grew up, and surveyed the block and the general state of disrepair of houses along my street. The four-unit apartment building across the street from where I sat had burned and was standing in ruin, the roof caved in.

Fragments of memories bobbed to the surface like jetsam, but nothing coherent floated by. My mind drifted as I studied the houses and tried to remember which of my friends lived where. Then I glanced down the dirt road toward the quarters. It was now paved and ended with a turnaround at the railroad. Houses had been built almost all the way to the tracks, and, surprisingly, there was a small brick church next to the rails. I was amazed at how close the tracks were. As a child, it had seemed a mile or more through the underbrush to the railroad. I blinked, and, like a mirage, the image of James came to me, trudging up the road, dragging his skatiemobile, his face as inscrutable as ever. Stunned by the visualization, I realized I had not thought of him nor had I remembered the event in more than sixty years.

What else could I have forgotten? What else could I now remember? I couldn't remember if all those years ago I had even driven my car to the Miller's home to show them or if I told them I'd won the car. I didn't even remember if I said goodbye to them when I gave up my paper route on finishing high school at the end of May 1957, the month after I won the car. I suppose I simply moved to the next stage of my life and they disappeared from view. Not that I had forgotten them, as I did James and his skatiemobile. I had thought of them from time to time, of course, but I had never taken any action to find them in my effort to thank them.

I soon discovered a few visits to my childhood were not enough to unpack the dusty trunk of memories that I'd failed to open for more than a half-century. Another visit soon followed, and, then, another.

I would slowly drive along my paper routes, stopping here and there, as memories emerged from the depths, and the newness of it all—as well as the oldness—began a life of its own.

I rediscovered the neighborhood I had abandoned so long ago.

Norwood has changed in many ways over the past fifty years. The commercial areas along Twelfth Avenue are no longer vibrant, and abandoned buildings and houses blight the landscape. But the people who live there, now mostly black, seem as committed to the community and its betterment as the residents a half-century ago.

As I traveled the neighborhood and reminisced over the past and my coming of age in those years, I could feel something tugging at me, something I hadn't felt in a long time. It felt a lot like home—much like the homesickness of my first year of college in Nashville—and it soon became apparent to me that the arc of my life had been cast not only by those people who cared about me and each other, but also by the community, the place itself. Norwood.

We Americans are a rootless lot. We almost never seem to wind up in the place we started or the place we feel we belong.

I am often reminded of Robert E. Lee Prewitt in James Jones's powerful novel *From Here to Eternity*, published in 1951, yet another book from my college days. Prewitt, a career enlisted man in the U. S. Army immediately prior to World War II, was stationed at Schofield Barracks near Honolulu. Prew, as he was called, was from a coal-mining town in eastern

Kentucky and an orphan. The Army was home to him, even as it had broken him to the rank of private for his refusal to join the boxing club, a refusal based on a remarkable personal code of honor. He later killed a sergeant in vengeance over the death of his friend, and, then, because he himself was injured in the clash, failed to return to base. When the Japanese attacked Pearl Harbor and his base, he realized he must return to his unit even though the island was then under martial law, and he knew it would be dangerous to do so because he was AWOL. It was not mere loyalty to the United States that drew him back. It was the Army. That's where he belonged. It was his *community*.

I've always thought that Jones's book, which in 1953 was made into one of perhaps the greatest films of all time, is also one of the great American novels. It's much more than a war novel. It carries many themes. I think of it in part as a statement about the rootlessness of society in America and the need for community and belonging. Homesickness is about far more than mere longing for a place, though that's part of it. And it's only partly about people, who in my case are mostly gone. And it's not just about the memories either—the nostalgia—though that's certainly a part of it as well. No, homesickness is about the desire to return to the place you feel you belong, regardless of whether you were happy or fulfilled, or whether it was a heart-rending experience.

Mine had not been an idyllic childhood or adolescence. It was filled in large measure with loneliness and agonizing self-doubt. I felt I never fit in. Yet there was something about the closeness of the boundaries of our community, surrounded and isolated by industry, which gave me comfort. Norwood and its people had provided me with everything a young boy needed to grow into a man—boundaries and the secure feeling of adult supervision, and an excellent neighborhood school. I was one of the neighborhood kids. The neighbors knew every one of us. We knew the merchants who operated the shops in our community. They, too, had names and faces and smiles.

As I sit here, writing out the last few pages of my story in longhand, as every word of these stories has been written—trying to put in some kind of perspective the feeling of homesickness I experienced—I recall something else from long ago, something I haven't thought about since my interview with Mr. Berkowitz a lifetime ago. As I sat before him, tell-ing him something of my background, I told him in the briefest terms about having delivered newspapers and the importance I placed on that experience.

He then asked me, with that grandfatherly, benign smile I came to love so, "Tell me," he began, "tell me about Norwood, where you delivered all those papers."

I remember now, so clearly, what I told him, the man across the desk I had met only a half-hour earlier.

"I have a son, Mr. Berkowitz," I said, and I then told him I wanted my boy to grow up as I did, in a neighborhood where he can get to know all kinds of people, old and young, rich and poor, white collar and blue collar. Where the people are all mixed up, urban and country, long-time citizens and immigrants, and people of different religions. Different colors, good people, grouchy people, even bad people. That's how a child learns how he fits into the world around him, seeing all the kinds of folks he'll encoun-ter later in life, out in the real world, the way I did. And that's the kind of place Norwood is, where I delivered papers and learned about life and what was expected of me.

When Mr. Berkowitz looked surprised by the intensity of my emo-tion, I backed off a little. "I'm sure Norwood is not unique. It's just one of many urban neighborhoods where people live close to where they work."

Mr. Berkowitz smiled and said he preferred neighborhoods like that, too.

For all these many years I've lived as a professional among the affluent. I was too busy with career and family to think much about where I had come from, but in truth, as the years passed by, I did occasionally drive through Norwood with, first, my own children, and then my grandchil-dren. It was fruitless of course. To them, it was just another place, while for me the neighborhood would come alive with each visit. It's now as if a railcar has been sidetracked to my front door carrying a load of regret—regret for having abandoned the neighborhood and the people who had shaped me so long ago into who I became.

Not that I could have prevented the social patterns from developing as they did—of course not—but I could have contributed some small thing to stabilization, just as Abe Berkowitz had made his voice count at a critical time in Birmingham's history; just as the Millers had pressed against a rising tide of hatred and intolerance by teaching at least this one soul the truth at a critical time in his own moral development.

When I was a senior at Birmingham-Southern College, I read *The Death and Life of Great American Cities*, Jane Jacobs's then-recently-published (now, classic) work about urban development and what makes a community livable. At the time, I had never been to New York City and had no idea what Greenwich Village, Jacobs's model neighborhood, might have looked like. But from her description, I was reminded of my neighborhood, Norwood, and it occurred to me then that Jane Jacobs—if she were to have traveled with me on my paper routes for a few days, and if she could have met some of the people on my routes, and if she could have seen how insular and self-contained Norwood was, like a village—she might well have said, "This, too, is my kind of place."

Jane Jacobs's book about New York urban life made a significant impact on me, a college senior in Birmingham, Alabama, at a time when these two worlds were worlds apart. The thought even crossed my mind that I might someday become an urban planner, but in those days as a senior in college my mind was not focused on my career—I was bound for induction in the military service only a few months ahead.

Fifty years have passed since I read Jane Jacobs's landmark work. Though she recently died, she and her theories and writings about urbanism continue to be cited in current books, as, for example, *Walkable City* by Jeff Speck (2012). I never became an urban planner, but my nascent interest in what makes a community livable has taken on new life.

And it was just about the time I had begun my periodic visits to Norwood in pursuit of my memories that I became aware of a man named Barack Obama and his quixotic tilt toward the presidency. Fascinated by the little I was able to learn about him in the newspapers, I read his memoir, *Dreams from My Father*.

It was there I learned of a young man with a degree from Columbia University who qualified for a high-paying corporate job but opted instead to become a community organizer for nominal pay. In that position, he helped his adopted, impoverished community on Chicago's South

Side to organize themselves and solve their own problems to improve their lifestyles. He wrote in his memoir, "Communities have to be created, fought for, tended like gardens."

While some have denigrated President Obama for beginning his career as a "mere community organizer" when he could have been a Wall Street tycoon or business leader, I find it heroic that a talented young man eschewed a high-paying career to devote his time and talent to a poor community and its people.

I was immensely impressed with his story and how he had turned toward the kind of communities I had unconsciously abandoned. His story reminded me of another one of my heroes, Myles Horton, of the Highlander Folk School in Monteagle, Tennessee.[8] Horton attended Columbia's affiliate Union Theological Seminary, where he studied under Reinhold Niebuhr. Then he established his school in Grundy County, the poorest county in Tennessee, and committed his life (his autobiography is appropriately titled *The Long Haul*) to organizing poor communities and working for their betterment.

While I have no dream to change the world—as President Obama and Myles Horton have done—there may be time yet to contribute something back to the community that nurtured me to maturity, time to be helpful in tackling the problems facing Norwood and its people. I'm interested in finding an effective and popular way to deal with vacant and abandoned homes and buildings which blight all urban neighborhoods in the city of Birmingham.

I dream of droves of our people of all ages—black, Hispanic, white, Asian—taking on the challenge of moving back to downtown Birmingham and to its urban communities to work and to establish a truly colorblind community of residents of all demographic groups—a truly diverse neighborhood of the young and the old, the rich and the poor, blue collar and white collar, as a community should be.

About five years ago, my granddaughter, Maxie, and I had left my office and were driving a few blocks away from downtown Birmingham. An older lady was slowly hobbling along the sidewalk with a cane and a large shopping bag. I stopped and asked her where she was headed and whether I might give her a ride. She peered through the car window and saw Maxie, relaxed, and got in the car with us. She immediately began a delightful and sunny soliloquy about her day and all that was right in her life—who she was going to visit and how nice it was that we were going her way.

We traveled in her direction for about a mile and she directed me to the curbside at a federal housing project. There, she slowly extracted herself and her bag from my car. She leaned inside and thanked me, then turned to Maxie in the back seat and said, "Always remember, Honey, be cheerful. I always told myself, all my life, to bloom where I'm planted, and I've always tried to do just that."

She paused for a moment, then continued, addressing Maxie with a grandmother's warmth, "Bloom where you are planted, young lady. It will always keep you young."

Then she flashed a one-hundred-watt smile, turned, and hobbled toward the building, leaning on her cane, counter-balanced by the shopping bag.

Samuel Ullman, perhaps, said it best:

Youth is not a time of life; it's a state of mind.[19]

Younger people may say that folks her age, and perhaps my age as well, are "over the hill" or "washed up." But that's not true. This beautiful woman bubbled with life and just the memory of her sharing her truth with my granddaughter makes me feel more alive today than I've felt in years—alive at the prospects that lie before us all.

Epilogue

George Leighton had it largely right when he wrote in his 1937 article in *Harper's* magazine that Birmingham's future had been preordained by . . . "a group of speculators and industrialists in 1871 [who had] founded a city and peopled it with two races afraid of each other." Certainly, that pattern of segregation had been exploited over several generations of industrialists and capitalists, allowing both races to be harnessed for the benefit of the bottom line, most of the profits for which, not co-incidentally, went north to absentee owners and bankers. Among Leighton's conclusions? "The evil done by years of Jim Crow poison is incalculable; the social cost of 'keeping the nigger in his place' is beyond computation."

This Jim Crow evil continued well beyond the date of that 1937 article for another twenty-five years in Birmingham, Alabama, in particular. Under the leadership of Eugene "Bull" Connor, a useful pawn in an ugly political game, the rank and file white working man stiffened his back and was instructed not to yield to the growing social consciousness influencing change across the nation. Thankfully, this cancerous form of public control fueled by suspicion and hatred was defeated, in part, due to the inspired leadership of Rev. Fred Shuttlesworth and his constant, vigilant attack on segregationist maneuvering after *Brown v. Board of Education*, and, in part, by a rising class of local, deeply concerned businessmen and lawyers in Birmingham, including the growing presence of the University of Alabama Medical School and the University of Alabama in Birmingham.

Yes, the good citizens of Birmingham, of which there were many of all stripes and colors, had finally had enough when the unimpeded beating of the Freedom Riders in May 1961 was broadcast to the nation and to the world and the full implication and awareness of such unrestrained hatred prodded them into action. The account of how Bull Connor was finally removed from office is a fascinating story, the details of which is little known to the public, but it is worthy of study in our high school civics classes. It would not have happened as it did but for the action of key white and black community leaders coming together.[19]

David J. Vann, one of the primary participants in these efforts, later wrote a paper in 1978, fifteen years after the change in city government which forced Connor from office. He entitled that paper, "Birmingham, Alabama: From the Commission to the Mayor-Council form of Government," down-playing in the title the high drama that took place during the almost one year it played out, and which included mass marches of children, police dogs and fire hoses, with thousands of marchers in jail and other holding facilities. As Vann met with Martin Luther King at the final settlement bringing an end to the protests and marches on Birmingham's streets, Vann quoted Dr. King as saying he believed that we would live to see the day when Birmingham would be the symbol for some of the best race relations in America.

Four months later, on Sunday, September 15, 1963, events occurred in Birmingham that broke Dr. King's heart—and the heart of any other person of conscience. The day began with the bombing of the Sixteenth Street Baptist Church in which four little girls were killed. Then as the day wore on two more black youths were murdered in separate incidents. Six children, all on a single Sunday. Dr. King must have thought his prophecy that Birmingham would become the place of the best race relations in American was no longer even a remote possibility.

This year—2013—fifty years since Dr. King's prophecy—Birmingham is poised to memorialize and honor the fiftieth anniversary of a year of tragedy and triumph. While race relations in Birmingham may not yet have reached Dr. King's prophecy, the City has clearly moved light-years ahead of where it began. We work together today, blacks and whites; we are friends, and we recognize the commonality of us all. But that camaraderie does not continue around the clock. We largely live in separate neighborhoods and attend separate schools and churches.

The individual leaders in 1962-63, black and white, had a vision for a better community, one free of fear and discrimination based on race. Their dreams for our community have been realized in part, but we have miles yet to go.

One contemporary leader who has taken concrete steps to influence a new era of reconciliation in Birmingham is my friend Jim Rotch, a lawyer who drafted the *Birmingham Pledge* and is chairman of The Birmingham Pledge Foundation. *The Pledge*, now over fifteen years running, is intended as a public commitment by each signee to do his or her part in excising *all* prejudice from the daily life. To sign on to this remarkable public initiative, as quoted below, go to the website at www.BirminghamPledge.org.

- I believe that every person has worth as an individual.
- I believe that every person is entitled to dignity and respect, regardless of race or color.
- I believe that every thought and every act of racial prejudice is harmful; if it is my thought or act, then it is harmful to me as well as to others.
- Therefore, from this day forward I will strive daily to eliminate racial prejudice from my thoughts and actions.
- I will discourage racial prejudice by others at every opportunity.
- I will treat all people with dignity and respect; and I will strive daily to honor this pledge, knowing that the world will be a better place because of my effort.

It falls to each of us, individually—man, woman, and child—to make this commitment, this *Birmingham Pledge*. If we, all of us, purge the fears and prejudices and insecurities of the past, perhaps we might revitalize our city and its urban neighborhoods and become neighbors around the clock. Then Birmingham might well become the model of the best race relations in America, finally realizing Dr. King's prophecy. If Birmingham, the crucible where much of the Movement occurred, could pull that off, could we not become the beacon city for the world?

And is that not, after all, why we are here? To leave our community and the world a little better than we found it?

*   *   *

Recently, my friend, Walter Henderson, whom I hadn't seen since high school, and I spent several hours touring Norwood and reminiscing. We rolled around the Boulevard, following the sinuous path as it curves and rises and falls with the contours of the gentle hills and valleys. We passed the school and slowed to a stop. We laughed as I recalled for him my Halloween antics of long ago, when I raced across the Boulevard toward the school for refuge.

No, the community's not the same as we remembered it, yet it feels so right when I now visit, like the way an old pair of shoes fits one's feet, like an old friendship after a fifty-year lapse picks up the beat. I now find myself thinking about Barack Obama's statement that "Communities have to be . . . tended like gardens," and the lady's advice to my granddaughter Maxie, "to bloom where you are planted."

After working for myself, my small family, and my law firm for a lifetime, I am now faced with the ultimate question: Why, in the world, am I here? Is it not now time that I contribute something to the larger community?

And so my story has come . . . full circle. Perhaps it is my time to tend the garden, to get my hands dirty—perhaps even to bloom.

I look back now, back to the magic place it started, where a blameless child so long ago rolled his spool in the dirt on the edge of a neighborhood called Norwood, and now, as an older man, revisits the streets of his youth, haunted by gratitude for the undeserved gifts of others . . . happy to have a second chance . . . and hungry to play out the next chapter.

End Notes

1. Theophilus Eugene "Bull" Connor (page 3)

As I grew up in Birmingham in the forties and fifties, the name Bull Connor was a constant presence in my life, much as the name "Roosevelt" must have been during the Great Depression, though I don't recall Connor ever inspired any hope.

By 1963, Connor had served as one of three members of the Birmingham City Commission since 1937 (but for one term he sat our as a result of a person indiscretion). During that time as Commissioner of Public Safety, he consolidated his power over the police and fire departments. By 1963, he was virtually a dictator, the other two Commissioners rarely failing to vote with him.

Following the court decision in 1947 striking down Birmingham's racial zoning patterns, there followed about forty bombings of houses in the City as the Ku Klux Klan tried to prevent any encroachment into white neighborhoods. The City jokingly became known as Bombingham. The Police Department, riddled by members of the KKK and operating under Connor's leadership, never made any arrests during that period.

Connor believed that segregation of the races was both legally and morally correct and he enforced the Jim Crow laws with reckless authority. Such a position put him in good stead with Birmingham's industrial base which had endeavored from the beginning of the City's history to keep Birmingham's workers, black and white, absolutely separate so they could be played against each other in order to keep production costs down. Any attempt to change the order of things was branded as "Communistic."

Because of his inflexible attitudes about race and his commitment to maintain segregation of the races regardless of changes in the law, he became the perfect foil for Reverend Martin Luther King Jr. in his attempts to break down the Jim Crow order by passive resistance to "unjust" laws.

As a consequence, African Americans have Bull Connor to thank for the legislative action in Washington, D.C. that improved their status as citizens, namely the Civil Rights Act of 1964 and the Voting Rights Act of 1965. Of course, Bull Connor had something very different in mind. But anyone can see the direct line between those desperately needed legislative acts and the non-violent protests in Birmingham in May 1963 led by Rev. Martin Luther King Jr., Rev. Fred Shuttlesworth and others, which caused a violent reaction on the part of the police and fire departments led by Connor, as Public Safety Commissioner.

An interesting footnote to the story of the Civil Rights marches in Birmingham reflects how brilliantly Reverends King and Shuttlesworth "threaded the needle" relating to timing. (For more detail, see Endnote No. 18, *infra*.) At the time of the protests in May 1963, Connor had been voted out of office through a referendum which changed the City government from a Commissioner form to a Mayor-Council form. And after a series of elections, Albert Boutwell had been elected as Mayor over Connor on April 2, 1963, but Connor and the other Commissioners appealed to the courts to remain in office for the balance of their terms. The protests known as Project C (for confrontation) began on April 3. Had the preachers acted more quickly, they surely would have disrupted the voting, and Connor may have been elected as Mayor. Or by acting more slowly, the protestors might have missed their opportunity, as Connor and the other Commissioners were removed from office by the Supreme Court of Alabama on May 23, 1963. The confrontation they had planned with Connor would probably not have worked against Boutwell, who had been elected at least in part to tone down the race rhetoric.

Nunnelley, William A., *Bull Connor*, University of Alabama Press, 1991.

2. Hank Williams (page 61)

For the hard-scrabble folks of Alabama and the Deep South in the late 1940s, Hank Williams was one of their own. He sang of love gone bad and loneliness, of personal regret and the "lowdown" blues. Hank Williams gave voice to the themes that country folk held dear. His lyrics were simple and straight-forward and hit common people where they lived. This fragile young man from Alabama burst into creative flame for a breath-snatching moment, like a comet, the flame fizzling into the darkness on the first day of 1953. Hank Williams was dead at twenty-nine.

All his accolades came after his death. In 1987, he was inducted into the Rock & Roll Hall of Fame. He was named to CMT's 40 Greatest Men of Country Music second only to Johnny Cash. He is listed in the Songwriter's Hall of Fame.

On April 12, 2010, the Pulitzer Prize Board awarded Williams a posthumous Special Citation, presented to his daughter, Jett Williams. The award paid tribute to his "craftsmanship as a songwriter who expressed universal feelings with poignant simplicity and played a pivotal role in transforming country music into a major musical and cultural force in American life." For an excellent biographical sketch of Hank Williams, see *www.pulitzer.org/awards2010*. See also *Encyclopedia of Alabama* at *encyclopediaofalabama.org* for a more detailed biography.

Hank Williams's music continues to inspire and influence music enthusiasts not only within our own country, but in other parts of the world as well. See, for example, Sivert Bjordal of Norway, who dedicates his website, *www.sivertbjordal.com*, as "My tribute to Hank."

I have quoted from two of Hank's songs, one in Chapter 11 and the other in Chapter 35, both with permission of his daughter, Jett Williams.

3. Jim Crow Laws (page 69)

The pejorative term "Jim Crow" was used well before the American Civil War (1861-1865), at a time when slavery was legal in the Southern States, and referred to persons of African descent. It was based on a character by that name developed by a white actor and playwright, Thomas D. Rice, who performed in blackface during the 1830s, and this, the name "Jim Crow," came to refer to the caste system primarily in the Southern states that assumed white supremacy. It was more than the imposition of segregation laws. It was the Southern way of life.

Prior to the Civil War, there was no need in the South to subordinate by law persons of African descent—the fact that they had been brought here as slaves had done that. And then, in 1857, the *Dred Scott* decision by the United States Supreme Court held that they were not citizens of the United States, thereby sealing the permanency of that lower caste. The class difference, however, did not cause them to be separated from whites. On the contrary, there had been close contact, sometimes an intimacy, between the superior and subordinate races prior to the Civil War.

All that changed with the defeat of the Confederate States in the Civil War. The emancipation of the slaves frightened the whites, who felt the existential threat of two races living together, particularly as they believed the blacks to be beneath them.

Then came the hardships of defeat. Their cities and lands lay in devastation. They faced long years of occupation by Federal troops during the Reconstruction era. And to their dismay, blacks were given the vote and placed in positions of authority.

It was during Reconstruction that those amendments to the U. S. Constitution were passed by Congress to perpetuate the new order established by the War. The Thirteenth Amendment, ratified in 1865, abolished slavery. The Fourteenth Amendment, ratified in 1868, granted citizenship to every person born in the United States (thereby over-ruling the *Dred Scott* decision), and provided for due process and equal protection by the states for its citizens. The Fifteenth Amendment, ratified in 1870, granted voting rights regardless of "race, color, or previous condition of servitude."

For a time, blacks had reason for optimism. They held political offices widely in the South, even serving in state legislatures and in various state and local offices. A handful of blacks were elected from the Southern states to Congress. Free public schools were assured to blacks. Transportation facilities were available to black and white by and large without regard to race.

Unfortunately for the blacks, the political will of the North could not be sustained indefinitely and Reconstruction came to an end in 1877. Thereafter, and despite the three Amendments only recently adopted, the whites in the South over the next generation clawed their way back into a position of white supremacy through various means, including a reign of terror by the Ku Klux Klan, in a process they called "Redemption." While the slaves had been freed on paper, they soon found themselves in another form of bondage through share-cropping with their former masters. In many places in the Deep South, the enforcement of vagrancy laws was turned into a leasing program whereby black prisoners were leased to timber companies, coal mines and other industries to work off fines they could not pay. This enormously profitable system created a condition worse than slavery, as the lessee industry had no incentive to adequately feed, clothe or take care of workers they did not own. Hence, thousands died in such service.

Whites quickly assumed control of their state legislatures, and fearing a free black race and believing in white supremacy, enacted a web of laws, state and local, that provided essentially for two separate societies. These laws establishing segregation of the races became known generally as "Jim Crow laws."

Then came the landmark decision of *Plessy v. Ferguson*, 163 U.S. 537 (1896) which upheld the constitutionality of racial segregation laws under the principle of "separate but equal." It was followed ten years later by *Berea College v. Kentucky*, 211 U.S. 45 (1908), which upheld Kentucky's law prohibiting black and white students in the same school.

With the approval of segregation by the Supreme Court, the Southern states were encouraged to expand and embellish their Jim Crow laws until they controlled all aspects of life, including education, transportation, work, recreation, health and burial. There was even a Birmingham City Ordinance that made it unlawful "for a negro and white person to play together or in company with each other in any game of cards or dice, dominoes or checkers."

Overlaying those laws, elaborate rules of "etiquette," or customs, were developed by which blacks and whites were to conduct themselves. For examples of those rules, a black male should never offer his hand to a white male for a handshake; blacks and whites should not eat together; blacks were to address whites by their formal names using Mr. and Mrs., but whites were to call them by their first names; and no black person given a ride in an automobile could sit in the front seat with a white. The list went on and on.

In my own experience, until grown, I never went to school with a black, never attended church with a black, never had a conversation with a black, except as reflected in these stories. All aspects of life for blacks and whites were strictly separated and it would have been possible in Birmingham to live one's life without any personal contact with a member of the other race.

I used the separate water fountains for whites only, and witnessed the relegation of blacks to the back of the bus, but most other aspects of segregation occurred outside my sight. As an adolescent, I never questioned the fairness of such laws or the order of things, except for one instance that I recall. I read in the newspaper of a black accident victim who died waiting for an ambulance to arrive from a black ambulance service. Unfortunately, the call for emergency service had been timely but had gone to a white ambulance crew who, upon arrival, refused to help because the victim was of the wrong color and to intervene would have violated the law. That struck me as hideously wrong.

But, in general, I believed that things were the way they always would be. That is, until I met Mrs. Miller.

Blackmon, Douglas A., *Slavery by Another Name: The Re-Enslavement of Black Americans from the Civil War to World War II,* Doubleday, 2008 [Pulitzer Prize for Non-Fiction, 2009].

Woodward, C. Vann, *The Strange Career of Jim Crow*, Oxford University Press, NY, 1955, Third Revised Edition 1974.

4. *Brown v. Board of Education of Topeka*, 347 U.S. 483 (1954) (page 70)

In this landmark case, the United States Supreme Court overturned *Plessy v. Ferguson,* the 1896 case that established the principle of "separate but equal" facilities for whites and blacks. *Brown* held that segregated schools are inherently unequal and deprived blacks of the equal protection of laws guaranteed by the Fourteenth Amendment.

As I read about the decision in the newspaper, my fear for the future was palpable. Segregation of the races was all I had ever known. How could that be reversed without monumental social upheaval? In re-reading the newspaper article, my heart sank farther as I noticed that the decision by the nine justices had been unanimous. That meant Alabama's own Justice Hugo L. Black, one of the nine, had supported the decision. As a consequence of that betrayal, Black came to be vilified in his home state.

Clerking for Justice Black at the time of *Brown* was David J. Vann, a native of Alabama, who, following his two-year clerkship, returned to Alabama to practice law. Because he had served as a law clerk on the Supreme Court at the time it had done the unthinkable, he too, was villainized by the white supremacists as he worked across the color line to bring down Bull Connor, Birmingham's infamous Police Commissioner, and the Jim Crow laws, which Connor enthusiastically enforced.

Ten years after *Brown,* in 1964, my son, Hewlett C. "Hugo" Isom III, was born, and from the date of his birth has been called "Hugo" in respect for Hugo Black, who had the insight and courage to rise above his cultural background and do what had to be done.

And three years after that, in May 1967, I took a job with a law firm in which David Vann was a partner. (See Note 18, *infra.*) David became my close friend and one of my mentors, a man for whom I had the greatest respect.

5. Asa Earl "Ace" Carter (page 87)

Ace Carter was one of the most enigmatic characters in Alabama history. He was deeply involved in the Ku Klux Klan, but saw the need to organize the business community and ordinary citizens in a lawful, grassroots resistance to the efforts to abolish those Jim Crow laws in the South which upheld segregation of the races, and for this purpose he became the leader of the White Citizens Council in Birmingham and north Alabama.

Later he became an ardent supporter of George Wallace in his quest to become Governor of Alabama in 1962. Carter became his principal speech writer and was the author of his "Segregation Forever" inaugural speech, his declaration at the University of Alabama as he "Stood in the School House Door" and later his lectures as he ran for president, spinning the Alabama story.

In 1968, he split with Wallace, who he thought wasn't radical enough on the race issue. He tried his own hand at running for Governor in 1970, but ran a poor race, placing fifth in the field of candidates. *Fighting the Devil in Dixie, How Civil Rights Activists Took on the Ku Klux Klan in Alabama*, Wayne Greenhaw, Lawrence Hill Books, 2001, Pages 105-106, 154-155, 271-272.

One of Carter's favorite Confederate generals was Nathan Bedford Forrest. Unlike Robert E. Lee, who accepted the inevitable and did his utmost to persuade his men and the people of the South to act nobly in defeat, Forrest became embittered by Reconstruction. He eventually joined the Ku Klux Klan in Pulaski, Tennessee, became for a time its Grand Wizard, and staged a resistance to Reconstruction.

Carter, having labored for years to defend white supremacy in the South, probably realized that he, too, had lost a war. Disillusioned, he left politics and the State of Alabama behind in 1974, moved West and changed his name and his persona. He became Forrest Carter, named for his hero, and denied any connection to Asa E. Carter. He wrote a novel, *The Rebel Outlaw: Josey Wales*, from which a popular movie was made starring Clint Eastwood. He also wrote *The Education of Little Tree*, published in 1976, as an autobiography in which he claimed to be a Cherokee Indian raised by his grandparents. *Little Tree* became well-known, selling millions of copies until the truth of Carter's double identity became public. Wayne Greenhaw wrote an article, "Is Forrest Carter Really Asa Carter? Only Josey Wales May Know for Sure," in the *New York Times*, Aug. 26, 1976.

Greenhaw, Wayne, *My Heart is in the Earth*, 2001, River City Publishing, LLC, pages 41-59.

Eskew, Glen T., *But for Birmingham: The Local and National Movements in the Civil Rights Struggle*, UNC Press, pages 114-118.

6. Ace Carter Speech (page 88)

The speech I've quoted is an actual radio address by Carter in Carter's own voice contained on a reel of microfilm and an LP record album archived in the Birmingham Public Library, Department of Archives and Manuscripts.

I do not remember in any detail the speech Ace Carter delivered on that occasion. As I recall, he told the story of the South's misfortune in losing the War and the humiliation suffered by Southerners at the hands of the Federal Government during Reconstruction. The occupation of the South after the war by Federal troops—often colored troops— was particularly degrading to those left to pick up the pieces. And then came hordes of carpetbaggers and scalawags to make their fortunes on the misfortunes of the Southern people. He spoke of the Southern people—Anglo Saxon people, he said—as the greatest fighting people on the face of the earth, and how they not only endured but eventually prevailed.

In the year 1956, only seventy-five years had passed— just three generations—from Reconstruction, and memories in the South were long. Carter's speeches, which roused and magnified those memories, cast the darkening shadow of another Federal take-over complete with Federal troops. Then he extolled the Anglo-Saxon fighting spirit. He pictured a South after the breakdown of segregation when the Anglo-Saxon race would have been "mongrelized" by race mixing. His speeches yanked followers from their chairs shouting for justice.

7. *Clacker*: term used for a type of trade token (page 155)

Roy J. "Jack" Wood, my uncle, wrote a book called *Alabama Trade Tokens*, published by the Birmingham Public Library Press in 1995. "Trade tokens" were used by workers and their families to pay for goods in the many "company stores" across the nation. In the book, Wood mentions the term "clacker" along with a number of other fanciful names (e.g., scrip, brass, flickers, good fors, goo-ga-la), each being used, in one or more regions of the country, for the generic catchall term "tokens." In the coal mines of Alabama, in particular, such tokens were called clackers.

8. The Highlander Folk School, Monteagle, Tennessee (pages 162 & 323)

As a teenager, I was shocked by the articles I read about Highlander, a communist Training School located in Monteagle, Tennessee, right in the middle of the South. Those articles appeared in pamphlets I'd pick up at meetings of the White Citizens Council, and would invariably show a picture of an interracial group at Highlander, pointedly identifying those who were Jewish. They were all, of course, thought to be communists or "fellow travelers." How can it be, I thought at the time, that such a disloyal organization is allowed to exist in our country?

How wrong I was to have been misled by such propaganda.

Formed in 1932 by Myles Horton, a Tennessee native who had studied at Columbia University's Union Theological Seminary under Reinhold Niebuhr, Highlander was founded as a school to teach impoverished mountain people basic skills, including how to organize themselves to solve their own problems and to work collectively toward a democratic and equitable society.

For more than twenty years, Highlander conducted workshops to train organizers for the CIO, a union which had not before been effective in organizing workers in the South. The workshops at Highlander were interracial. Though Highlander was successful in its approach, it became apparent that one of the difficulties in union organization in the South was the Jim Crow laws preventing the two races from conducting meetings under the same roof in their home towns.

In the early fifties, Horton began conducting workshops on civil rights and peaceful protests. Bill Moyers writes in his preface to Myles Horton's autobiography, *The Long Haul:*

> Highlander was now the principal gathering place of the moving forces of the Black revolution. Martin Luther King Jr. came. So did Rosa Parks, Andrew Young, Julian Bond, Stokely Carmichael, and scores of others. The state tried to close it down, the Klan harassed it, state troopers raided it. But Highlander was indestructible.

Actually, it was not indestructible. During the virulent McCarthyism of the fifties, the Tennessee legislature, believing Highlander was a communist organization, revoked its charter finally putting the school out of business and confiscating its property in 1960. Horton said in response to that action:

> You can padlock a building. You can't padlock an idea. Highlander is an idea.

By 1961, Highlander had re-opened in Knoxville under the name "Highlander Research and Education Center, Inc." where Horton continued his work until his death in 1990 at the age of eighty-five.

Elisabeth Sifton, Reinhold Niebuhr's daughter, wrote a book about her father published in 2003 entitled *The Serenity Prayer: Faith and Politics in Time of Peace and War.* There, she tells of seeing on television in the spring of 1981 Bill Moyer's interview of an old gentleman in a rocking chair—a Southern gentleman.

> Tears of happiness bolted from my eyes. It was Myles Horton. Just to hear his voice touched my heart, but my nostalgia for his robust, unpretentious political courage nearly broke it. This was just what I remembered from my childhood—these intrepid marvelous people! The crucible that was the Great Depression had been an experience that for some had forged real character . . . .

> It was at Highlander . . . that the first workshops were held to train black and white students and ministers in Gandhi's techniques of nonviolent civil disobedience.

> These were the vanguard civil-rights protesters who went on to challenge the evil racial laws and customs of the South. Horton had always been courageously committed to changing what had to be changed, and mercifully he lived to see some of his efforts bear fruit in the Civil Rights and Voting Rights Acts passed during the Johnson administration. And there he was, reminding us of how he had started.

> A direct line ran from his Union [Seminary] classes in 1930 to Birmingham and Selma—that he made clear. He had gone north to Union in the first place because he wanted to study with theologians who were exploring ethical and religious issues that were going unheeded in the white South." ***Pages 149-150.***

Highlander today continues its operations from New Market, Tennessee, where it works with grass roots leaders on a wide variety of social concerns, including Civil and Human Rights, Humane Immigration Policy and Economic Justice and Worker's Rights, to name a few. See *www.Highlander-Research.org*.

Horton, Myles, with Judith Kohl and Herbert Kohl, *The Long Haul, an Autobiography*, Teachers College Press, New York, N.Y., 1998.

Adams, Frank, with Myles Horton, *Unearthing Seeds of Fire: The Idea of Highlander*, John F. Blair, Publisher, 1975.

Horton, Myles and Paulo Freire, Edited by Brenda Bell, John Gaventa and John Peters, *We Make the Road by Walking: Conversations on Education and Social Change*, Temple University Press.

Jones, James B. Jr., "Myles F. Horton, Tennessee's 'Radical Hillbilly': The Highlander Folk School and Education for Social Change in America, the South and the Volunteer State," posted by James Jones April 2, 2007.

Morris, Aldon D., *The Origins of the Civil Rights Movement: Black Communities Organizing for Change, The Free Press*, 1984 (Pages 139-157).

Sifton, Elisabeth, *The Serenity Prayer: Faith and Politics in Times of Peace and War*, W. W. Norton & Company, 2003.

9. The Interstate Commerce Commission (ICC) (page 169)

The ICC was established by the Interstate Commerce Act by the United States Congress in 1887. The primary purpose of the Act and of the ICC was the regulation of the railroad industry in order to prohibit unfair and monopolistic practices. The Act was extended in 1935 by the Motor Carrier Act to cover interstate bus carriers and trucking.

The Interstate Commerce Act included a non-discrimination clause which prohibited any railroad from subjecting any person "to unreasonable or undue prejudice or disadvantage whatsoever." A similar clause was written into the Motor Carrier Act. This provision probably was intended to prohibit discriminatory freight rates and similar unfair practices, but was broad enough to command the attention of those who objected to the Jim Crow laws in the South.

Even with that non-discriminatory clause in place, the ICC did not buck the prevailing laws of the South requiring separation of the races on railroads and common carriers. After all, it was the U. S. Supreme Court which had, in 1896, established the "separate but equal" rule in *Plessy v. Ferguson,* 163 U.S. 537. Based on that case, the Southern states enacted railroad segregation statutes and expanded the concept of separate accommodations to every form of transportation, such as buses, street cars and even taxi cabs, and, indeed, every aspect of life in the South.

For sixty years, the Jim Crow laws were challenged but held firm based on *Plessy* and the "separate but equal" principle, though some plaintiffs were granted relief based on inequality standards. Then came the landmark case of *Brown v. Board of Education of Topeka,* and four other similar cases decided by the U. S. Supreme Court on May 17, 1954, which expressly overruled *Plessy* and held separate but equal educational facilities "inherently unequal." While relating only to educational facilities, it was clear that *Brown* had cut the ground from under the Jim Crow laws.

The following year, in November 1955, in an eight man majority opinion, the ICC in *Keys v. Carolina Coach Company* prohibited "separate but equal" accommodations in bus travel across state lines. The defendants were ordered to abandon their Jim Crow policies for interstate travelers by January 10, 1956, both on the buses and in waiting rooms.

Most carriers responded to that ruling by removing their "white" and "colored" signs and instituting a policy similar to that of Southeastern Greyhound Bus Lines with respect to interstate passengers. (See Note 9, *infra*) As to *intrastate* passengers, local Jim Crow laws continued in force, thereby creating a cumbersome system in which it was unlawful to separate "interstate" passengers, and also unlawful to allow the mixing of "intrastate" passengers. This untenable situation prevailed until the Montgomery bus boycott case, *Gayle v. Browder,* 352 U.S. 903 (1956), held invalid Montgomery's Jim Crow law relegating black passengers to seating in the rear of the bus.

Even though Jim Crow laws in the South relating to transportation should have been settled by the end of 1956, there was substantial resistance to desegregation from political leadership and White Citizens Councils in the Deep South. Bus and train terminals and restaurants were slow to comply, particularly the restaurants which often were owned by third parties, who argued they were not bound by ICC rules, thereby setting the stage for the Freedom Rides into the Deep South in 1961.

The ICC no longer exists, having been abolished by Congress in 1995.

Greenberg, Jack. *Race Relations and American Law*, Columbia University Press, 1959.

Barnes, Catherine A., *Journey from Jim Crow: The Desegregation of Southern Transit*, Columbia University Press, 1983.

Arsenault, Raymond. *Freedom Riders: 1961 and the Struggle for Racial Justice*, Oxford University Press, 2006.

10. Greyhound Directive (page 171)

On November 7, 1955, the Interstate Commerce Commission decided two cases, both of which rested heavily on the Supreme Court's decision in *Brown v. Board of Education*. In *NAACP v. St. Louis-San Francisco Ry. Co.*, the ICC banned white and colored signs in railway stations. And in *Keys v. Carolina Coach Co.*, the ICC held that requiring Negro *interstate* passengers to sit only within specified portions of buses amounted to discrimination and undue and unreasonable prejudice and disadvantage in violation of Section 216(d) of the Interstate Commerce Act.

Following *Keys*, the president of Southeastern Greyhound Lines, my father's employer, issued the following instructions to company personnel:

TO: ALL COACH OPERATORS AND STATION PERSONNEL

SUBJECT: SEGREGATION

The recent orders of the Interstate Commerce Commission compel us to issue the following instructions concerning the segregation of passengers on buses and in stations. Therefore, effective January 10, 1956, Executive Bulletin No. 50, dated August 16, 1955, will be modified to the following extent:

1. Interstate passengers must not be asked to seat themselves in any particular part of the bus.
2. Intrastate passengers may be courteously requested to comply with the law of that particular state, but if passenger refuses to comply, then no further action should be taken.
3. Existing signs and separation of waiting rooms and restaurants will be maintained as at present, but station personnel

must not take any steps to enforce segregation in the use of these facilities.

I know you can be depended upon to handle this delicate situation with tact and understanding to the end that trouble and misunderstanding can be avoided.

Greenberg, Jack, *Race Relations and American Law*, Columbia University Press, 1959, page 124.

11. *The Southerner* (page 189)

The Southerner was a monthly magazine published by the Alabama White Citizens Council during 1956. Each issue contained on the front cover a photograph of a famous Confederate general along with a biographical sketch of several pages in which the virtues and deeds of the officer were extolled. The balance of the publication was given over to various articles about the plight of the white man in the South, the successes of the Citizens Councils, and the dangers of communism.

Microfilm copies of *The Southerner* are stored in the Birmingham Public Library, Central Office, Department of Archives and Manuscripts. I understand that the only archived copies of the publication survive in the New York City Public Library. My copies, which I cherished as a teenager, were discarded later with other trash.

12. Ed Salem's Drive-In (page 237)

Ed Salem's Drive-In was owned by Ed Salem, a former All-American football player at the Univeristy of Alabama. His restaurant was located near downtown on Highway 31 (Twenty-sixth Street North), only a couple of streets south of my Norwood neighborhood and a few blocks east of Phillips High School. It was a high school hang-out and cruising spot where teenagers sported their cars, listened to music, and ate hamburgers and french fries.

The Jim Crow laws in Birmingham so thoroughly segregated the races that it was almost impossible for any relationship to develop between members of the two races. The resulting distrust, suspicion and fear marooned the members of each race onto islands so remote from one another that no bridge could link them. It was the music floating on waves of air that began the first cross-cultural connections, and the jukebox at Ed Salem's carried that music. I wanted to describe how white teenagers in the mid- and late-fifties were moved by the music their parents abhorred. By the mid-fifties, rock'n'roll had captured white teenagers in the South and across the nation. It represented a cultural revolution that began in its own way to bridge the gaps between the white and colored races. White teenagers moved equally to the beat of Elvis Presley, Buddy Holly, Chuck Berry and Fats Domino. And where best to show that but the local hang-out, Ed Salem's Drive-In?

I have no recollection of where my conversation with Danny Kilpatrick occurred. It may well have been at Ed Salem's. Or perhaps a drug store or other local store. By placing the event at Ed Salem's, I gave myself the opportunity to describe the place and the music. The dialogue with Danny is exactly as I remember it, except with respect to the music which I've added.

13. William Bradford Huie (page 255)

For a biography of this Alabama author, see Encyclopedia of Alabama, *www. encyclopediaofalabama.org.*

14. William Golding, Nobel Prize Speech (page 266)

So far as I recall, Betty never followed up with me about the review of the book that evening and I never learned whether I had been too simplistic— until much later. In 1983, William Golding received the Nobel Prize for literature. After reading his acceptance speech, a truly remarkable statement of "faith," I learned all over again that there is very little about this life that is simple and easy. *www.nobelprize.org/nobel_prizes/literature/laureates/1983/ golding-lecture.html*

15. Joe David Brown (1915-1976) (page 269)

Brown was born and grew up in Birmingham, Alabama, and became a journalist. He worked for several newspapers across the South, and, in 1942, he joined the U. S. Army Air Corps and became a paratrooper. He was among the first to parachute into Normandy for the D-Day invasions, receiving a battlefield promotion to second lieutenant, and numerous decorations for his service.

He was for over ten years a foreign correspondent in various parts of the world. It was during that time that he published his first novel. Eventually, he would write five novels, three of which were made into movies.

Stars In My Crown (1947)

The Freeholder (1949)

Kings Go Forth (1956)

Glimpse on a Stage (1968)

Addie Pray (also known as *Paper Moon*) (1971)

Set in world War II and based on his own war experiences, *Kings Go Forth* was made into a movie in 1958. The protagonist, Sam Loggins, was played by Frank Sinatra, Britt by Tony Curtis, and Monique by Natalie Wood. Even though the movie was not true to the book in one major aspect—some of the tragedy had been supplanted by a hopeful ending—it was an excellent movie nonetheless.

I've always been fascinated by the titles of books and the sources from which they come. Brown elected not to attribute the title *Kings Go Forth* to a source. After a search, I found it comes from the Bible like so many titles:

> And it came to pass, after the year was expired, at the time when Kings go forth to battle, that David sent Joab, and his servants with him, and all Israel; and they destroyed the children of Ammon, and besieged Rabbah. But David tarried still at Jerusalem. (2 Samuel 11:1)

I then re-read the old, old story of King David and Bathsheba.

16. Ferrell E. Griswold (page 284)

Rev. Griswold was a Baptist minister in Birmingham, Alabama. He was a graduate of Howard College and Birmingham-Southern College, and earned a Master's Degree from Grace Seminary, Albany Georgia, and a Doctor's Degree from the University of Chicago. Born September 21, 1928, he died February 13, 1982. A eulogy posted on the internet by the Berea Tape Ministry states:

> He was very outspoken in his views on biblical creationism and reformed theology as well as the Christian heritage of this nation. His patriotism and views on constitutional government were always evident in his biblical, world and life views.

In Diane McWhorter's Pulitzer Prize-winning *Carry Me Home* (Simon & Schuster, 2001), a history of the Civil Rights struggle in Birmingham, she indicates that Ferrell Griswold was the spiritual leader of the United Americans for Conservative Government (page 514), an organization which was the Ku Klux Klan's respectable political front (pages 443-444).

17. *Rising Road* (page 288)

Birmingham was destined to be an industrial city, hungry for more and more workers to mine the coal and fire the iron ore, and they flowed into the city, the blacks from the deltas and flatlands of South Alabama, and the whites from the Appalachian foothills of north Alabama, two peoples to be played against each other, to be exploited, by the industrial barons. Into that volatile brew poured the mass of immigrants from Southern and Eastern Europe—the Italians, the Greeks and the Slavs—at the turn of the 20th Century. Most of the immigrants were Roman Catholic. The prevailing fear by white workers toward the blacks was expanded to include the foreign workers as well. Xenophobia ran amuck. The KKK put Catholics on their list only slightly below the blacks.

By 1920, weekly anti-Catholic publications spewed reports across America that it was the intention of the Church to take over America by force—that the Knights of Columbus were in fact an underground army whose arms had been stashed in their Churches. This hysteria took strong root in Birmingham, where immigrants abounded.

It was into this social hotbed that Rev. James Coyle was sent in 1904 by the Church to be the pastor of St. Paul's Cathedral. A young man, just thirty-one, he would mature quickly as he attempted to face down the prejudice toward Catholics he was destined to live with in this city.

Rising Road is a new publication, brought to market ninety years from the date of Rev. Coyle's death at the hands of Edwin Stephenson, a Methodist minister, on the porch of the rectory next door to St. Paul's, following a ceremony in which the priest married Stephenson's daughter to a Catholic. It is a story of the hate and fear and twisted love that led to Rev. Coyle's death and the trial that followed. Written by a Professor of Law, it is a particularly clear and cogent account of this interesting and distressing slice of Birmingham history, where Hugo Black, later to become a leading liberal light on the U. S. Supreme Court, led the team in defending Rev. Stephenson.

I recommend this powerful and well-written book that speaks of a time in America when a wave of hate and fear toward the Roman Catholic Church and its members turned deadly. Ninety years later, five members of the highest Court in the land—the court on which Hugo Black once served—are Roman Catholic, potent testimony that such hate and fear were unfounded.

Davies, Sharon. *Rising Road, A True Tale of Love*, Race and Religion in America, Oxford University Press, 2010.

18. Connerly, Charles E., *The Most Segregated City in America* (page 301)

The Most Segregated City in America: City Planning and Civil Rights in Birmingham, 1920—1980, The University of Virginia Press, 2005.

19. Berkowitz, Lefkovits, Vann, Patrick & Smith (page 324)

This law firm resulted from a merger in late 1963 of two firms, Berkowitz & Lefkovits which dated from 1928 when Mr. Berkowitz opened his law office in Birmingham, and Vann & Patrick which had been in business for only a few months. At the time of the merger, C. H. Erskine Smith joined the firm as a partner and Charles F. Zukoski became Of Counsel.

The merger arose from the following circumstances:

The City of Birmingham was governed by a three-person commission, one of whom was Public Safety Commissioner Eugene "Bull" Connor. Under his leadership, Birmingham's reputation had suffered nationally and internationally as he and his all-white police force brutally enforced the Jim Crow laws of Birmingham and the State of Alabama.

There were dozens of unsolved bombings, assaults and atrocities that occurred over many years on Connor's watch as police commissioner. They never caught anybody for crimes against the black community. But a particularly brutal event occurred in Birmingham on Mother's Day in May 1961 that did have consequences. Earlier that day, a Greyhound Bus with Freedom Riders was burned in Anniston, Alabama. Then on the same day, a Trailways Bus ridden by Freedom Riders pulled into the station in downtown Birmingham where a mob of white men were scattered about, waiting. As the Freedom Riders disembarked, they were assaulted with clubs and chains for fifteen minutes before the police arrived. Some of the Freedom Riders were severely injured. A local news photographer had made pictures of the beatings in progress. The photographer was beaten and his camera was smashed, but the photographs were intact, and they clearly showed the faces of the Klan members. Still, no one was arrested. That was Birmingham.

But the publicity bothered certain people in Birmingham. People began to ask, where were the police? It was apparent that Connor had an understanding with the Klan that they would have fifteen undisturbed minutes to do their work. Connor jokingly responded by saying, "It was Mother's Day. The policemen were having lunch with their mothers."

Sidney Smyer, the President of the Chamber of Commerce, was in Tokyo at the time for an International Rotary meeting. He read of the event and saw the pictures on the front page. He was embarrassed. Smyer, like many civic leaders of the time, was an old-school, status quo conservative who didn't want to rock boats—but his heart was even more committed to building Birmingham into a successful commercial city, not the one-horse steel town it had remained since its inception.

The report and photographs of that event produced such a national and international backlash that the Birmingham Chamber of Commerce and business interests quietly took notice.

Then on the heels of the Freedom Riders came another event in September 1961. The Federal Court ruled that Birmingham's public parks must be desegregated. In reaction, the Commissioners voted to close the parks. They filled in the swimming pools and shut down the City golf courses. The football fields would be closed, as would the City Auditorium and the Art Museum.

The white business community began to see that this was having serious consequences, not just on the black community, but on them as well. And it would adversely impact their ability to create new job opportunities in competition with Atlanta and other Deep South cities.

The business community had known for some time that Bull Connor and the Commission had become a virtual dictatorship, but now they had gone too far. The City was becoming an international pariah. This would hurt our business interests. No one in the Chamber of Commerce and other institutions could afford to publicly criticize Connor for fear of being branded a communist sympathizer, or worse. Even the newspapers treated Connor with kid gloves. But things did begin to happen behind the scenes.

In late 1961, the President of the Chamber of Commerce, Sidney Smyer, asked the President of the Bar Association to appoint a committee to study the form of government best suited for Birmingham. It would be a study about organization and efficiency, without regard to the persons who currently held the positions of power. It was a study in a vacuum, since everybody was afraid to say the real reason—to get Bull Connor out of office. The President of the Bar hand-picked a committee, which included Abe Berkowitz. In March 1962, that Committee made its report to the Bar Association that Birmingham would be better served by a Mayor/Council form of government than the old three-member City Commission. Abe Berkowitz then presented his report to the Young Men's Business Club and began touring the city speaking to other civic groups.

But the fly in the ointment was how to effect the change. It was good to talk about change, but he knew it would be impossible to actually make the change happen. The change required a referendum. In order to call a referendum to approve the Mayor/Council form of government, a petition signed by ten percent of City voters was needed. That would take time. Once before, in the 'fifties, an attempt was made to collect signatures on a petition, but the petitions had been stolen and destroyed by the police and Klan members. That's how things were done in Birmingham. How could a petition signed by ten percent of voters be accomplished under Bull Connor's nose?

Abe Berkowitz was not the only one agonizing about that question. So was David Vann. David had been the primary attorney, assisted by Erskine Smith and others, who filed a suit several years earlier in Federal Court to enforce reapportionment of the State Legislature. That case was *Reynolds v. Sims*, and Vann argued the case before the Federal Court. That case was then consolidated with *Baker v. Carr* for a hearing before the U. S. Supreme Court. The decision in that case came down in 1962 and established the "one man, one vote" ruling which changed the face of legislatures around the country. Pursuant to that decision, Jefferson County, our county, was allocated ten representatives instead of two and seven state senators instead of one. A special election was set for August 28, 1962.

Suddenly, it occurred to Vann how to get ten percent of voters to sign up before Connor could interfere. But it was only ten days before that election. Vann took his vision to Abe Berkowitz, who was touting the new form of government to Civic Clubs. He told Mr. Berkowitz how they could get ten percent of voters to sign the petition for a referendum before Connor could react. It was simple, he said. On election day, put a booth in front of each polling station and ask people to sign as they went in to vote. That might be done in one fell swoop before Bull Connor and the other commissioners could react. Later, David Vann, a brilliant politician who himself eventually became Mayor of Birmingham, said it was the best political idea he ever had.

A lot happened in a short time after that. There were only ten days to get ready. Abe Berkowitz called Sid Smyer, Chairman of the Chamber of Commerce. Philosophically, these two men were miles apart. But they had the same objective—to get rid of Bull. They discussed the organization of a committee of twenty-five top business leaders to be called "Citizens for Progress" to raise money and organize the efforts. Smyer agreed to get twenty-five leaders, but then reported to Berkowitz that after calling business leaders he couldn't get a single businessman to sign on. To the man, they all said, "Sorry, I can't afford to get involved." Smyer told Berkowitz, "To hell with them. If we can't get twenty-five silk-stocking people, let's get five hundred anybodies." David Vann called on the Unions and Erskine Smith called the leaders in the real estate industry. They quickly rounded up five hundred volunteers for the Citizens for Progress. David Vann and Erskine Smith were listed at the bottom of the five hundred because their names were controversial. Abe Berkowitz and Sid Smyer committed to raise money. It was imperative that the referendum be about better government—not an effort to get rid of Bull.

Vann made arrangements with the *Birmingham News* to put their plans in the paper on Sunday, August 26, two days before the election, urging citizens to sign the petitions. Instead the newspaper, seeing a scoop, published the story immediately, including the fact that Vann was behind it—the same David Vann who had been law clerk to Justice Hugo L. Black of the U. S. Supreme Court, the man who had participated in the *Brown vs. Board of Education* decision.

So the cat was out of the bag. When the Committee met at a public park to organize, Klan members were there intimidating people and gathering up the materials. When the day came for the vote, many of the volunteers failed to show up to man the booths at the polling stations. One who did show up was beaten by Klan thugs. Recognizing an emergency, Erskine Smith hired temporary workers from Kelly Girls on his own American Express card to man those booths without workers.

When the resolutions were brought in, the organizers were elated. There were far more than enough signatures to call a referendum. Erskine Smith gathered the resolutions and announced he would guard them overnight with his shotgun.

The Mayor, allied with Connor, refused to call an election, but the Probate Judge did so, as required by law.

The Citizens for Progress met a stone wall in advertising their position in favor of the Mayor/Council form of government. The radio and TV stations were afraid to publish material in opposition to Connor. When finally a TV station relented, cash was demanded. Vann and Smith borrowed money from the bank and paid for it.

Surprisingly, the vote for new government was approved. But only by a slim margin.

Then the election was set for March 5, 1963 for the new Mayor and Councilmen. Albert Boutwell and Connor had the highest votes in a four-man field for Mayor and a run-off was set.

To Connor's surprise The Citizens for Progress won! Albert Boutwell was elected as Mayor.

The new Mayor and Council were installed on April 15, 1963.

But Bull and the other Commissioners announced they were not going without a fight. He and the Commissioners had been elected for four years, Bull said, and they would serve out their terms.

The new Mayor and Council then filed suit to get them out of City Hall.

On April 23, 1963, the Circuit Court upheld the Mayor/Council position and ordered them out. But the Commissioners appealed to the Supreme Court and posted a bond to stay in office.

Meanwhile, all hell had broken loose in Birmingham.

On April 4, 1963, Martin Luther King and the Southern Christian Leadership Conference began its Operation C (Confrontation) on the most segregated city in America. King brought his team to Birmingham after a defeat in Albany, Georgia, where the police chief refused to play their game. There, the police force treated the protesters with respect. Nothing happened. King wanted Action! He knew Bull Connor would react violently and provide a public outrage. He also knew Bull would soon be out of office, and there was a narrow window of time to act. They began the Easter boycotts of department stores and sit-ins at lunch counters.

Connor, who had been voted out of office, continued in control over Public Safety while the case was in Court. He refused to grant any permits for marches.

The un-permitted marches began. Many were arrested.

On April 17, the Reverands King, Shuttlesworth, and Abernathy were jailed by Connor's police.

Eight local pastors, all in favor of changes in Birmingham, published a letter asking that the boycotts and marches be deferred, to give gradualism time to work. King responded with his famous letter from the Birmingham jail.

On May 3, Bull used dogs for the first time against the massive marches, and then the fire hoses followed. And on May 6, over eight hundred school children were arrested. By then over 2,600 protesters were in jail and other places in lockup. It began to look like concentration camps in Birmingham. This was front page news across America, but in Birmingham, the news of the marches was located on the back pages. While most ordinary citizens had little information about what was happening downtown, the merchants and business community knew.

It was jokingly said in those days that Birmingham was the only city in America to have two Mayors and a King and a parade every day.

Connor and the Commissioners were unwilling to meet with King and Shuttlesworth and negotiate.

Attorney General Robert Kennedy sent his team to Birmingham lead by Burke Marshall, Chief of the Civil Rights Division of the Justice Department to try to find a settlement. According to Diane McWhorter, in *Carry Me Home*, Abe Berkowitz was a close confidante of Marshall. There were numerous meetings in Mr. Berkowitz's office with Burke Marshall, merchants, business people, and black leaders, aimed at finding a solution.

It was David Vann who handled the final negotiations that brought an end to the protests. He did not speak for Bull and the existing City Commission. They would not negotiate. Nor did He speak for the new Mayor/Council. They had no power.

So who did he speak for in negotiating with the black leadership? He couldn't speak for the government.

It was the merchants who were suffering under the boycott. Not only had they lost the business of blacks, whites were afraid to come downtown to shop. And much of the demands of the black leadership was related to merchants: Because of Jim Crow laws, the merchants furnished to African Americans no restrooms, no dressing rooms, no facilities of any kind. But if the merchants gave in, they would be subject to boycotts by whites and reprisals by the Klan. Under pressure during the protests, some merchants had quietly painted over the "White Only" signs, including Pizitz Department Store. The Klan had dropped a stink bomb in Pizitz' ventilation system as a warning. Pizitz was out of business for several days. Bull sent inspection teams to those department stores that had indicated a willingness to be flexible. The Inspectors cited code violations which cost the department stores thousands of dollars. It was simply not possible for the merchants alone to solve the problem. They were vulnerable and helpless. Since the city government was paralyzed and the merchants were vulnerable, it was clear the business community would have to take the lead.

The Chamber of Commerce was desperate. They formed a Senior Citizens Committee of businessmen. The membership was secret. No one knows, even today, who they were. This was a complex problem to solve from the white position.

It was incredibly complex on the black side as well. The African American community was divided on the question of boycotts and marches. The business class and moderately wealthy were not interested in rocking the boat. They were worried about the aftermath, what the impact would be when King left town.

Reverend Fred Shuttlesworth was a local preacher who spoke for a blue collar constituency of blacks. He was a local hero to most blacks. His home and Church had been bombed twice each and he had narrowly escaped with his life. He had been brutally beaten by the Klan on two occasions, and severely injured by the fire hoses. He was in favor of the boycotts, but thought he, not King, should have been in control, and particularly in control of the settlement.

It was into this quagmire that Vann was drafted.

After tremendous efforts by all sides, including Burke Marshall of the Department of Justice, a settlement was finally reached on May 9, 1963 after a number of all-night misfires. The settlement provided a four-point arrangement:

    1. Department store fitting rooms would be desegregated within

three days;

2. Within thirty days after the new Mayor/Council took office, Jim Crow signs would be removed from restrooms and water fountains;

3. Within sixty days lunch counters would be desegregated; and

4. One black sales person or cashier (for each department store) would be hired.

Pretty mild medicine you probably think. But no one was happy. The Klan reacted with more bombings, almost causing race riots. And the blacks were particularly upset that so many protesters, including children, were still in jail and the settlement did not provide for their release. Connor would not release them without bail money. And there was no money. Robert Kennedy leaned on the Auto Workers' Union and money was sent to David Vann and Erskine Smith for bonds, but it came in the nature of a loan. David Vann and Erskine Smith signed the Note. Others raised money as well for the bonds for the several thousands of protestors held in jail.

The bonds were made and protesters were released.

Things looked better for Birmingham—although bombings by Klansmen continued to threaten the peace. But then they culminated on September 15, 1963, with the bombing of the Sixteenth Street Baptist Church where four little girls were killed.

It was at the end of that pivotal year that a new law firm was formed by six like-minded lawyers, each of whom had labored to bring about racial justice in our city. Abe Berkowitz and Arnold Lefkovits. David J. Vann and J. Vernon Patrick Jr., C. H. Erskine Smith. These were the partners in the firm. Joining them Of Counsel was Charles F. Zukoski Jr., the sixty-five year old head of the Trust Department of the First National Bank of Birmingham, who had been pushed into retirement because of his civil rights activities.

Each of these lawyers who formed the new firm had one thing in common: they had given their best to their community during that time we now call the Civil Rights Era. Two Jews, two former members of an elite, white shoe law firm, a real estate lawyer who represented the ACLU in his spare time, and a patrician bank lawyer and former long-term mayor of the wealthy, suburban city of Mountain Brook—an unexpectedly diverse cross-section of the Bar.

This is the firm I joined following law school in May 1967. Though Mr. Berkowitz died in December 1985, the firm continued to be identified by his name. Forty years after the founding of the firm, it merged in 2003 with Baker Donelson Bearman and Caldwell, P.C., a large firm with Tennessee roots. Because the continuation of the use of his name was imperative to us in Birmingham, the surviving firm added Mr. Berkowitz's name to its title and the firm continues to this day to be known as Baker Donelson Bearman Caldwell & Berkowitz, P.C., a firm with over six hundred lawyers and public policy advisors conducting a national law practice.

Estes, Glen, *But for Birmingham: The Local and National Movements in the Civil Rights Struggle.* The University of North Carolina Press, 1977.

McWhorter, Diane. Carry Me Home: Birmingham, Alabama, The Climactic Battle of the Civil Rights Revolution. Simon & Schuster, New York, NY, 2001.

Connerly, Charles E., *The Most Segregated City in America: City Planning and Civil Rights in Birmingham, 1920-1980*, University of Virginia Press, 2005.

Harris, W. Edward. Miracle in Birmingham: A Civil Rights Memoir 1954-1965. Stonework Press, Indianapolis, Indiana, 2004.

19. Samuel Ullman (Facing Title Page and page 324)

Samuel Ullman was born in Germany to Jewish parents. The family immigrated to America in 1851 to escape discrimination, and settled in Mississippi. As the eldest son, it fell to him to assist his father with the butcher business and he was unable to attend college. In 1861, at twenty-one years of age, he joined the Sixteenth Mississippi Regiment and fought in the campaigns in Northern Virginia. Wounded twice, he returned home. One of his injuries would lead to his permanent deafness.

He moved to Birmingham in 1884 and became a progressive leader, serving on numerous boards, particularly the School Board. As president of the Board of Education, he succeeded in providing a high school for black students. In George Leighton's article "Birmingham, Alabama: The City of Perpetual Promise," published in *Harper's Magazine* in August 1937, he mentioned several individuals, including Samuel Ullman, who would not remain silent in an "atmosphere where the word democracy was an 'obscene jest'...."

When his hearing loss forced his retirement, Ullman pursued his lifelong interest in poetry. He wrote the poem *Youth* while in his seventies. It was a favorite of General Douglas MacArthur, who, as Supreme Allied Commander in Japan, placed a framed copy of the poem on the wall in his office. The poem became a national favorite in Japan, and today many Japanese citizens travel to Birmingham to visit the renovated Ullman home, now owned and operated as a museum honoring Ullman's life by the University of Alabama in Birmingham.

In the words of the Alabama Department of Archives & History, "Alabama Moments" cited below, that museum "...is a fitting memorial for a man who fearlessly, and without fear of consequences, advocated progressive actions in an era when that was neither fashionable nor popular." Ullman died in 1924. Below is the entire text of his poem *Youth*.

YOUTH
by Samuel Ullman

Youth is not a time of life; it is a state of mind; it
is not a matter of rosy cheeks, red lips and supple
knees; it is a matter of the will, a quality of the imagination, a vigor of the emotions; it is the freshness of
the deep springs of life.

Youth means a temperamental predominance of courage over timidity of the appetite, for adventure over the
love of ease. This often exists in a man of sixty more
than a boy of twenty. Nobody grows old merely by a
number of years. We grow old by deserting our ideals.

Years may wrinkle the skin, but to give up enthusiasm
wrinkles the soul. Worry, fear, self-distrust bows the
heart and turns the spirit back to dust.

Whether sixty or sixteen, there is in every human being's heart the lure of wonder, the unfailing child-like

appetite of what's next, and the joy of the game of living. In the center of your heart and my heart there is
a wireless station; so long as it receives messages of
beauty, hope, cheer, courage and power from men and
from the infinite, so long are you young.

When the aerials are down, and your spirit is covered
with snows of cynicism and the ice of pessimism, then
you are grown old, even at twenty, but as long as your
aerials are up, to catch the waves of optimism, there
is hope you may die young at eighty.

For more information about this remarkable man:

Armbrester, Margaret (Author), and Miyazawa, Jiro M. (Forward), *Samuel Ullman and Youth: The Life, The Legacy*, University of Alabama Press, 1993.

See also http://alabamamoments.state.al.us/Sec31det.html.

Acknowledgements

Mr. B had been gone for almost twenty years before I felt an urge to write some of his stories. I tried my hand at a couple of stories that were important for me to remember and to share with others in my firm which still carried his name. But I wasn't happy with the way they turned out.

I noticed a Community Education Brochure from the University of Alabama at Birmingham. A creative writing course would be taught for a term of five weeks, one evening each week for two hours. The teacher was Carolynne Scott.

There was only one thing on my mind as I signed up for the course, and when Carolynne asked each of her students why are you here, I confessed to her and the class my limited goal. I said I wanted to learn fictional techniques to help me write several stories about my mentor, Abe Berkowitz.

The class was excellent. We were expected to bring a new story each week to read aloud, and I soon turned to my own life for material. The first story taken from my life that I read in that class was *Tobacco Road*. And then another followed. I found that I loved to write. Perfectly content, I could sit for hours at a time pushing words around.

After that class, I shared a number of my stories with Carolynne. She helped me strike the proper tone and worked with me to better use fictional techniques for telling my stories.

When I assembled most of my stories into a chronological arc, I sent them to my friend, Sonny Brewer, a talented writer and editor in Fairhope, Alabama. Sonny gave me tough but excellent advice on story-telling. He wrote in the margin more than once, "Don't be such a wimp." His tough love approach was effective in helping me find my voice.

Then, I took my assembled stories to Robert B. Frese to discuss publication. He read the stories and has been an advocate. He has given me confidence from the first reading. He suggested breaking the "Interview" with Mr. Berkowitz (now entitled "The Question") into two parts, with the earlier part to create the opening chapter of the book. I thought that was a stroke of genius.

So I owe a debt of gratitude to those three people who have helped me immensely in my writing skills.

My statement of gratitude would not be complete without a mention of my assistant, Ann McNew. She typed the stories from my longhand and now reads my handwriting better than I do. She has helped me through the entire process. A tough Tennessee woman, she has offered her unvarnished opinion about a word or a sentence, and has been immensely helpful to me.

My daughter-in-law, Lanier Scott Isom, an accomplished writer in her own right, has also encouraged me. Some years ago, as she showed me family photographs, I was struck by a photo of her uncle, John Knudson McCullough. He was caught by the camera at about the age of eight, a young boy intent on reading his book while sitting in a tire and propped against the outside wall of his family farmhouse near Birmingham. That picture of the uncomfortable-looking boy, taken in about 1929 and which is on the dust jacket of this work, is used to illustrate the very real importance of reading in the development of how we think about the important matters in life.

There were many others who encouraged me as I wrote my stories. My partners: Anne Mitchell, David Larsen, Pat Clotfelter, Lisa Borden, Andrew Potts, and Jed Beardsley; my writer friends: Billy Bishop, Richard Brooks, Alan Perlis, Barbara Bonfield, Tom Gordon, Lawrence Willson, Hoyt Wilson, Carolyn McKinstry, Teresa K. Thorne, John Sims Jeter, Sonya Bennett, Jim Herod, Jim and Liz Reed, and Cedrick L. Threatt; my Norwood friends: Carol Clarke, Robert Gilmore, George Likis, Walter Henderson, and Ray Stone; and other friends: Sam and Gwen Knowlton, Forrest Hinton, Bill and Martha Dawson, John Jasey,

Bob Kracke, Jim Rotch, David Carn, Bart Crawford, Emris Graham, Marc Eason, Camilla Turberville, Mike Parsons, Eric Darrington, Susan Lines, Lawrence Pijeaux, Kendra Key, Mike Graham, Steve Wallace, Elizabeth MacQueen, Andy Olds, Jim Baggett, Gregory Sheinfeld, Veronica Kennedy, and Luther Kale. All of them at various times have read something I've written and given me hope that my time has not been wasted. Some read my complete manuscript, others only a story or two. Some have offered criticism and suggestions. I'm thankful for the friendship of each and every one.

There are no doubt other friends not mentioned here who have read a story and given me advice over the past few years as I've tried to learn how to write, and for my oversight I apologize and express my gratitude to all of them.

And, of course, I'm grateful to my own family: my sister, Dale I. Hawkins, and my brother, Charles E. (Ed) Isom; my cousins, Jackie O. Isom, Woodson Isom and his wife, and Roy C. Green, Jr.; my nephew, Ralph K. Hawkins; my son, Hugo Isom, daughter-in-law, Lanier Scott Isom, and their children, Clint and Frances; and my daughter, Natalie Isom Sansom, and son-in-law, Ken Sansom, and their children Jake and Virginia Mackenzie (Maxie); and my wife, Martha. They have all read, criticized, encouraged and pushed me along. And to my wife, Martha, I'm grateful as well to her for suffering my moodiness over the last five years or so as I ruminated over how best to write and present these stories.

And finally to my law partner and good friend B. G. Minisman Jr., I acknowledge my many thanks for permission to reprint the poem *Youth*, written by his great-grandfather Samuel Ullman. In light of my age—and the tremendous medical advances in the ninety years since the poem was written—I hereby petition B. G., as great-grandson and family representative of Samuel Ullman, to re-publish the poem *Youth* with one significant revision—please delete the last word—*eighty*—and substitute in its place and stead the words—*one hundred ten.*

That would give me much satisfaction.

THE END